ELIOTT LERNER

DRAWING MANGA:

A Graphic Novel on How to Create Your Own Manga

rockynook

Acknowledgments

I would like to give a big thank you to Hélène Raviart and Barbara Janssens for their support throughout this project.

I also want to thank Chloé Eva and Clarisse Delande for the cover design, Loïc Audrain for his work on the layout, and Alexiane Bargiel for her proofreading.

CONTENTS (TECHNIQUES)

Foreword

For many people, manga drawing is a gateway into the world of drawing. Underneath its simple appearance, it hides meticulous know-how and specific knowledge, which is why it often proves to be very tricky.

The purpose of this book is to clear up the haziness and confusion around learning how to draw manga. This book is by no means exhaustive, but it offers a first approach to manga drawing and to the basic techniques and knowledge of which it is made up.

Because the process of drawing is chock-full of successes, failures, and questioning, the story that is told here could be anyone's story.

At the end of this book, it is possible that everything will still not be completely clear. However, I hope that it will have been clarified at least a little and that this book will have given you a boost in getting started drawing manga.

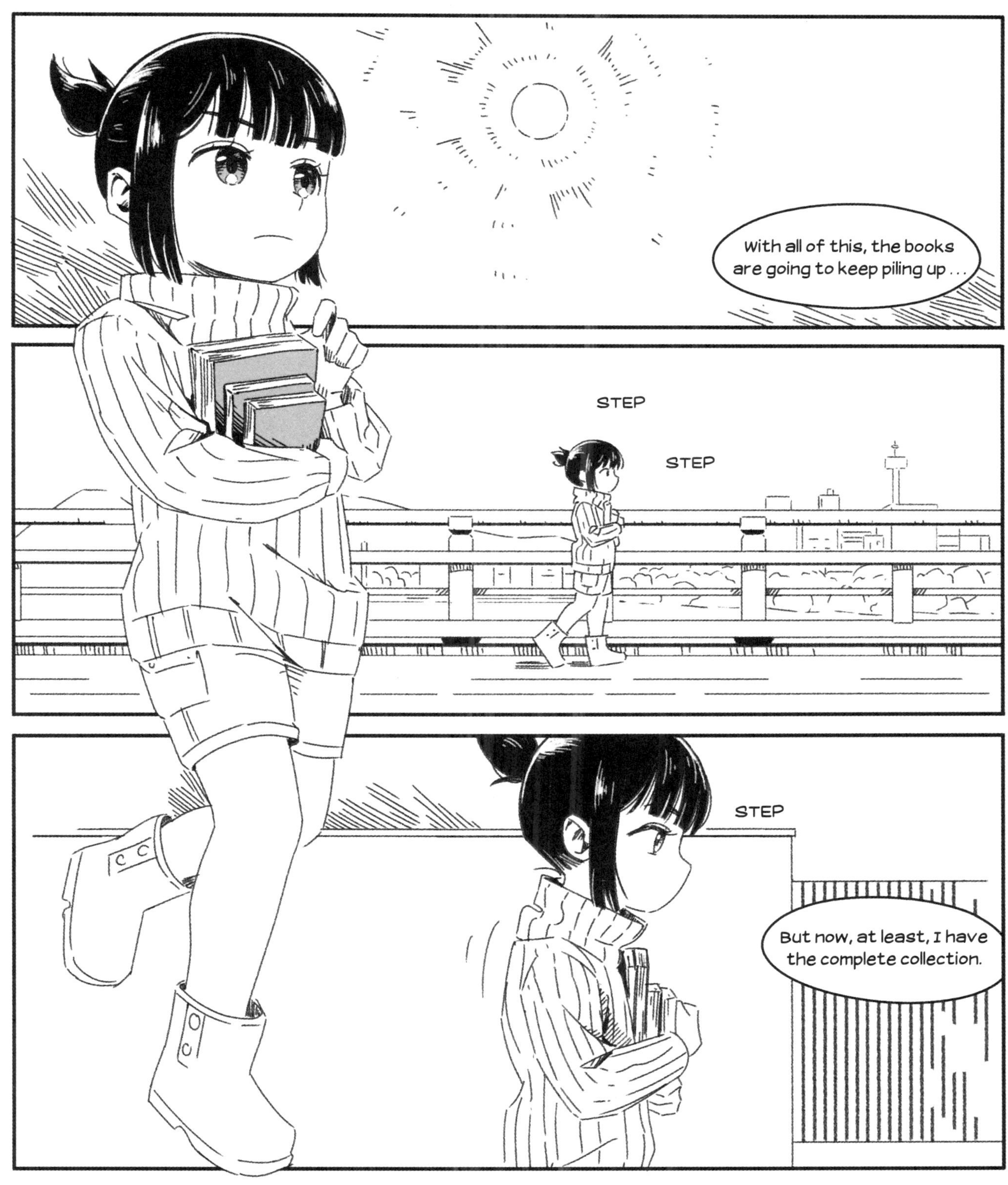
With all of this, the books are going to keep piling up . . .
STEP
STEP
STEP
But now, at least, I have the complete collection.

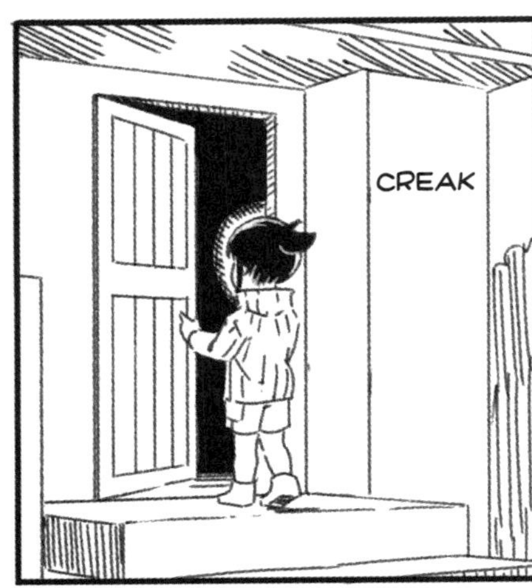

CREAK

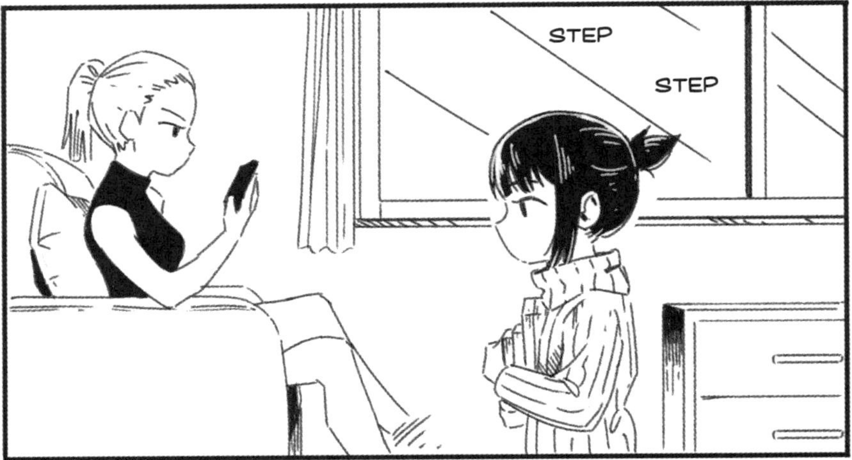

STEP
STEP

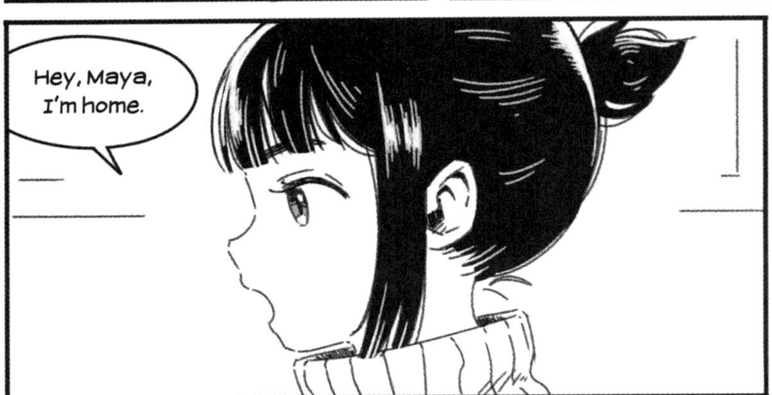

Hey, Maya, I'm home.

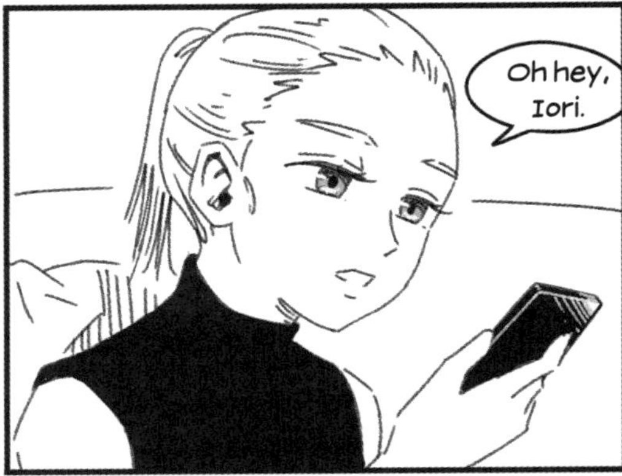

Oh hey, Iori.

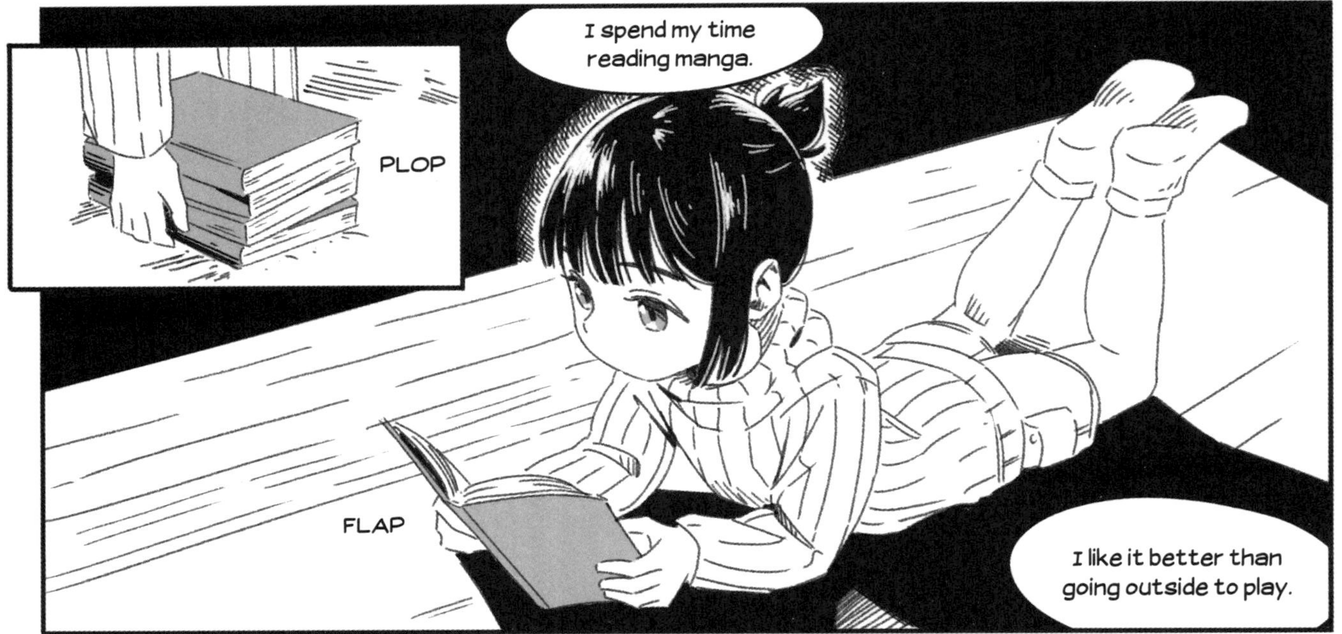

PLOP
I spend my time reading manga.
FLAP
I like it better than going outside to play.

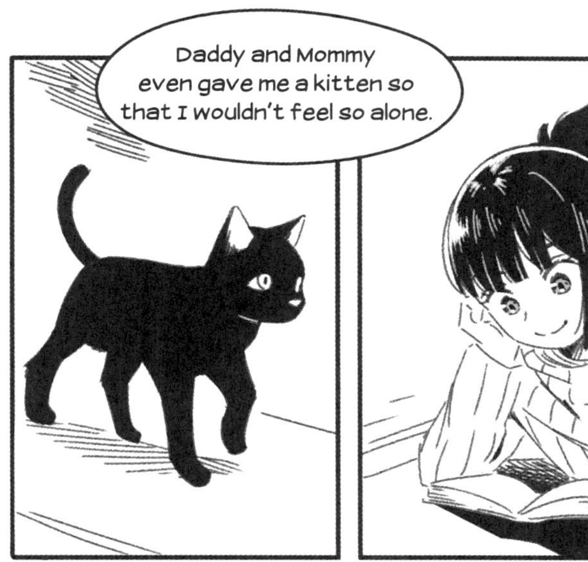

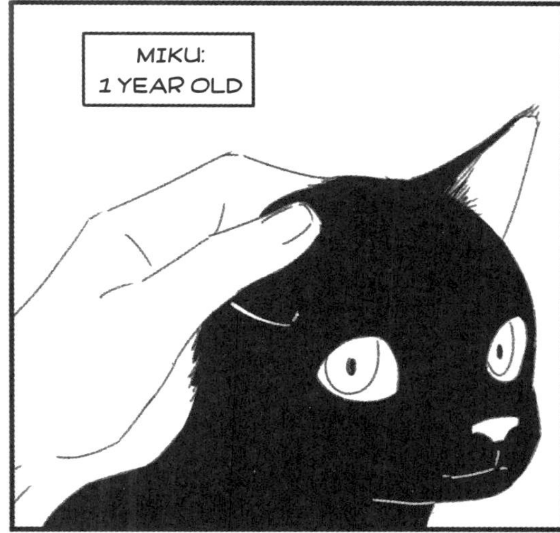

Then, little by little,
without even really knowing why
I was doing it, I started to draw.

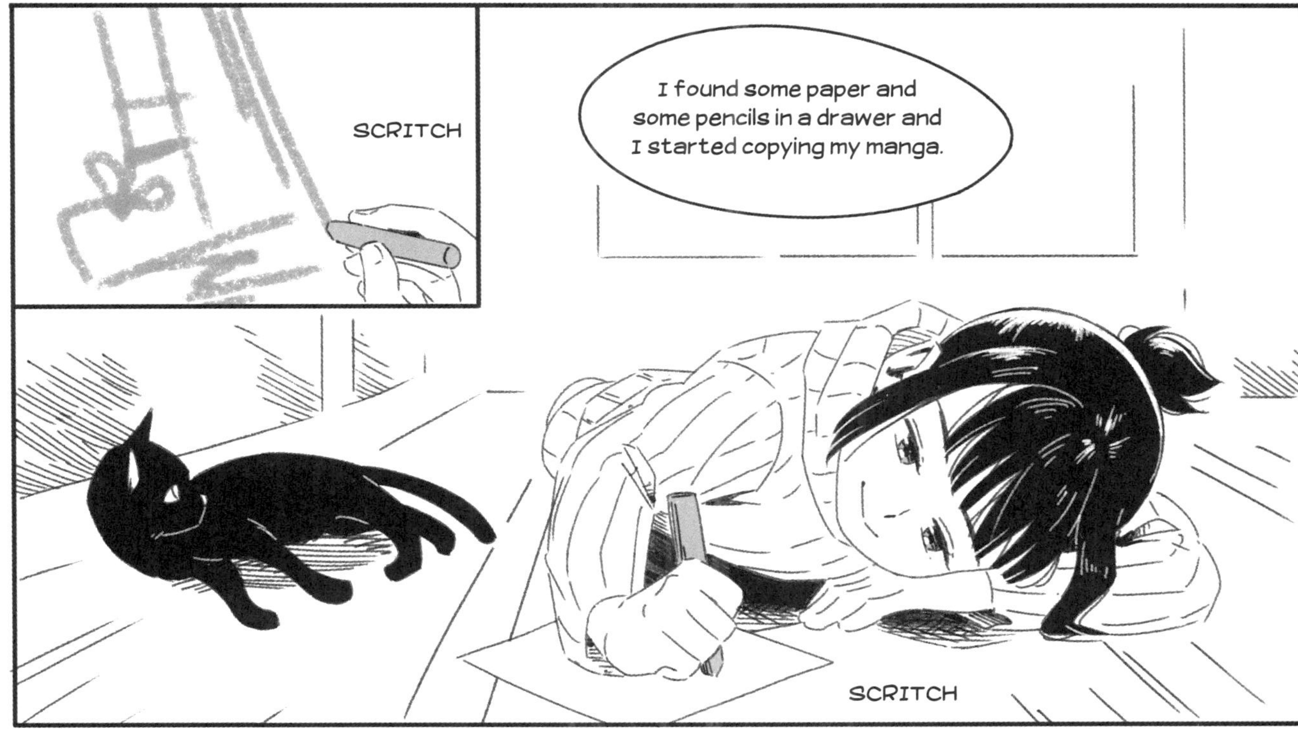

3

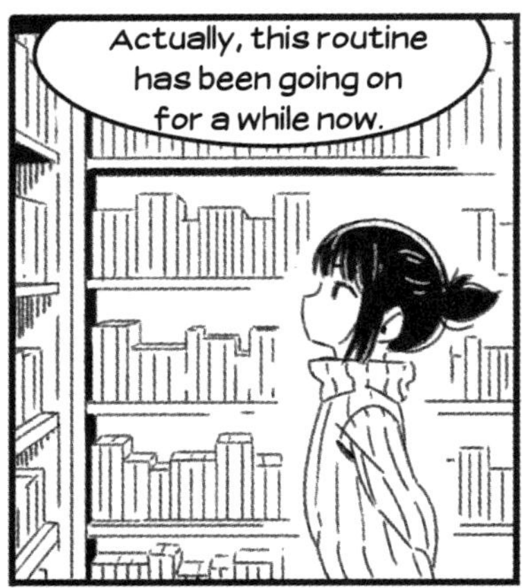
Actually, this routine has been going on for a while now.

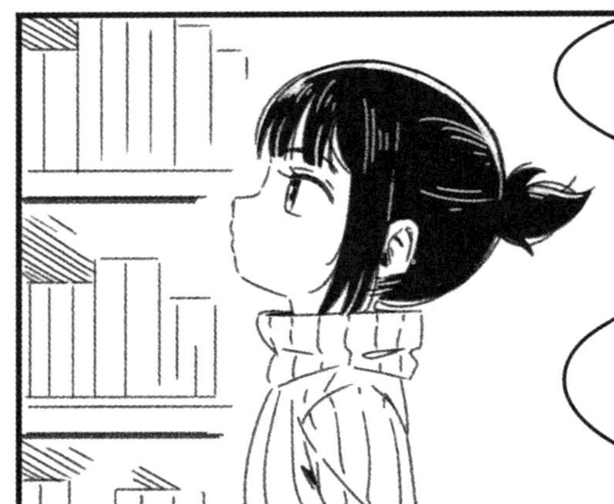
Daddy gives me a little bit of money every week during the holidays.
I spend almost all of it at the neighborhood *konbini* convenience store, buying manga. And magazines.

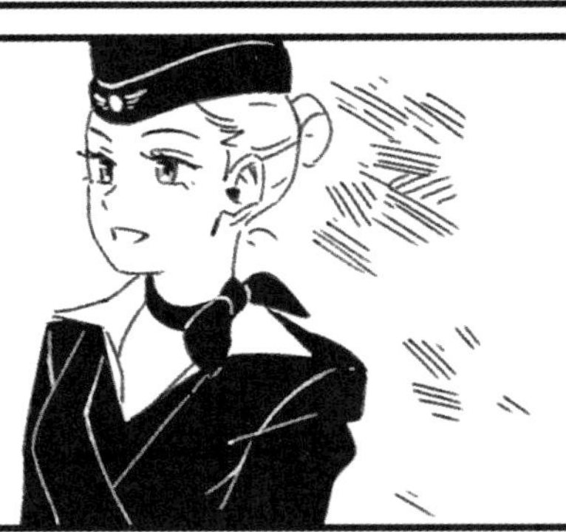
My mother is a flight attendant. She travels around the world a lot, so I don't see her very much.
She comes home every now and then, but she only stays for a few days and then she leaves again.

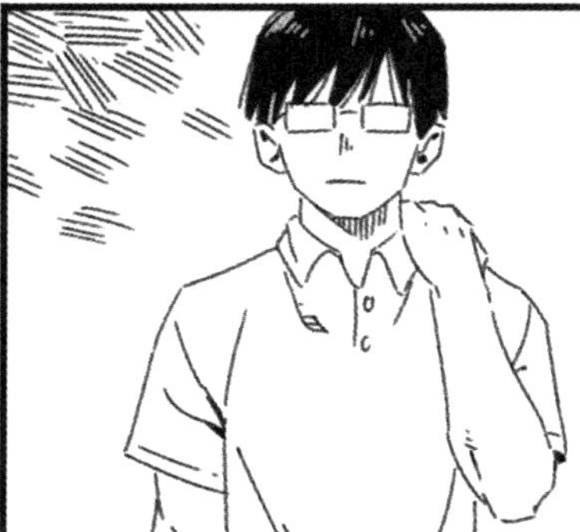
My father works a lot, and he's not on a time clock, so he gets home late at night.
There are even whole days when I don't see him at all.

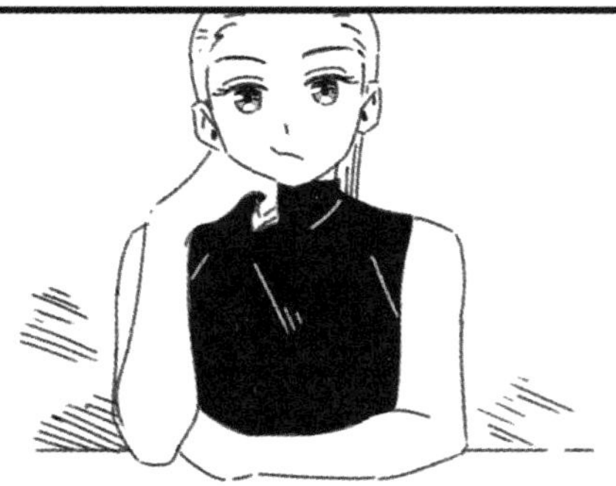
So, I have a nanny who takes care of me.
Her name is Maya, and she's nice and all but … I don't know … She just doesn't seem all that invested, if you know what I mean …

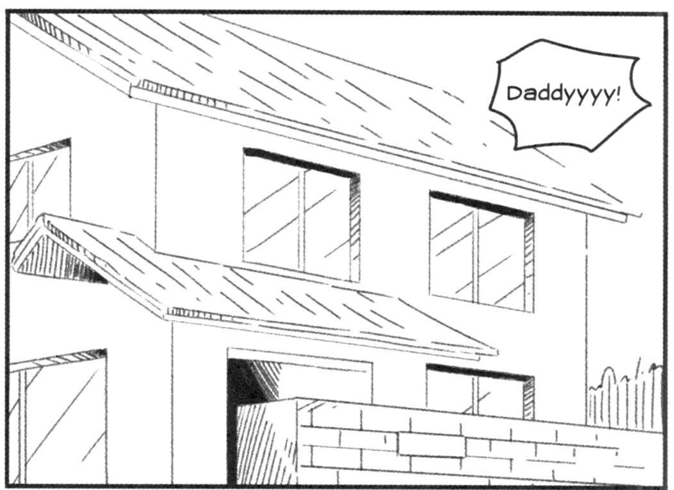
Daddyyyy!

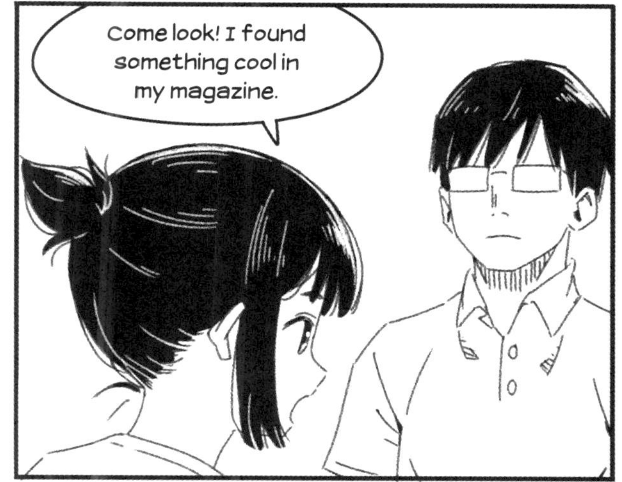
Come look! I found something cool in my magazine.

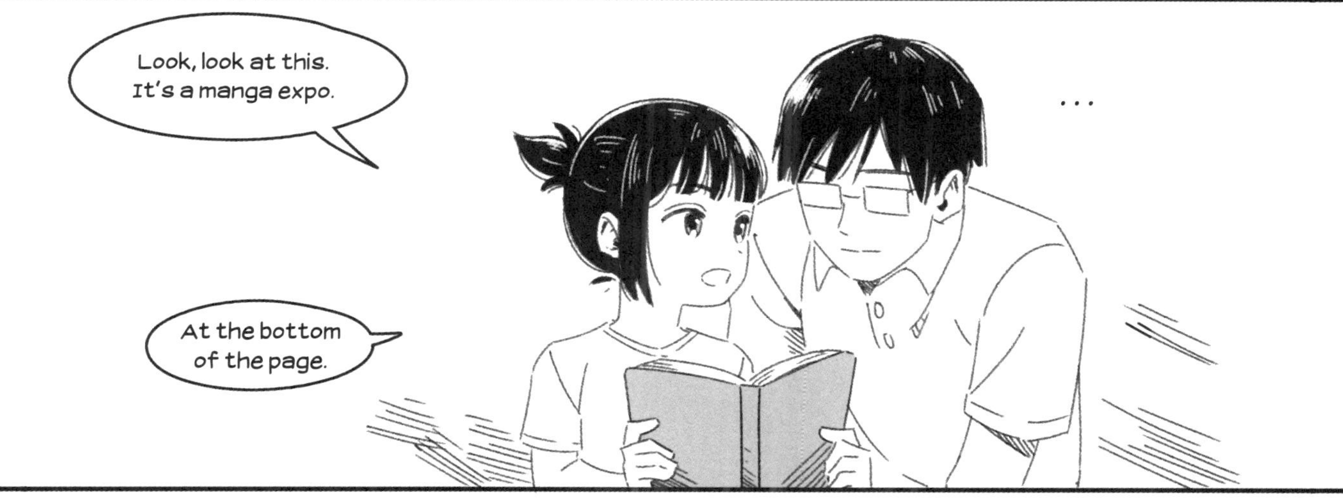
Look, look at this. It's a manga expo.
At the bottom of the page.
. . .

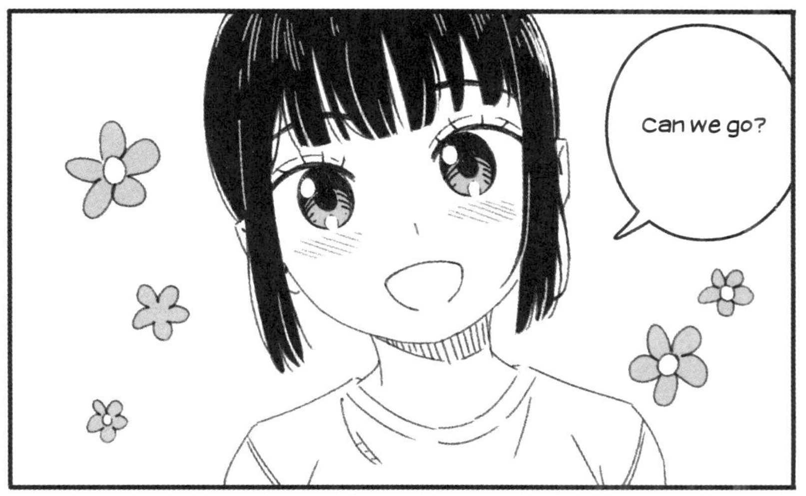

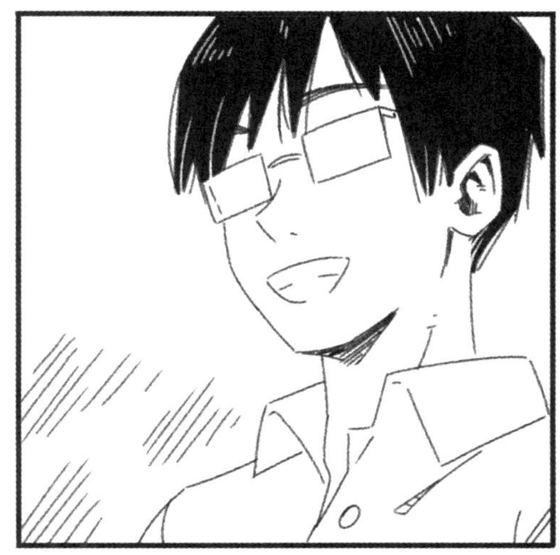
Can we go?

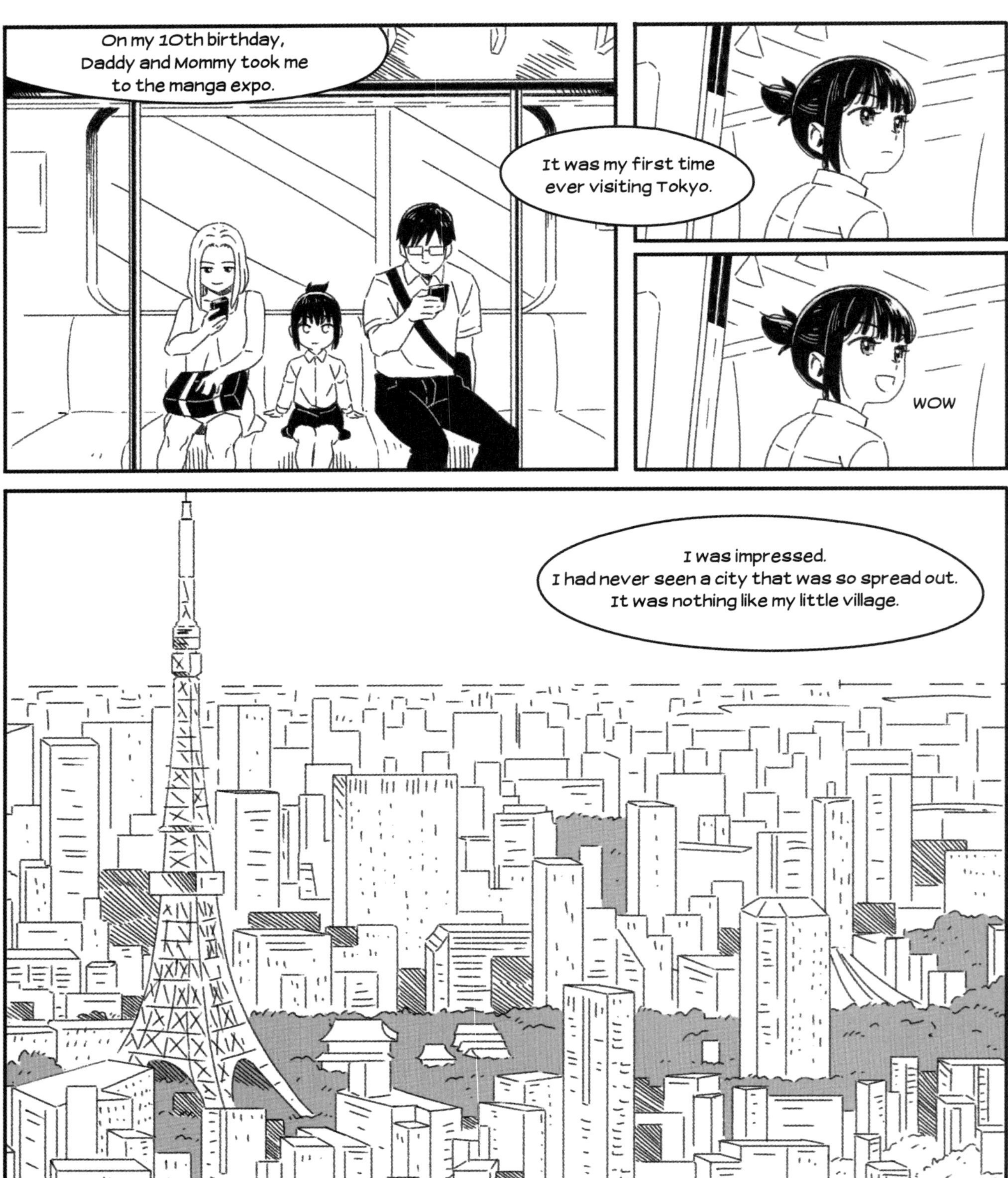

On my 10th birthday, Daddy and Mommy took me to the manga expo.
It was my first time ever visiting Tokyo.
WOW
I was impressed. I had never seen a city that was so spread out. It was nothing like my little village.

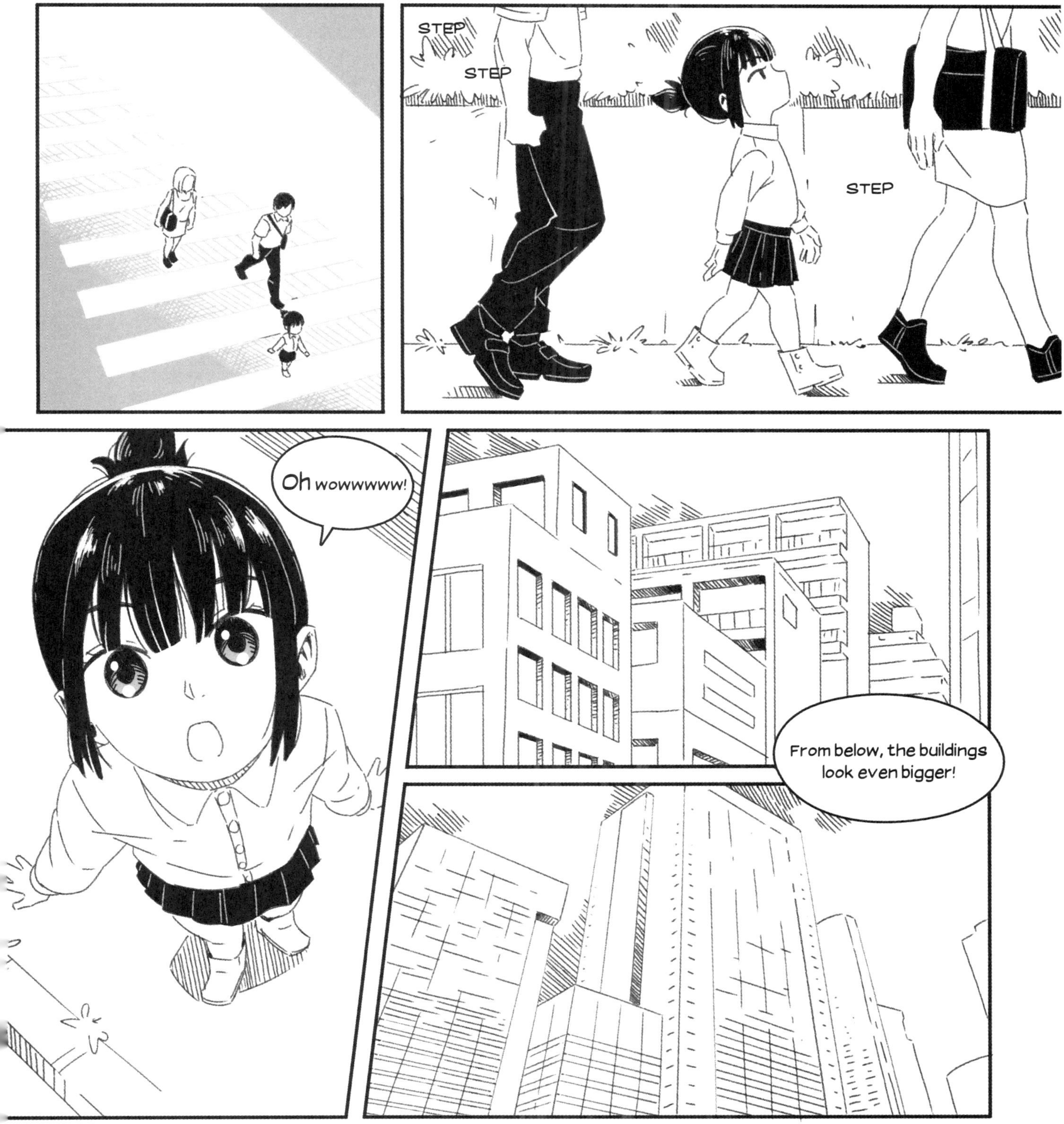

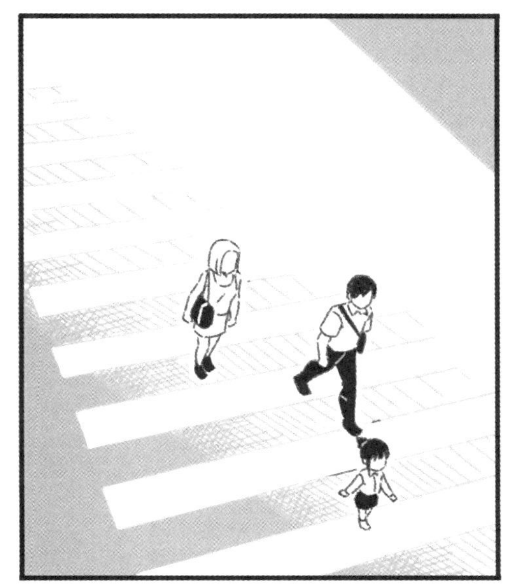

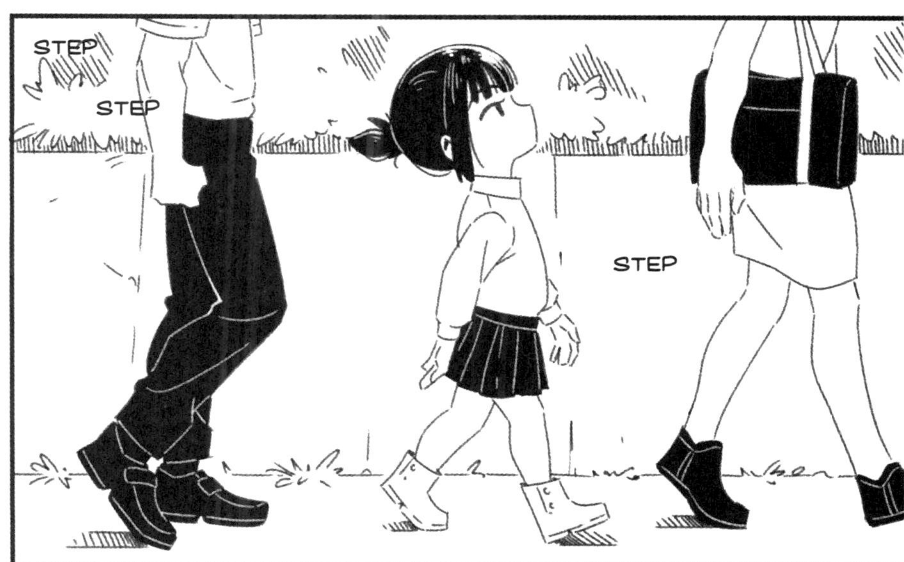

STEP
STEP
STEP

Oh wowwwww!

From below, the buildings look even bigger!

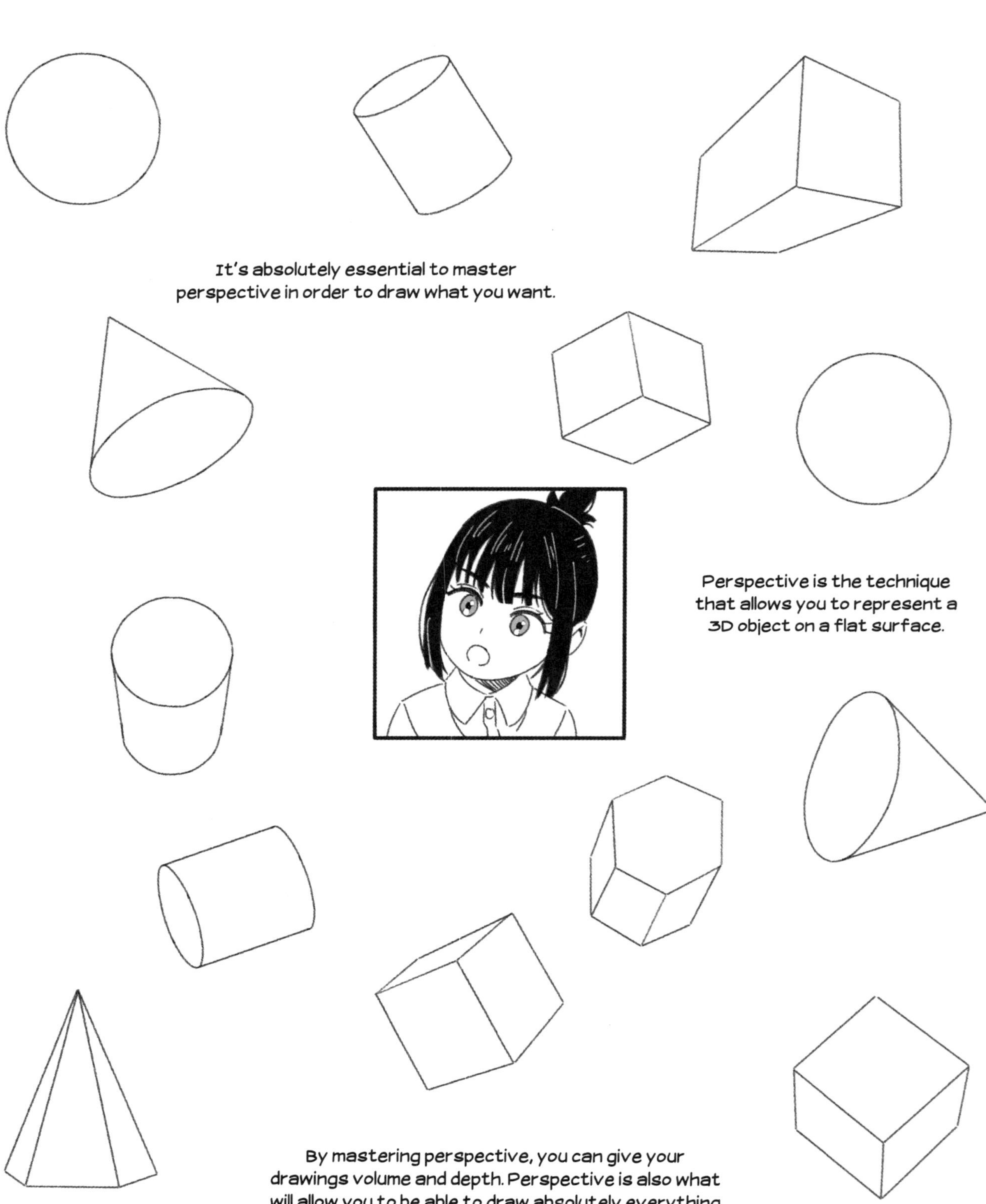

It's absolutely essential to master perspective in order to draw what you want.

Perspective is the technique that allows you to represent a 3D object on a flat surface.

By mastering perspective, you can give your drawings volume and depth. Perspective is also what will allow you to be able to draw absolutely everything (bodies, objects, landscapes . . .).

The horizon line represents the level of the observer's eyes.

Because the height of the observer can vary, the height of the horizon line can vary as well.

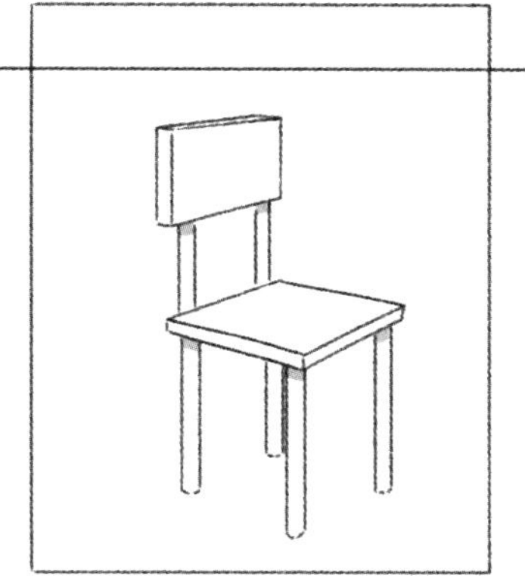

Adult's point of view: the chair is below the horizon line, so you can see the top of the chair.

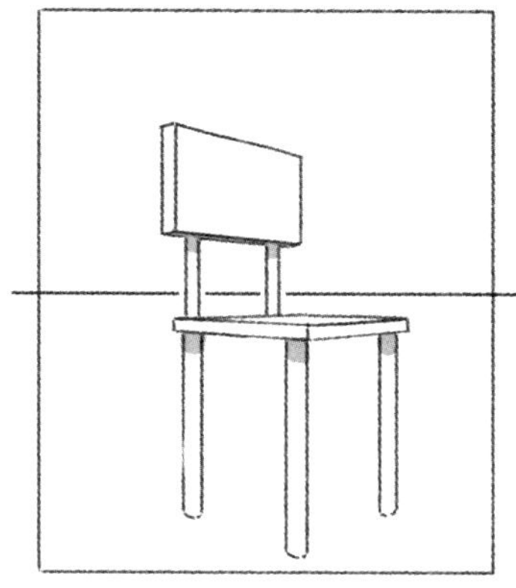

Child's point of view: the horizon line is lower, so you can't see the top of the chair anymore.

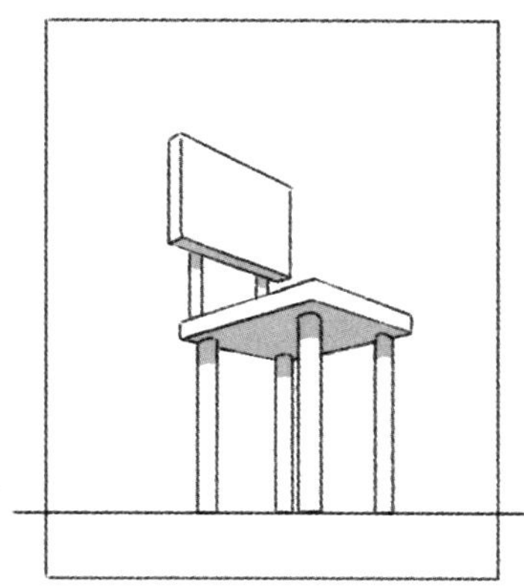

Insect's point of view: the horizon line is at floor level, so you see the bottom of the chair.

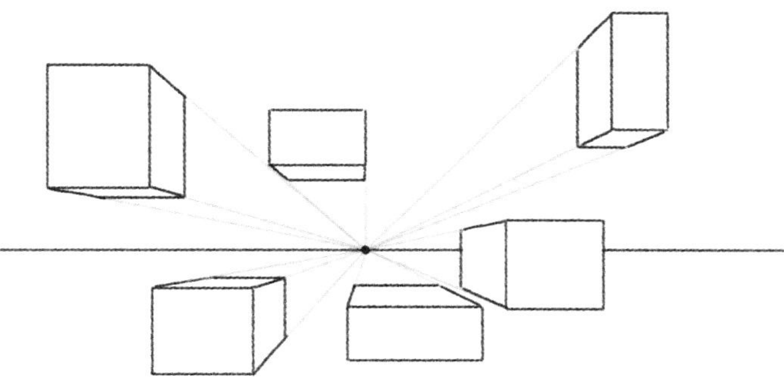

We use perspective with one vanishing point to represent an object we can see one side of.

The vertical and horizontal lines stay parallel to each other, while the depth lines appear to converge upon a vanishing point placed on the horizon line.

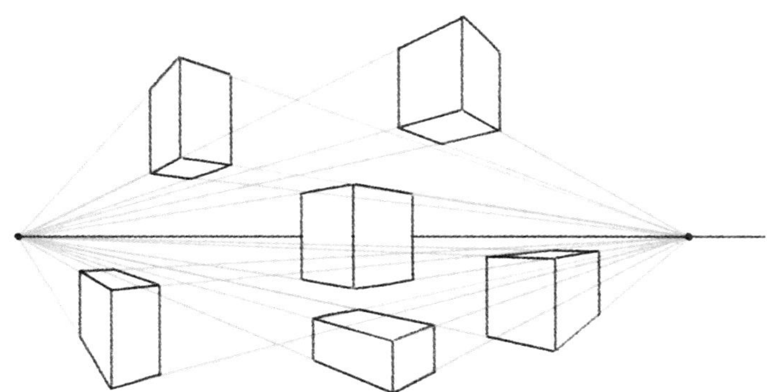

We use perspective with two vanishing points to represent an object we can see at an angle.

The lines on each side of the corner will converge toward their respective vanishing points.

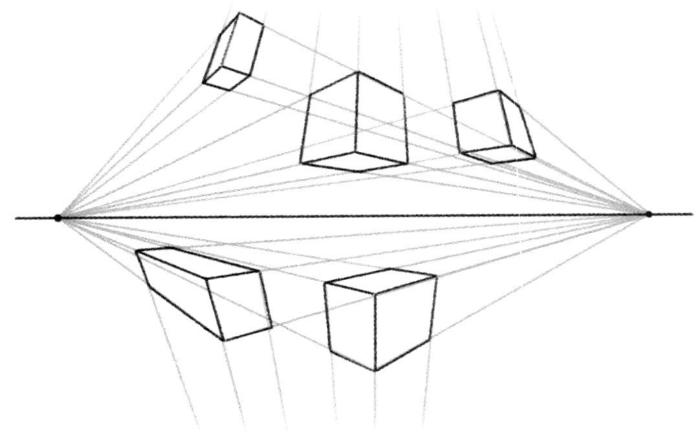

We use perspective with three vanishing points to represent an object seen from a bird's-eye view or from below.

The vertical lines converge toward a vanishing point positioned above the horizon (from an insect's perspective) or below the horizon (bird's-eye view).

The closer the third vanishing point is to the horizon line, the more noticeable the sense of depth.

Third vanishing point

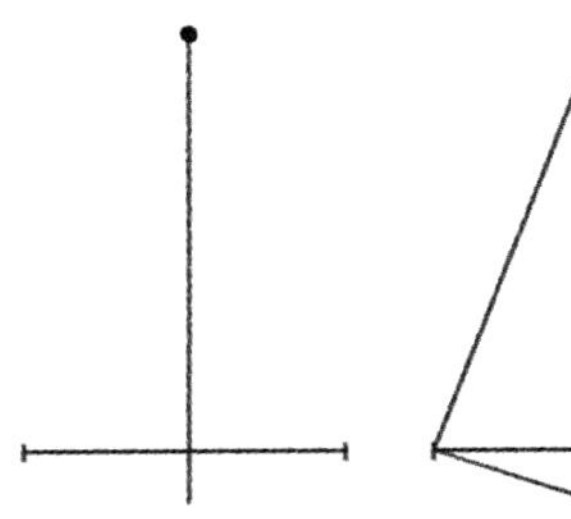

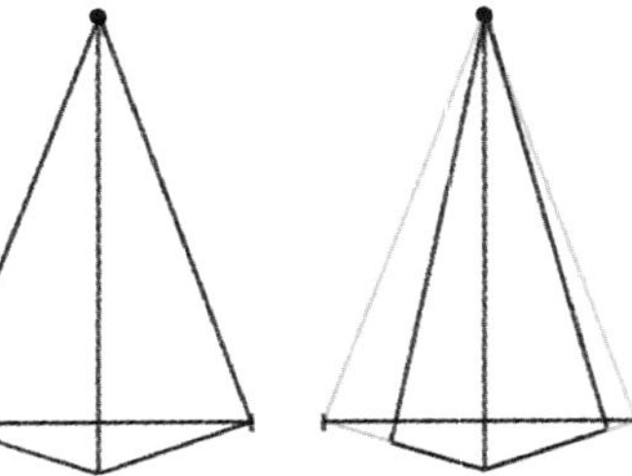

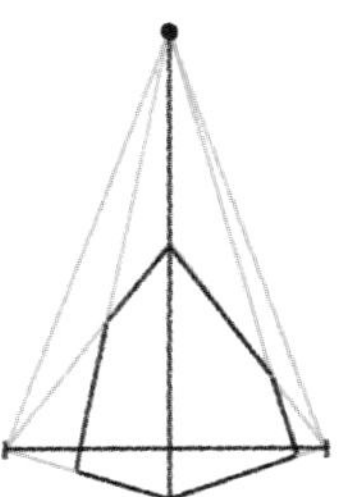

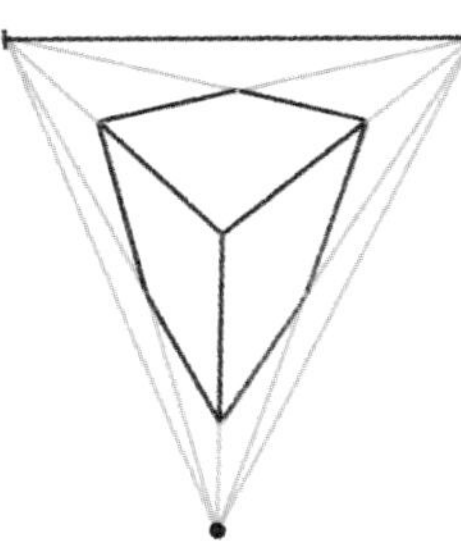

The vertical lines meet at the third vanishing point.

Draw the sides of the object.

Draw the contours of the object.

The technique for the view from above is the same!

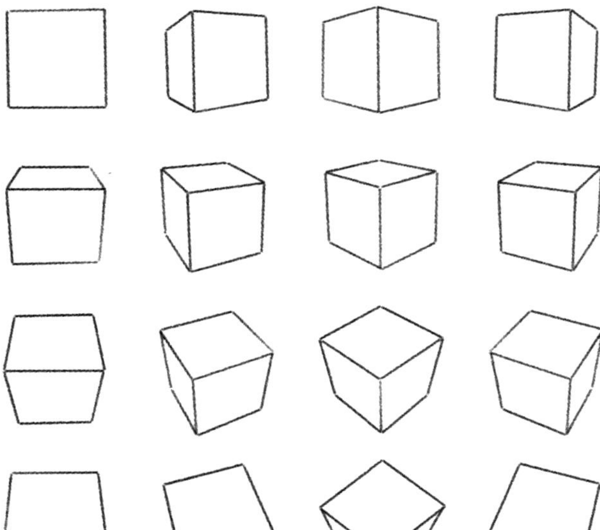

A good exercise to help you make progress with perspective is to draw as many cubes as possible, from all different angles.

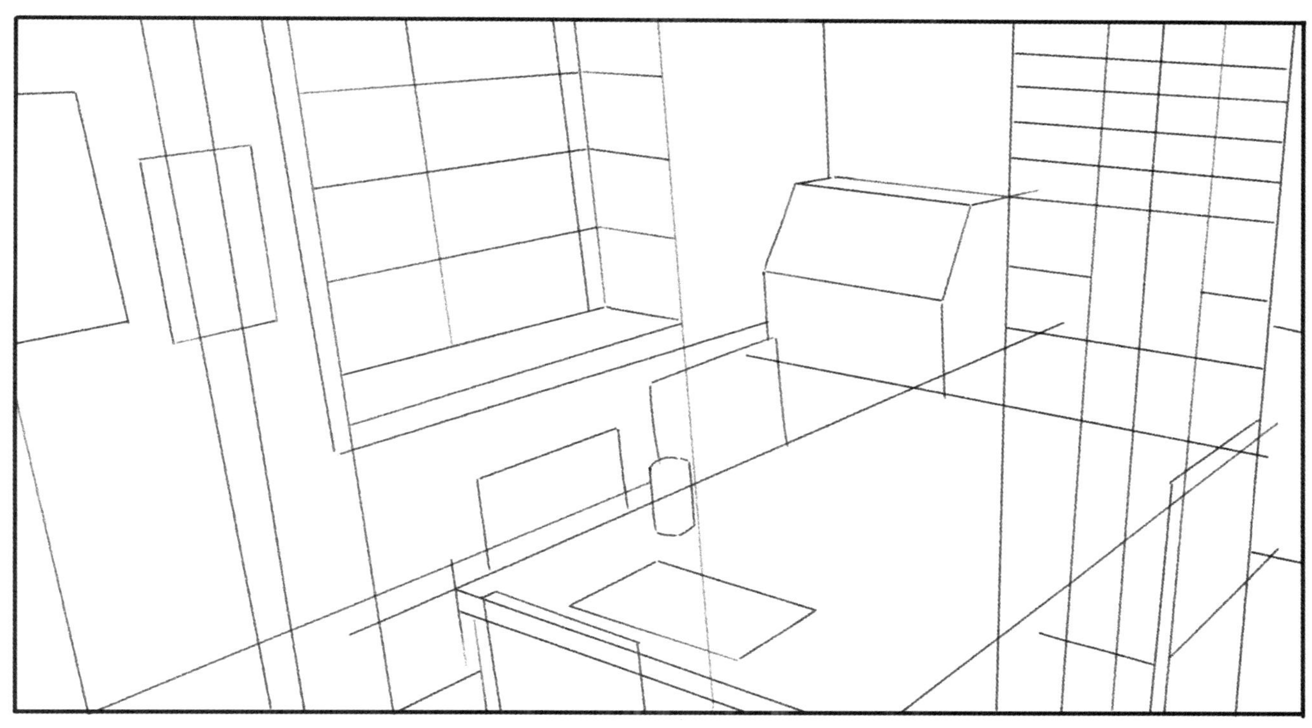

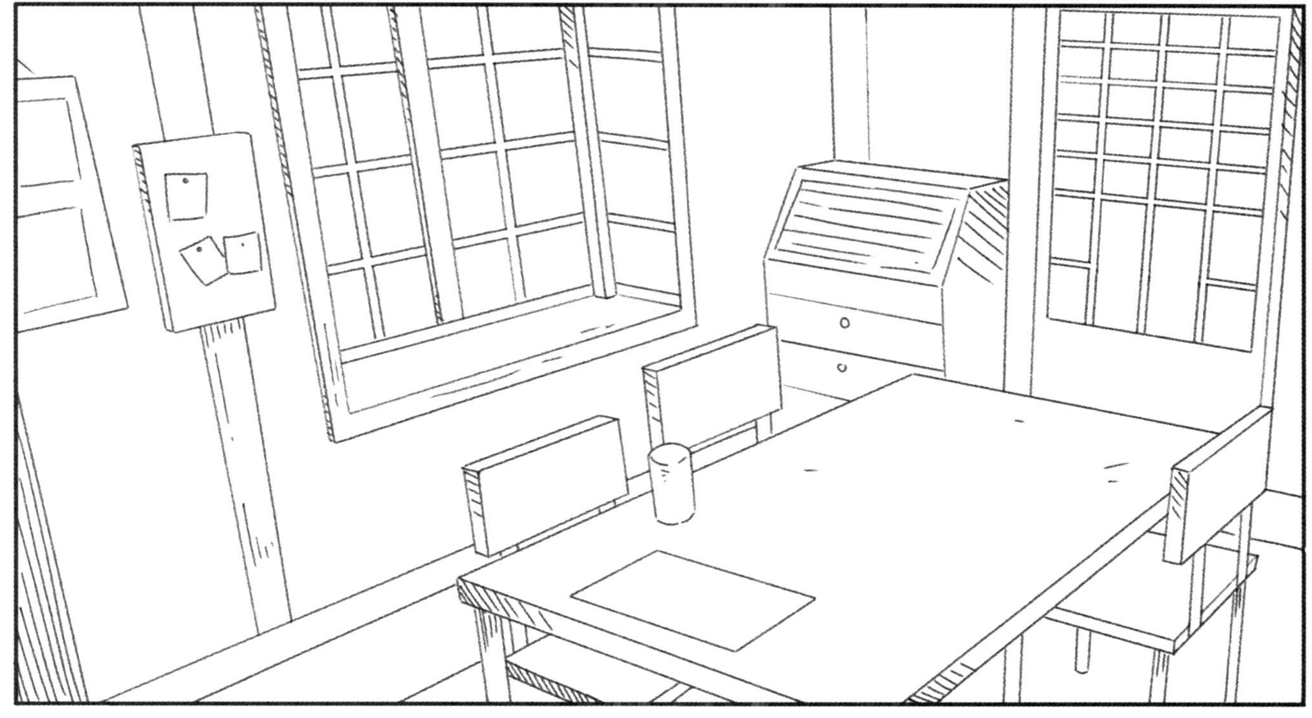

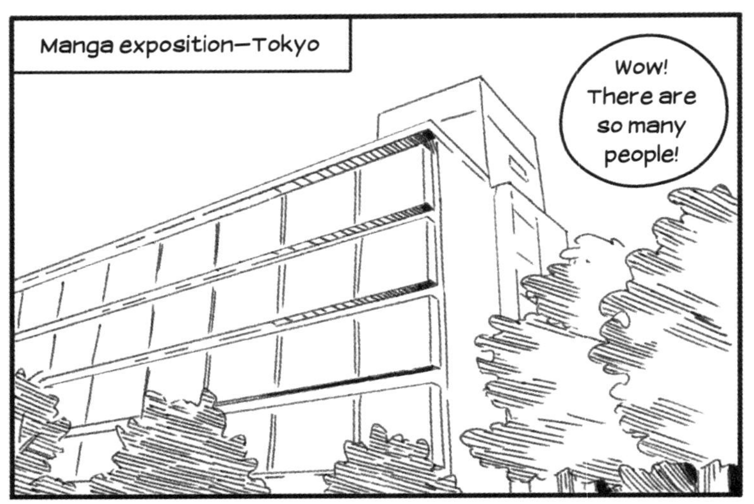
Manga exposition—Tokyo
Wow! There are so many people!

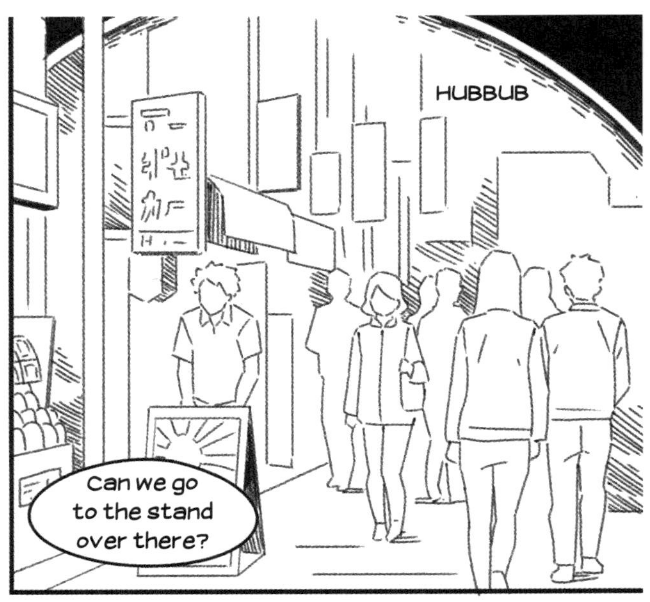
HUBBUB
Can we go to the stand over there?

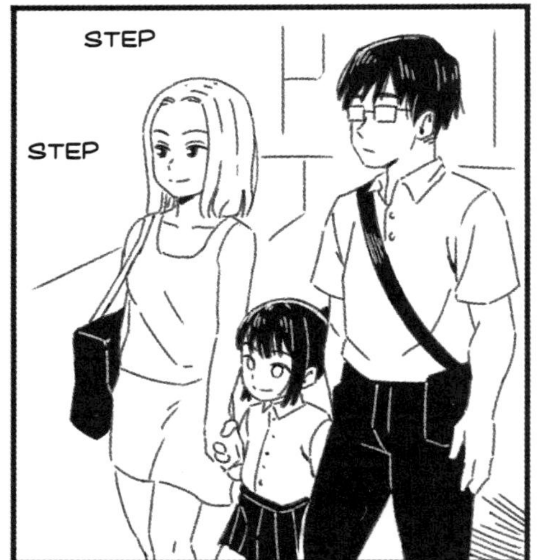
STEP
STEP

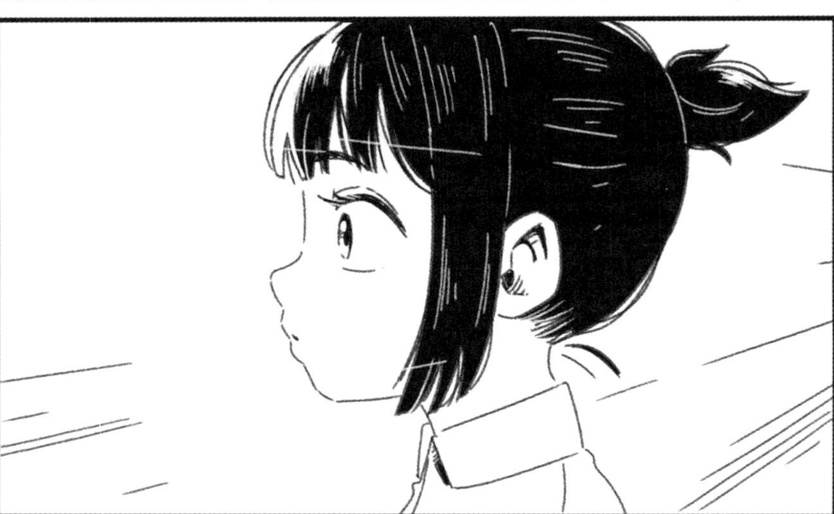

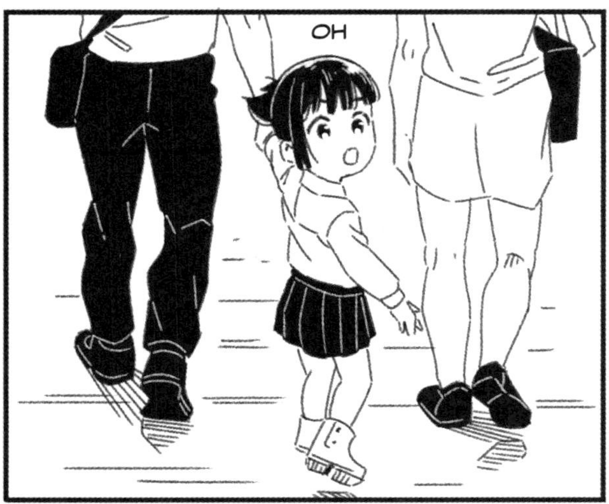
OH

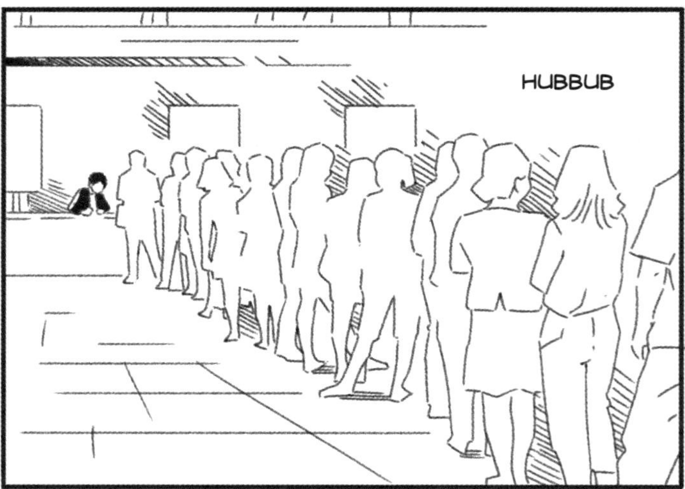
HUBBUB

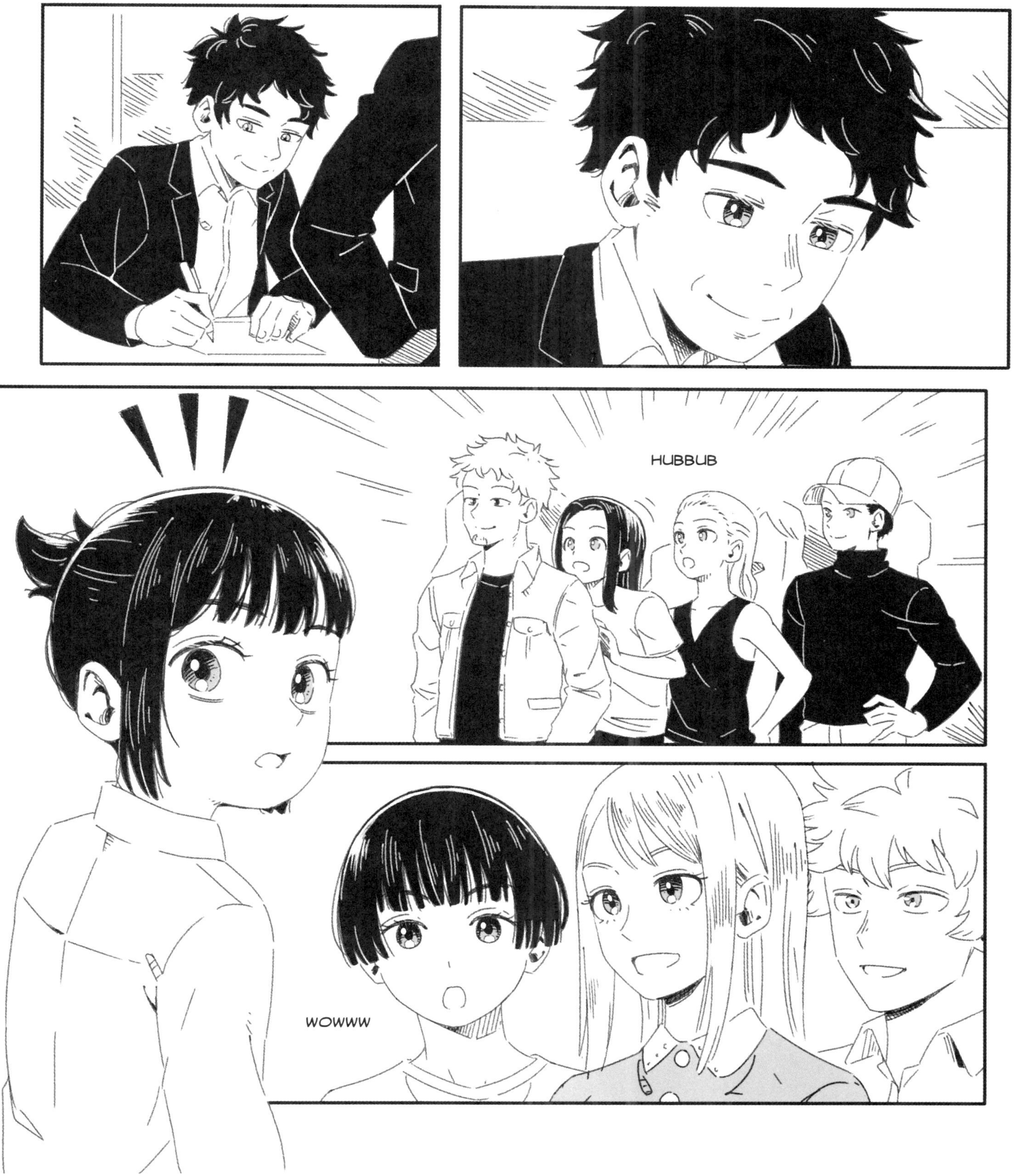

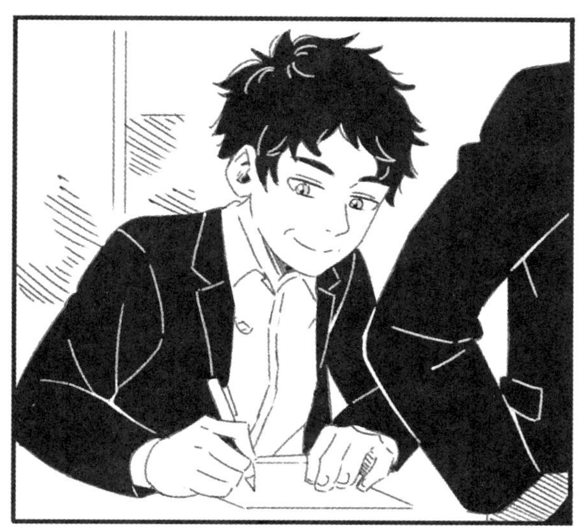

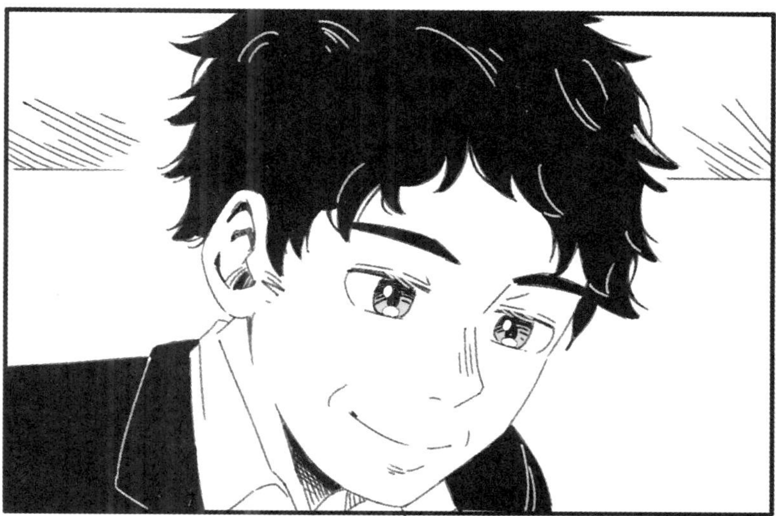
HUBBUB

WOWWW

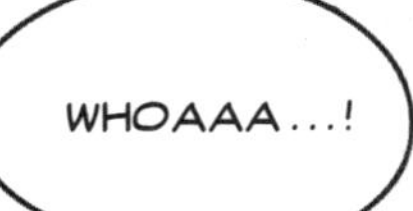

WHOAAA...!

You can get that famous just by drawing??

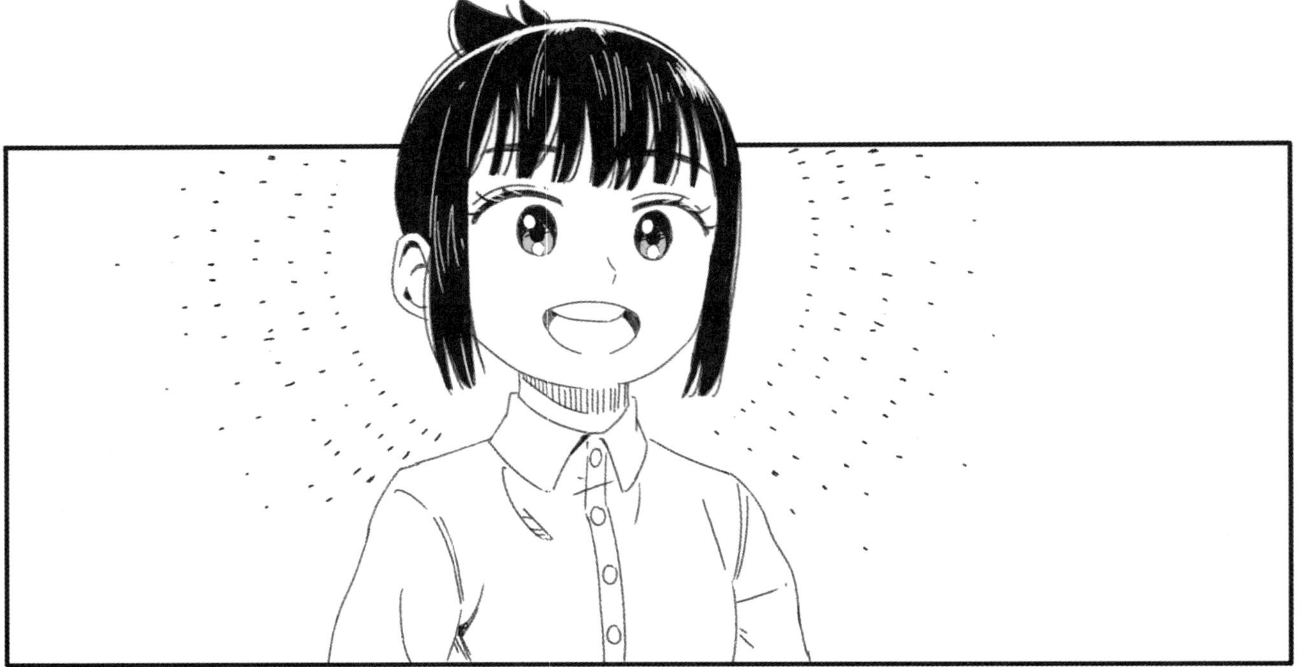

I've made up my mind!
I want to be like him!

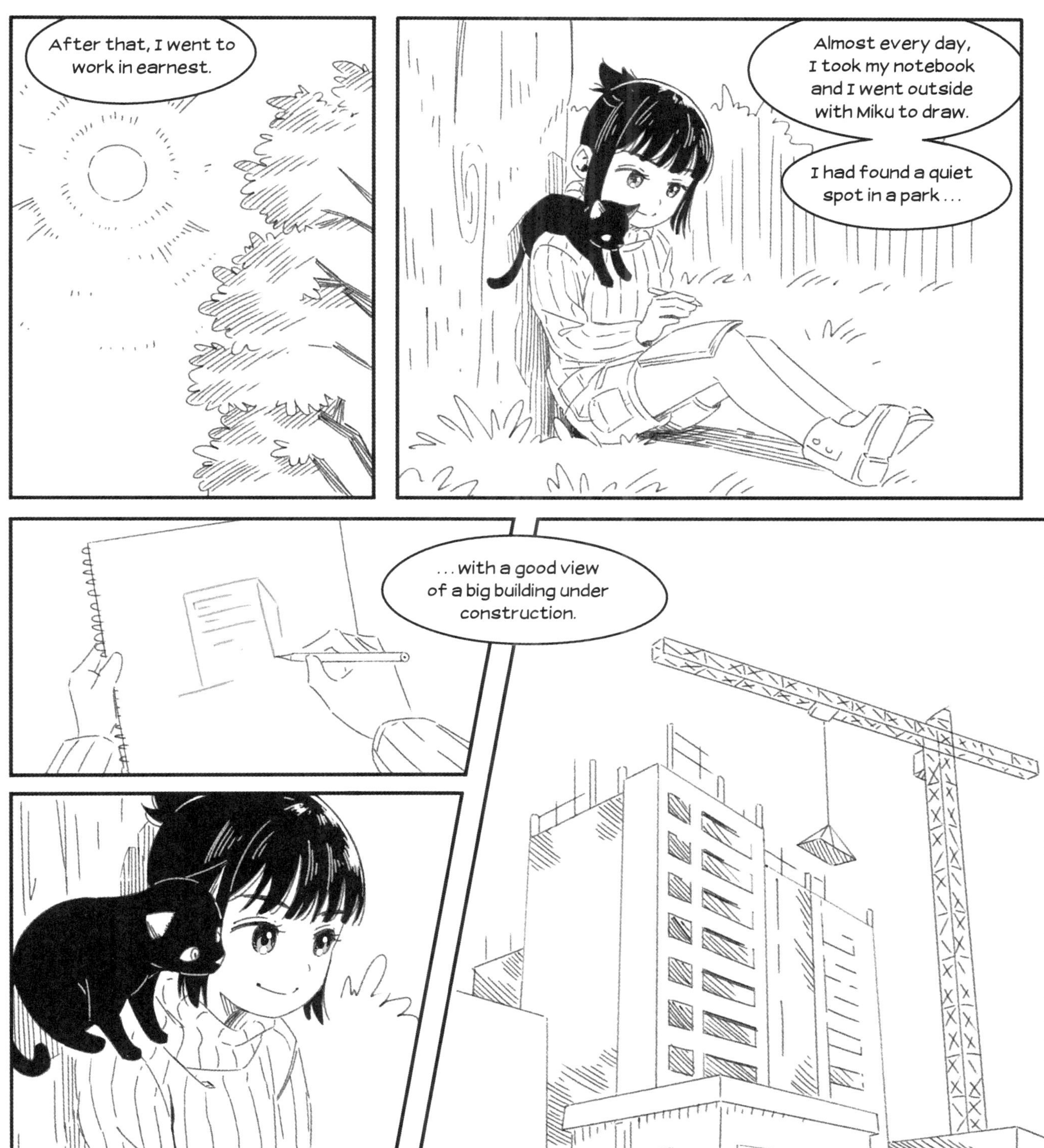
After that, I went to work in earnest.
Almost every day, I took my notebook and I went outside with Miku to draw.
I had found a quiet spot in a park . . .
. . . with a good view of a big building under construction.

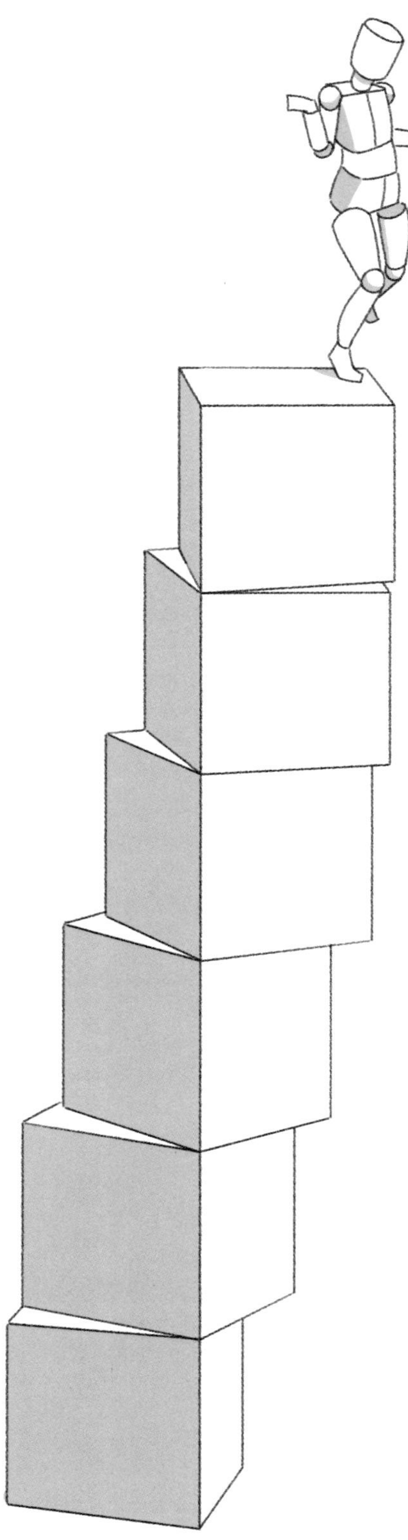

Just like a building, a drawing is constructed from the bottom to the top, from the framework to the finishing touches. Start with a solid framework before placing your bricks. Otherwise, everything might just collapse.

To put it more simply, you have to make a sketch before you start in on the actual drawing.

This is one of the most important rules: "Start with the global, then go to the details."

Respecting this rule will allow you to draw complex things, like the human body.

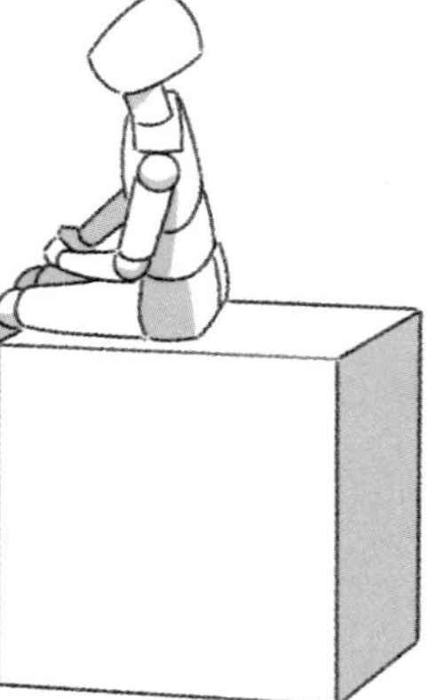

To define the proportions of the human body, we use some basic rules of thumb in our drawing. Use the head as your unit of measurement. This will make your life easier when you have to measure the different parts of the body.

On average, the human body is eight heads high.

The crotch separates the body into two equal parts.

When the arms are down along the length of the body, the wrists reach the level of the crotch.

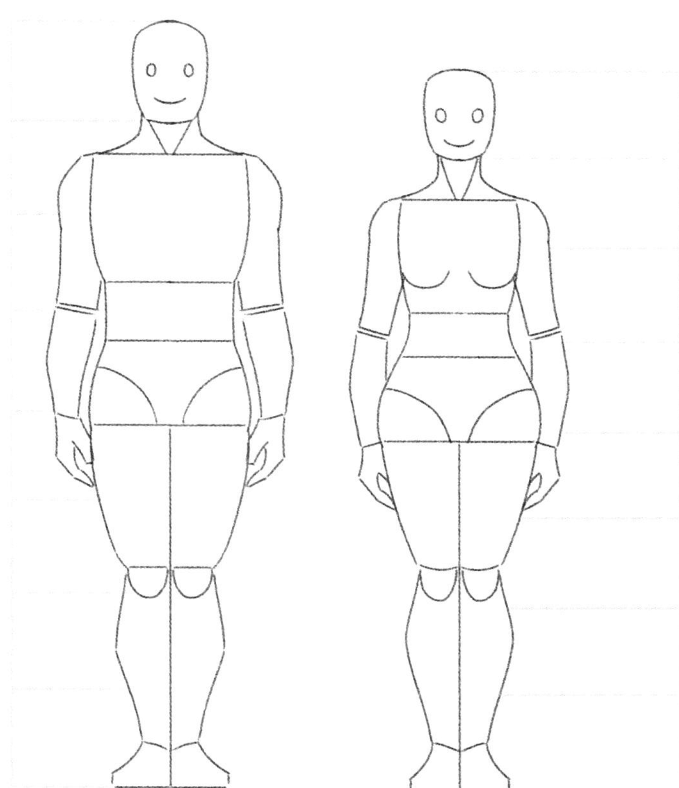

A woman's body follows the same rules as a man's body.
The positions are the same, but some of the ratios are different.
For instance, the pelvis will be wider than, or as wide as, the width of the shoulders.

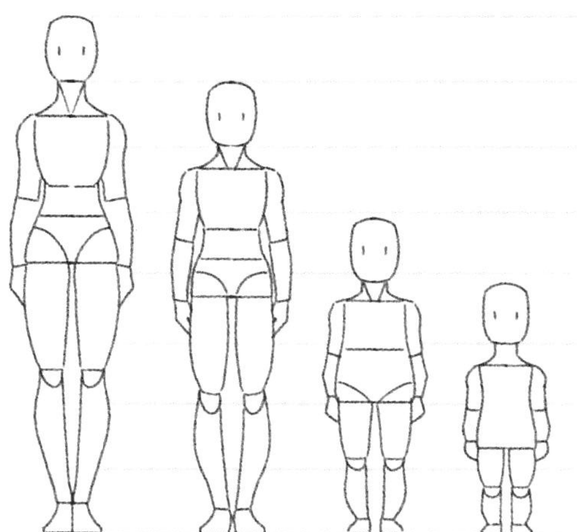

Proportions for a child: from four heads (young child) to seven heads (teenager).

The key is to simplify what you see into basic volumes. The human body is very complex, but when you simplify, it is easier to draw it.

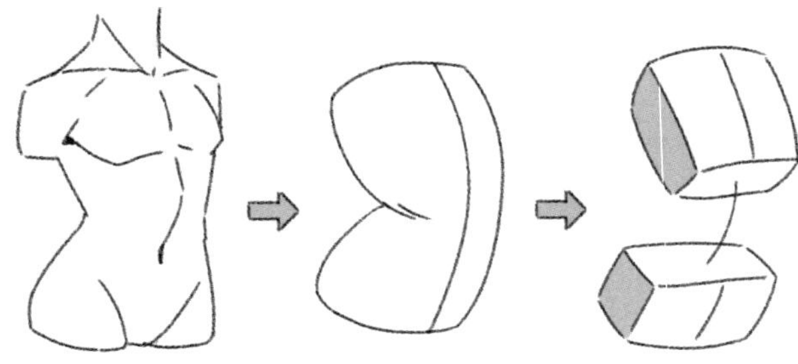

The first step is to simplify the torso.
It is represented by two boxes, one
for the rib cage and one for the hips.

Note that the upper box is much
taller, while the lower one is short.

Mastering this step will greatly simplify the
rest of the process. Train yourself to draw
the two boxes from different perspectives.

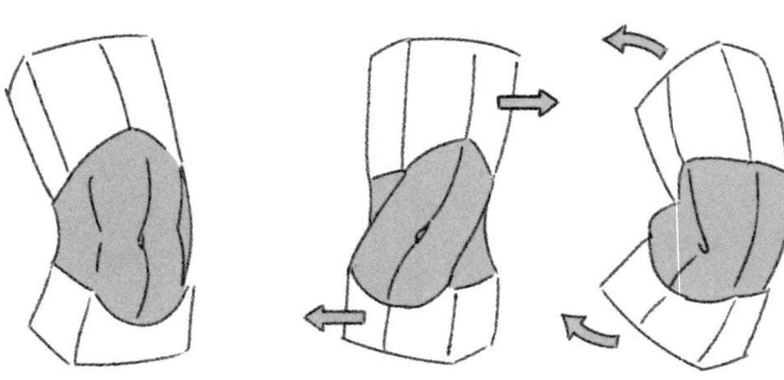
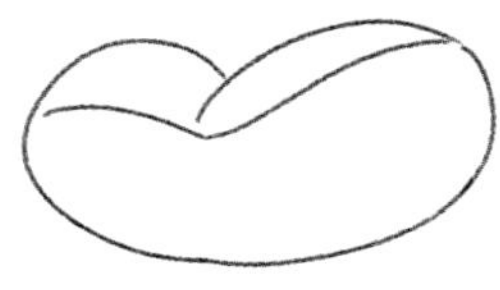
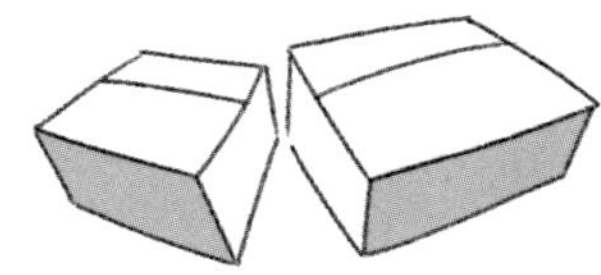

These two shapes are connected to
each other by a soft section: the stomach.
You can play with the different shapes by making
them turn in different directions to create twists
and compressions, just like on a real body.

Practice drawing the simplified torso
from a variety of positions and perspectives;
this will make what follows much easier.

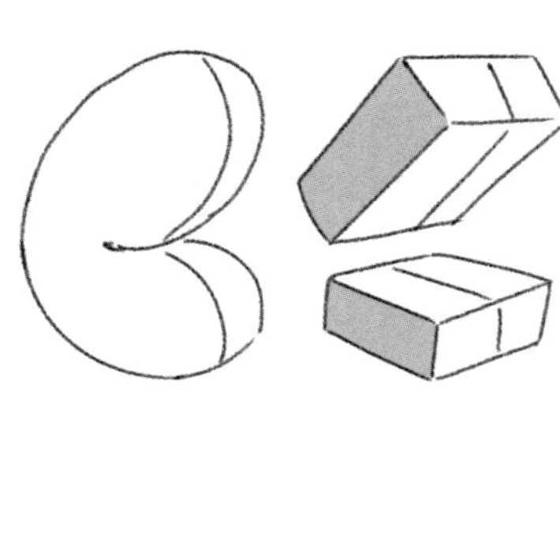
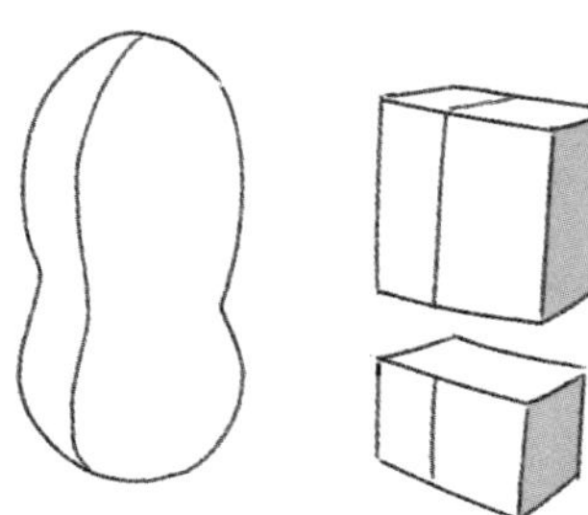
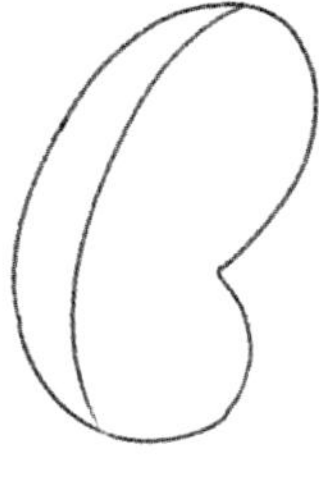
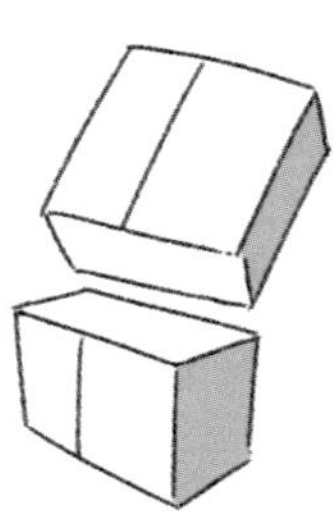

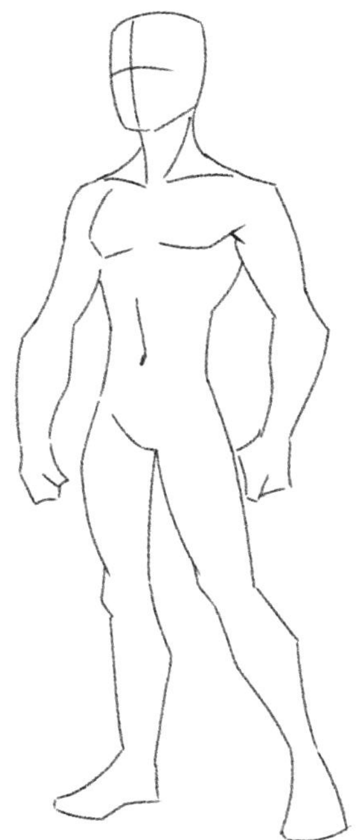
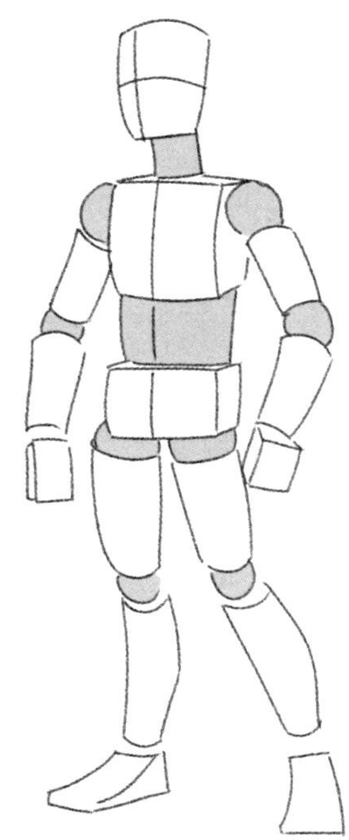

The arms and legs will be simplified into two cylindrical shapes connected to each other by a sphere (representing the elbows and the knees).

The hands, feet, and head are simplified to a simple box. This book devotes a section to them later on (see p. 57).

By varying the proportions of your shapes, you will produce a wide range of possibilities for your characters.

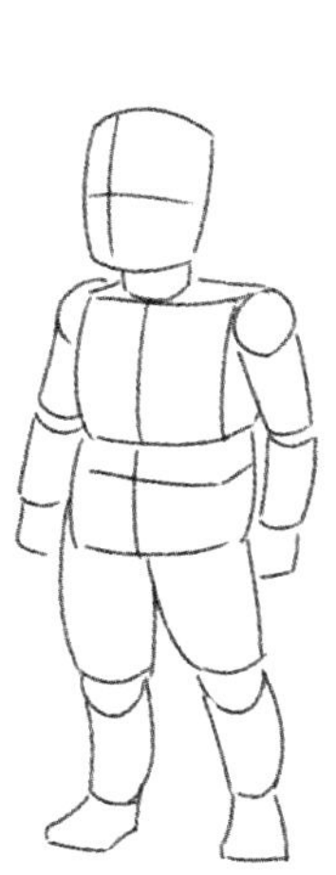
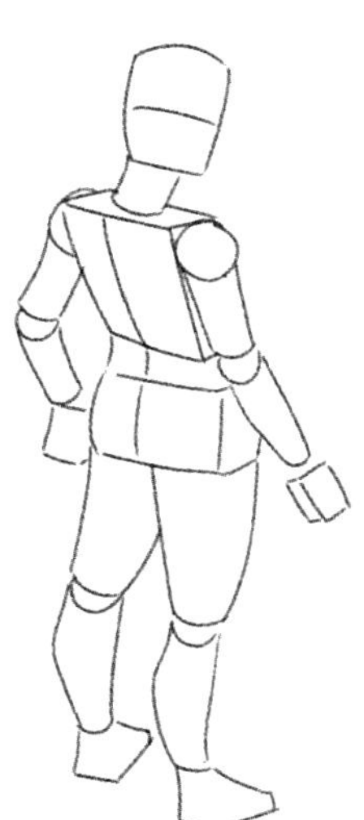
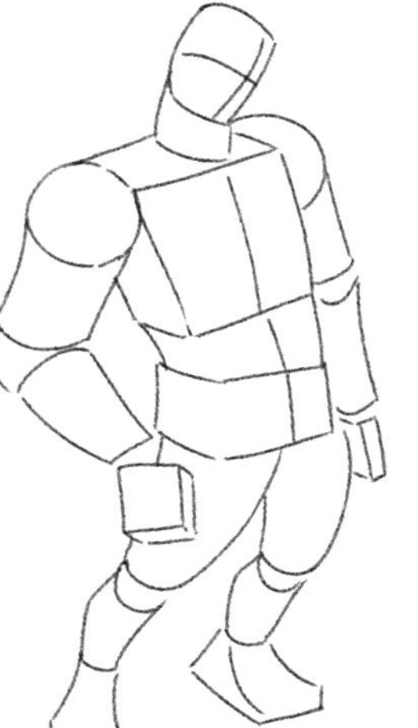
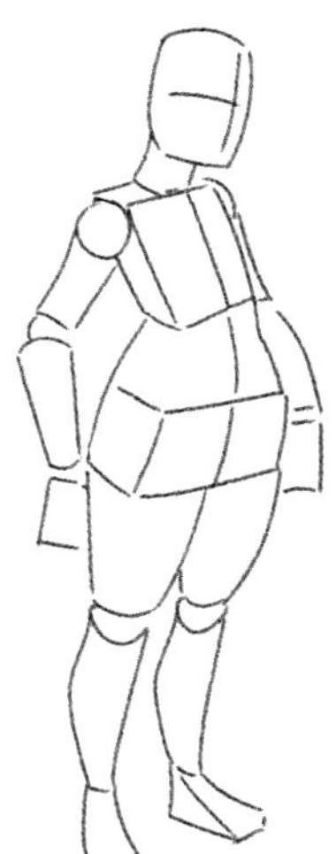

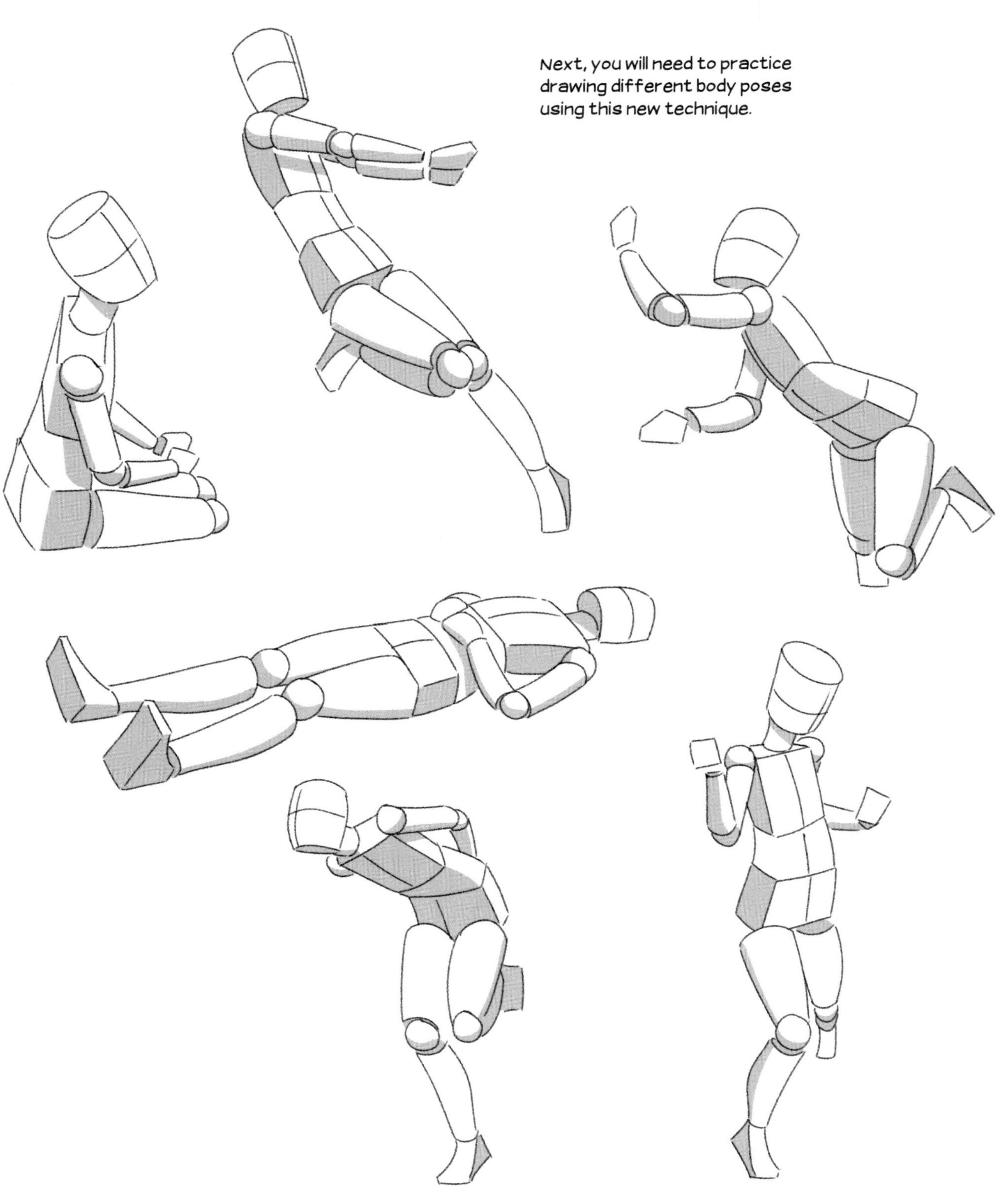

Next, you will need to practice
drawing different body poses
using this new technique.

20

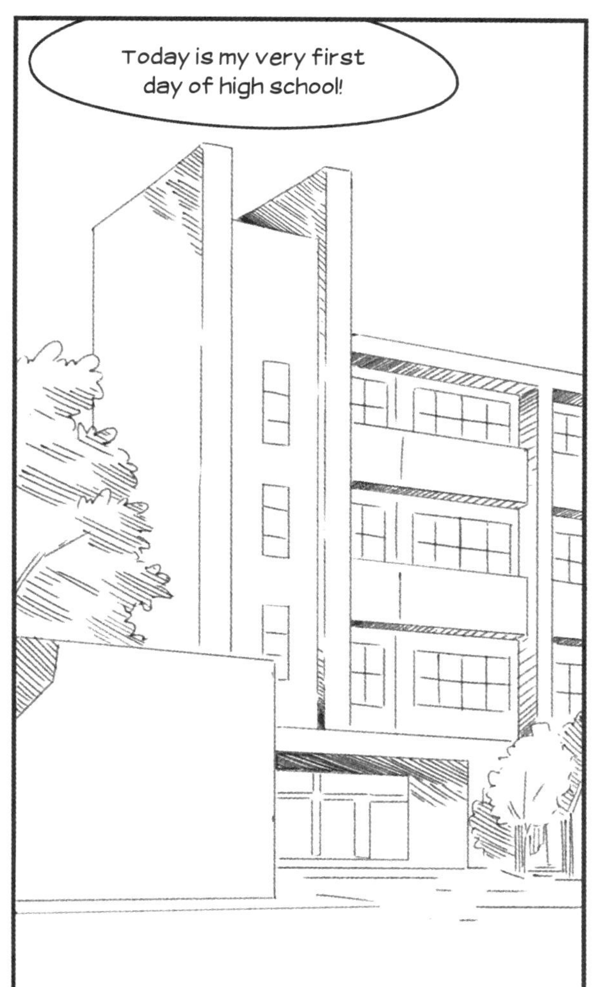

Today is my very first day of high school!

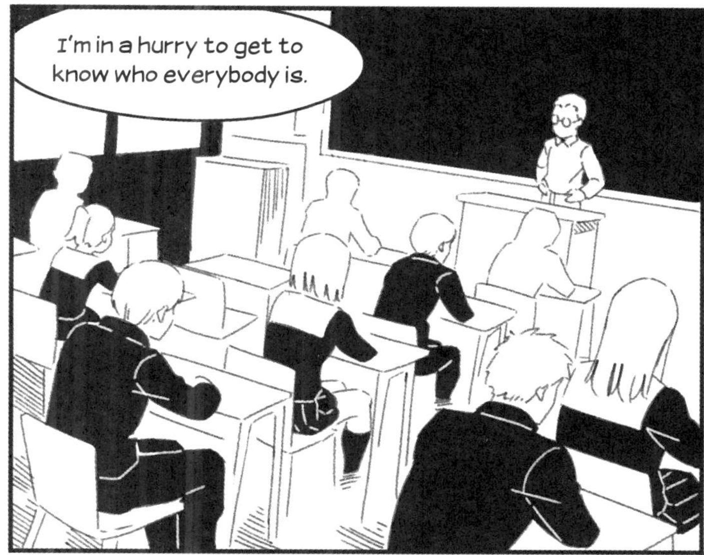

I'm in a hurry to get to know who everybody is.

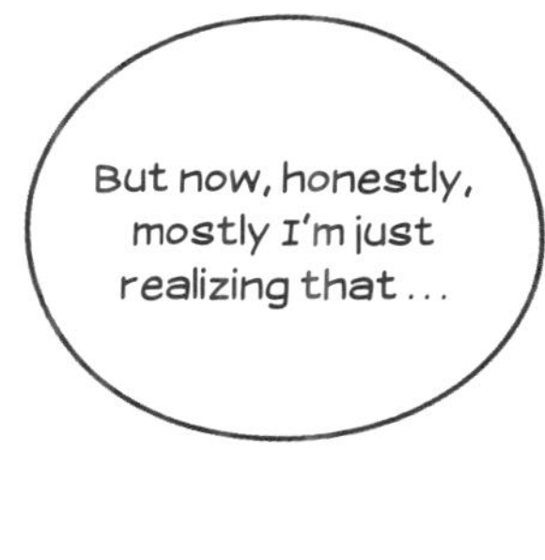

But now, honestly, mostly I'm just realizing that...

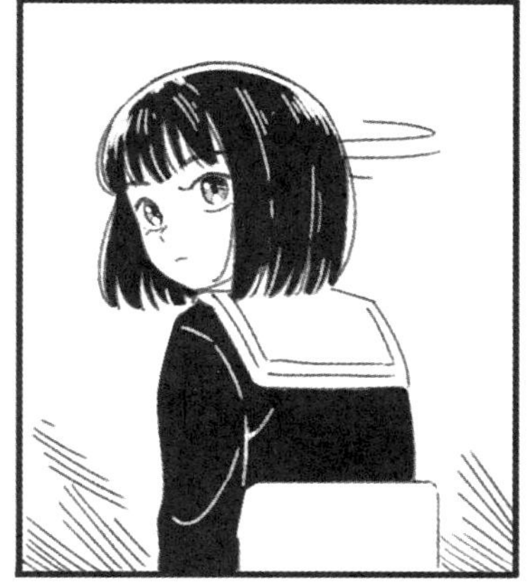

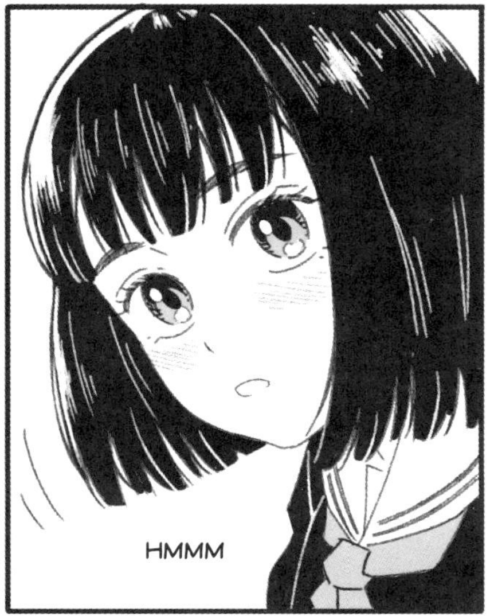

HMMM

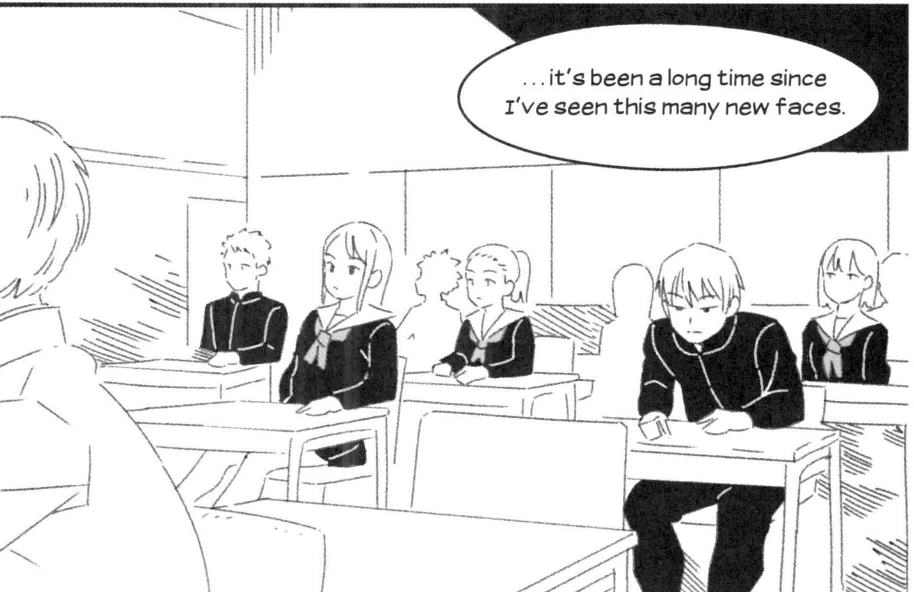

...it's been a long time since I've seen this many new faces.

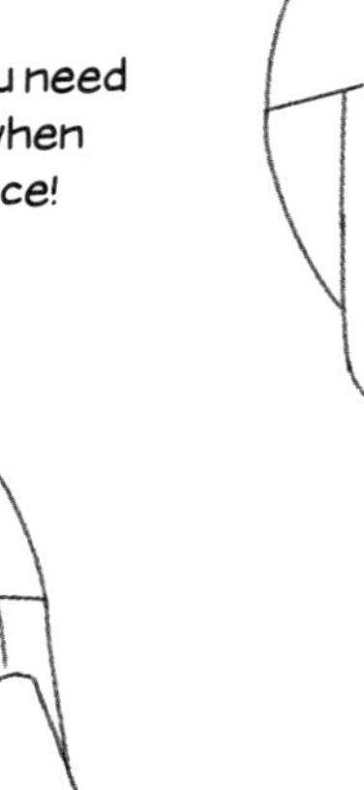

If there is one element that you need to take particular care with when drawing a person, it's the face!

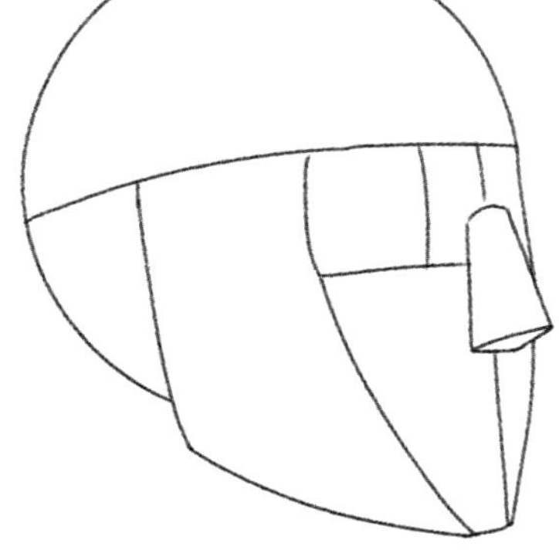

Because we are social beings, the face is the first thing we look at on a person. And it's the same thing with a drawing.

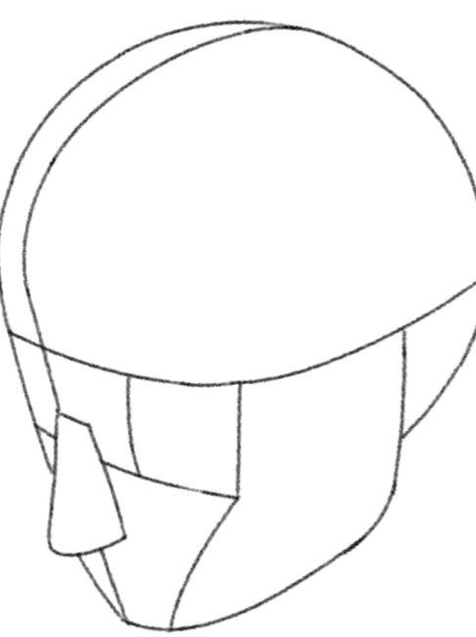

The face is what gives us our individual character, and so there are all kinds of different faces.

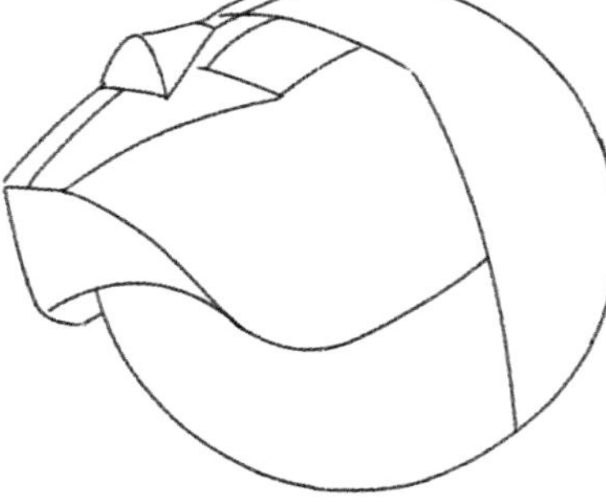

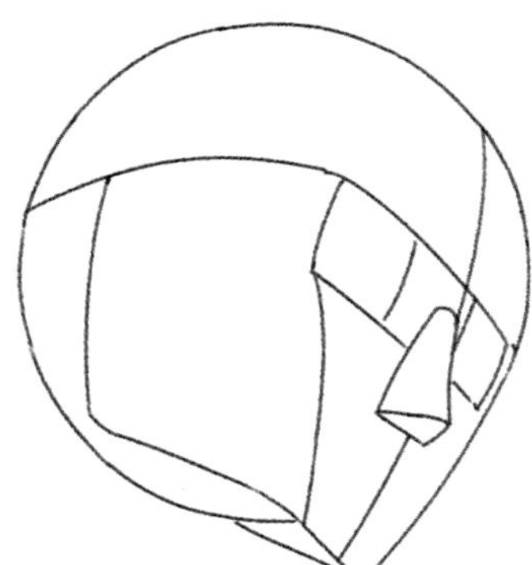

Fortunately for us, the structure almost always stays the same.

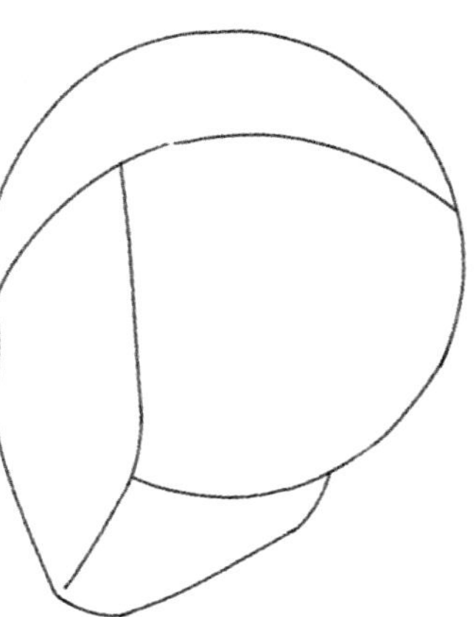

22

To be able to draw the head from every angle, you first have to understand its basic structure. Once that has been correctly established, it becomes much easier to add the elements of the face in the right place.

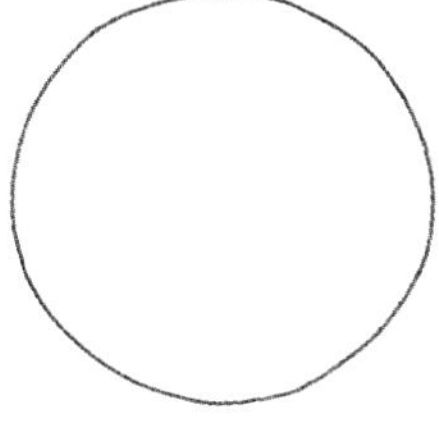

Draw a circle for the skull.

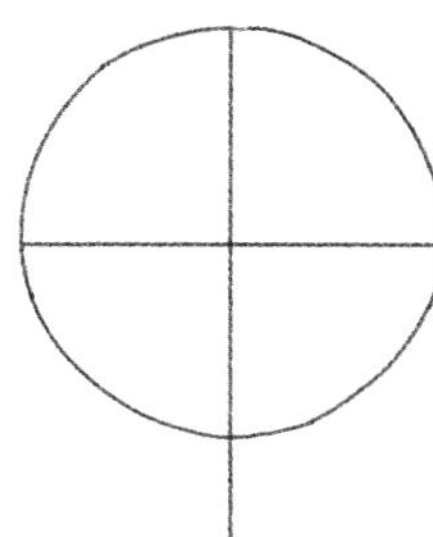

Draw a horizontal line for the line of the eyebrows and a vertical line for the face's axis of symmetry.

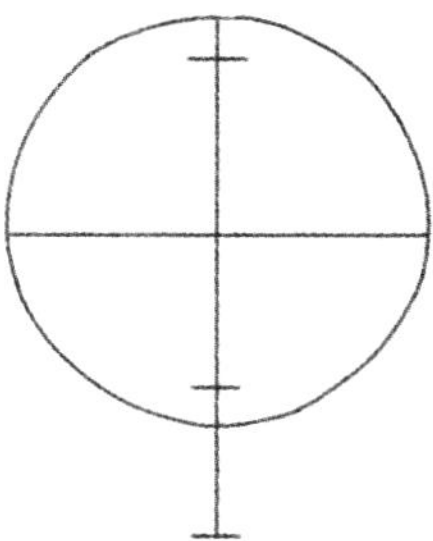

Divide the face into three sections. The distance from the hairline to the eyebrow line is the same as the distance from the eyebrow line to the base of the nose. The little line at the bottom indicates the chin.

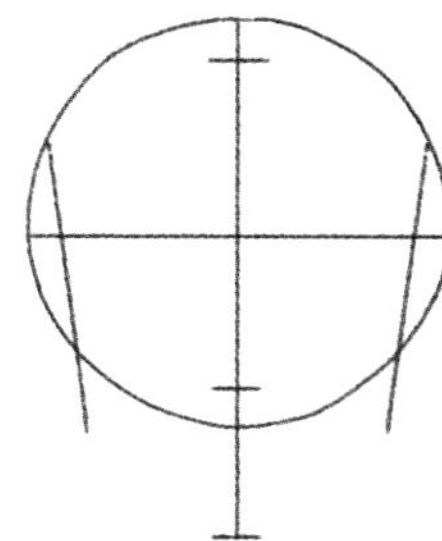

Cut off the edges of the circle, because the skull is flat at the temples. Extend these two lines to form the beginning of the jaw.

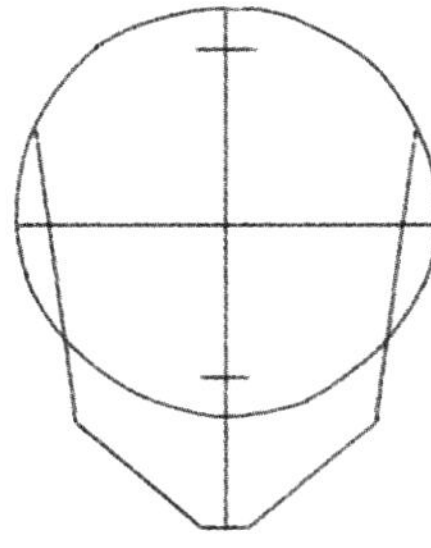

Connect the jaw to the chin. The jaw starts a little below the line of the base of the nose.

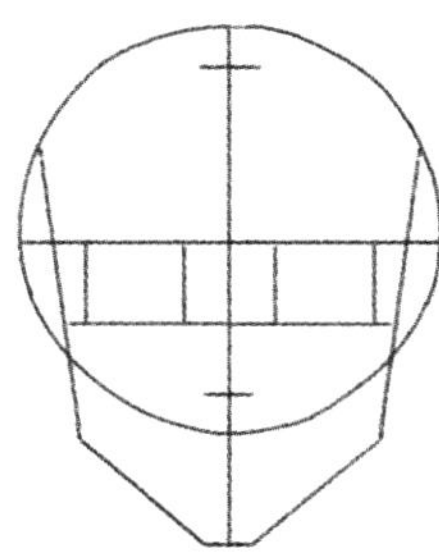

Draw a line halfway between the eyebrow line and the line for the base of the nose. Draw squares as reference marks for the eyes.

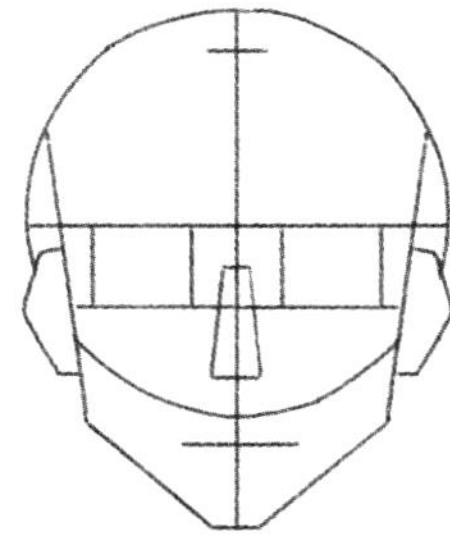

The mouth is situated between the line for the base of the nose and the chin line. Add a shape for the nose.

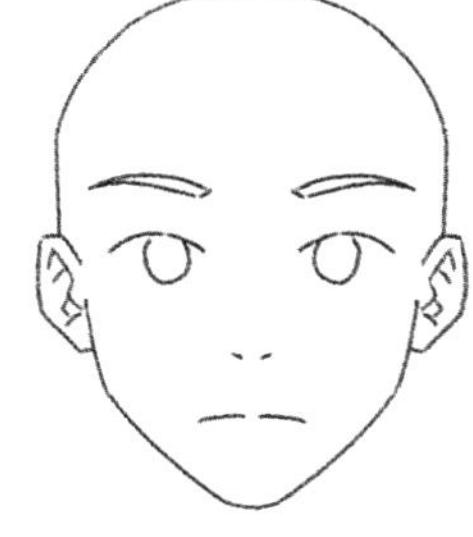

And there you have a face! You can draw two shapes for the ears. They are positioned between the nose and the eyebrows.

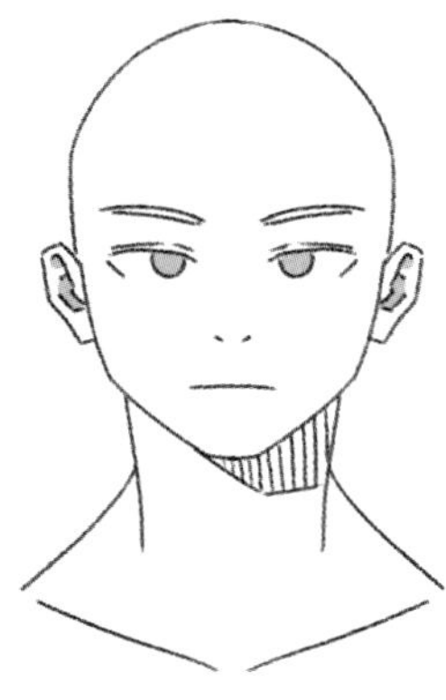

For a more masculine face, you can draw a wider chin and jaw.

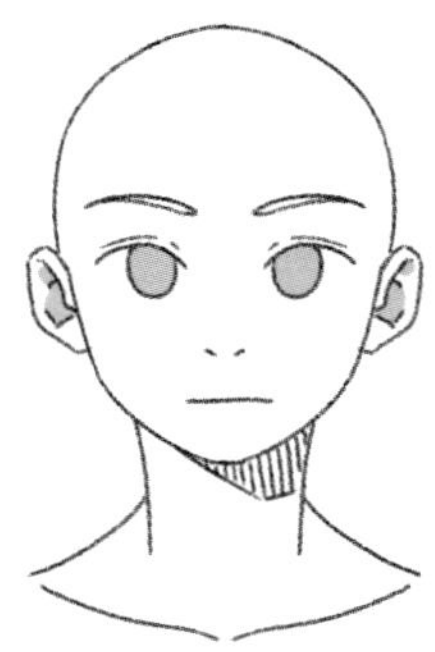

For a more feminine face, draw a smaller nose, narrower jaw, and bigger eyes.

You get different kinds of faces by varying the size of the three sections and the proportions. Big jaw, small eyes, huge nose, narrow forehead . . . anything is possible.

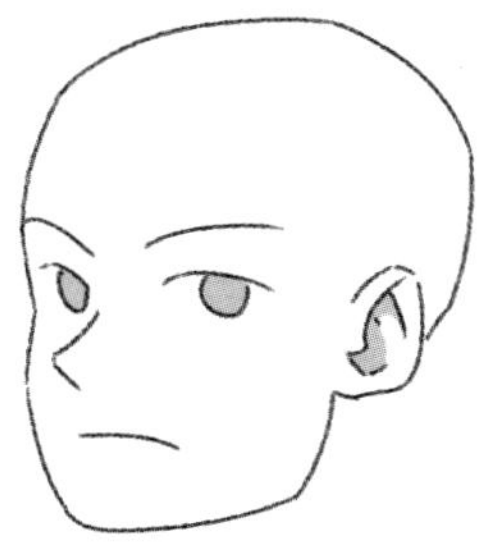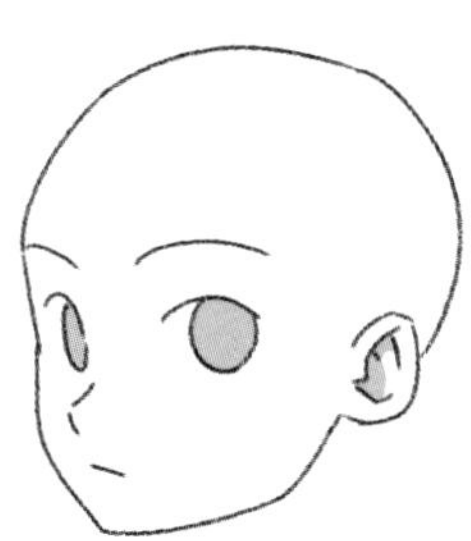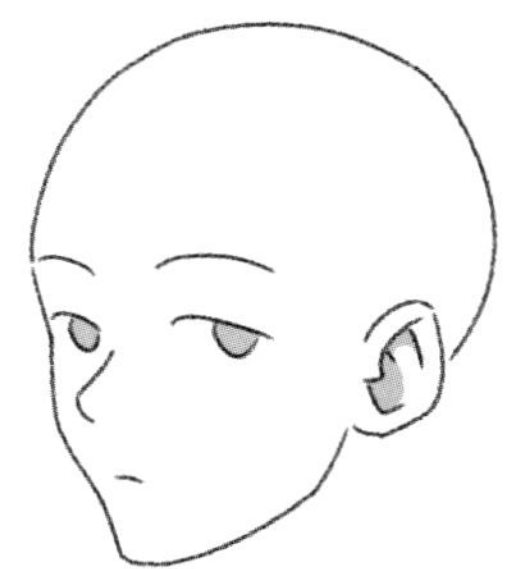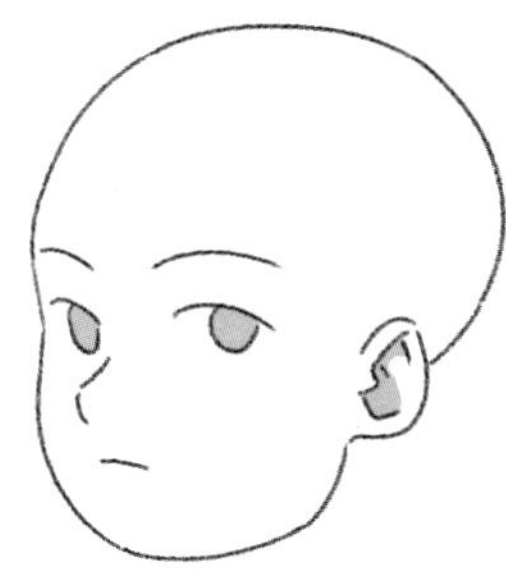

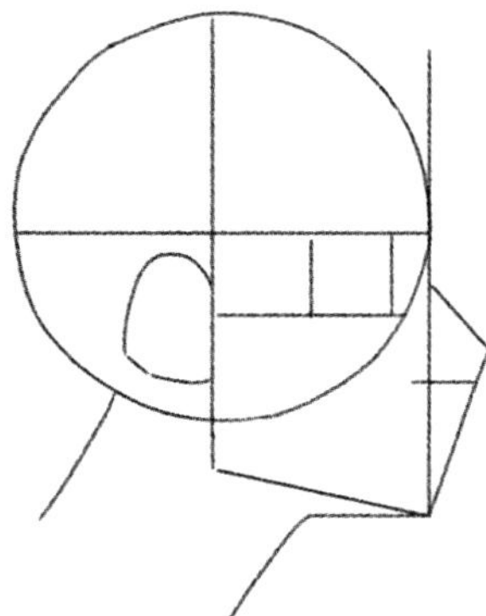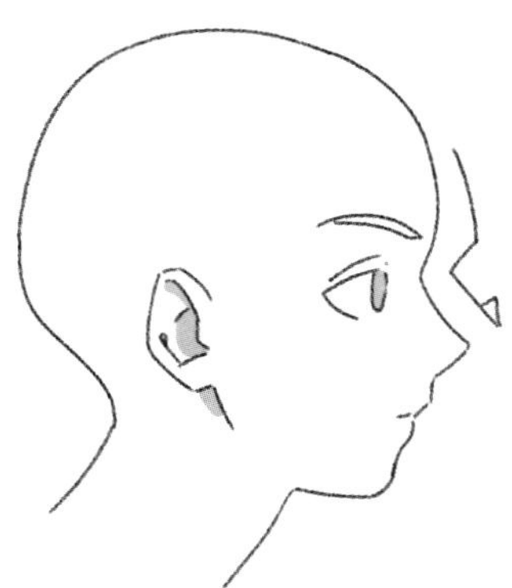

In a side view of a face, the line marking the sections is placed on one side of the face and the jawline faces us.

In profile, the eyes become triangles.

There is a small gap between the eyebrows and the beginning of the nose.

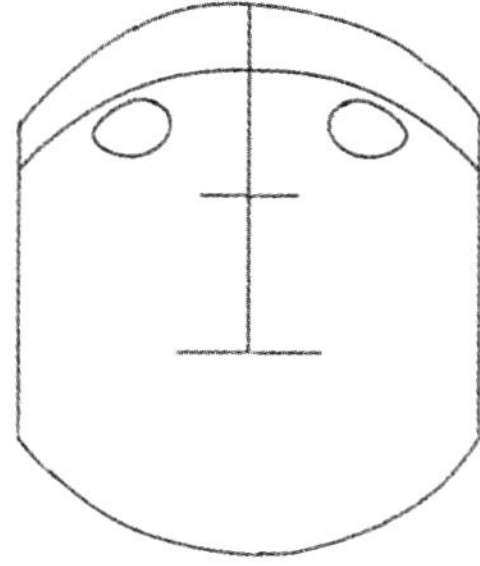 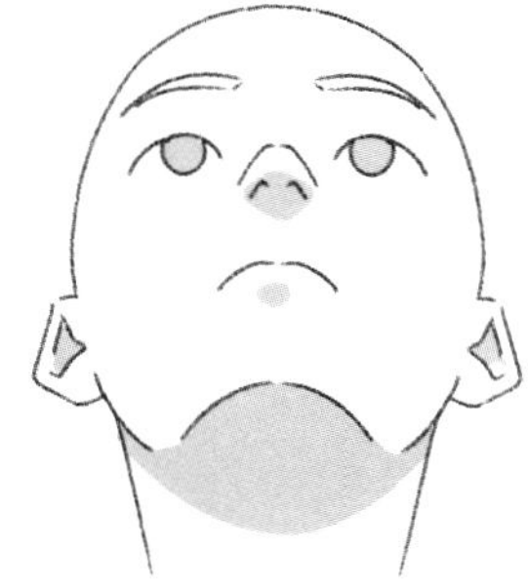

The rules of perspective
also apply to the face!

In a face seen from below,
the first section (from the chin
to the nose) can seem to be
longer than the last two.

The bottom of the
nose forms a triangle.

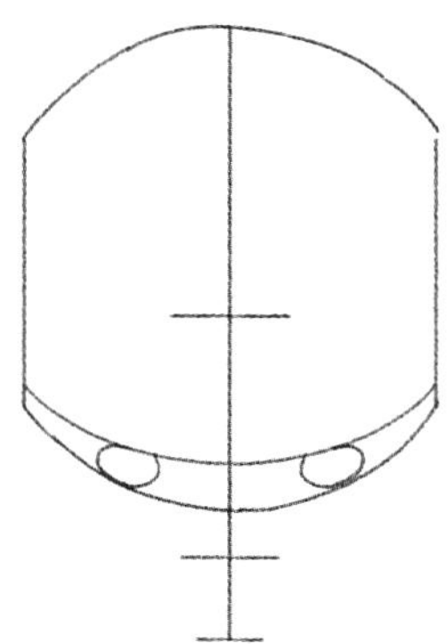 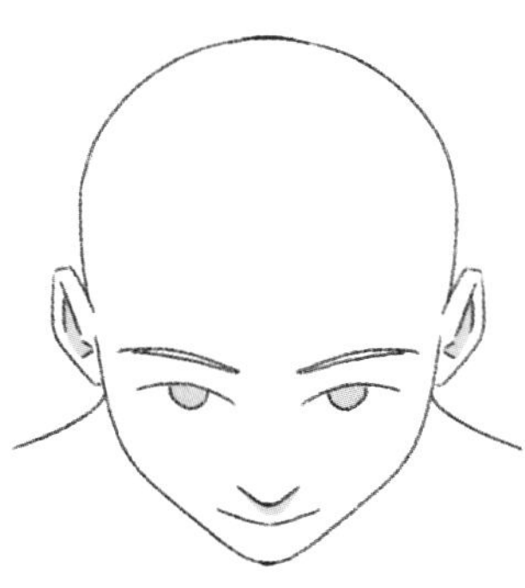

In a face seen from above, it is
the other way around. Now it is the
forehead that seems to be longer.

You can now have fun drawing faces looking in lots of different directions.

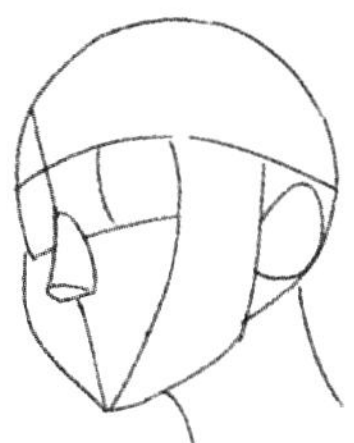 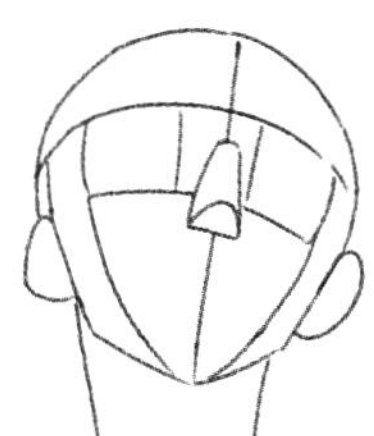 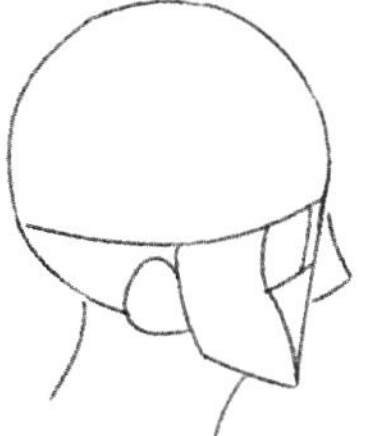 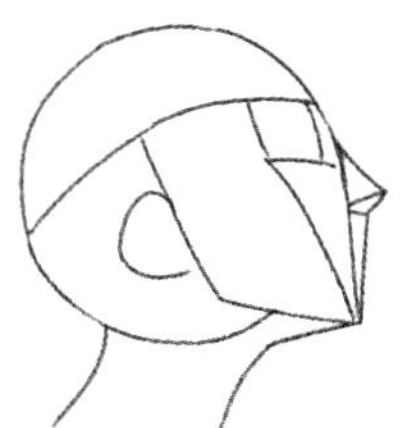 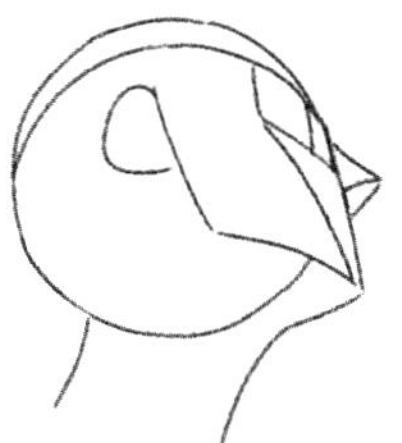

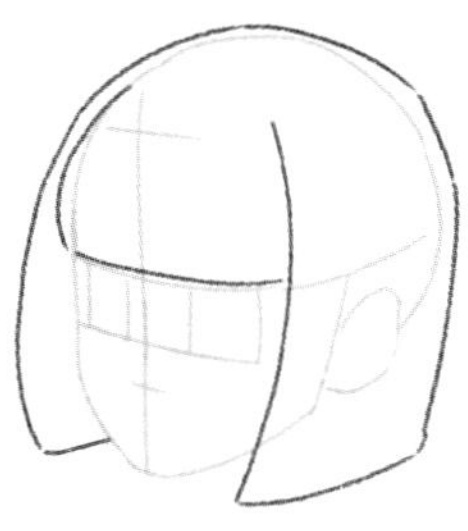

Let's think of the hair as a single mass, made up of one whole shape. Think of an overall 3D shape for it. It doesn't matter what kind of hair you want to draw; the idea is to think of it as a single shape.

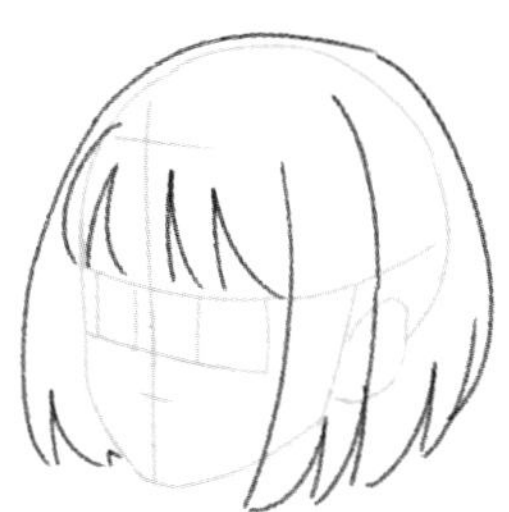

Once you have defined the overall shape of the hair, separate it out into several different portions to give it volume and depth.

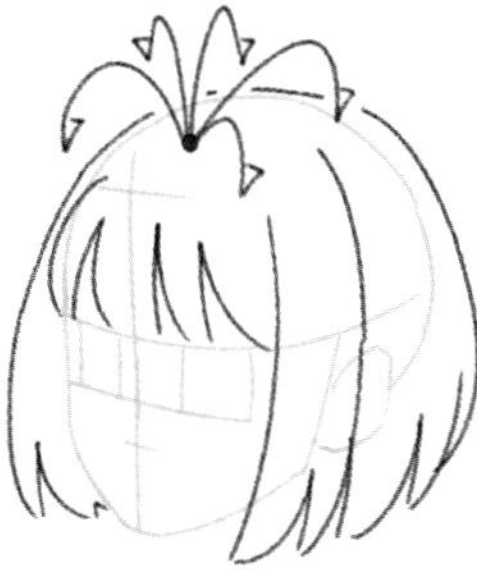

Then you can draw more detailed strands, starting at the root line. Its position varies from person to person, depending on their haircut.

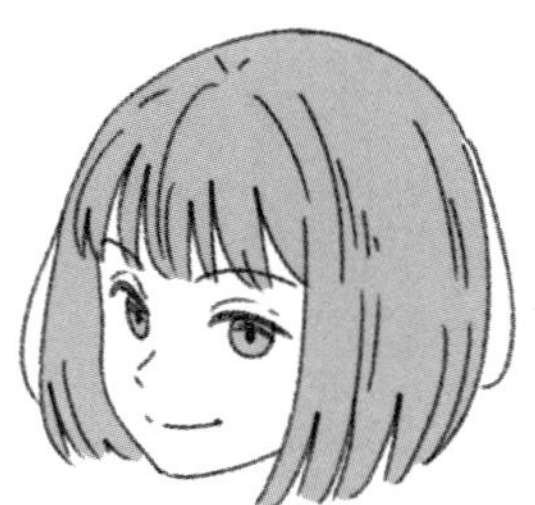

And here you have a beautiful head of hair!

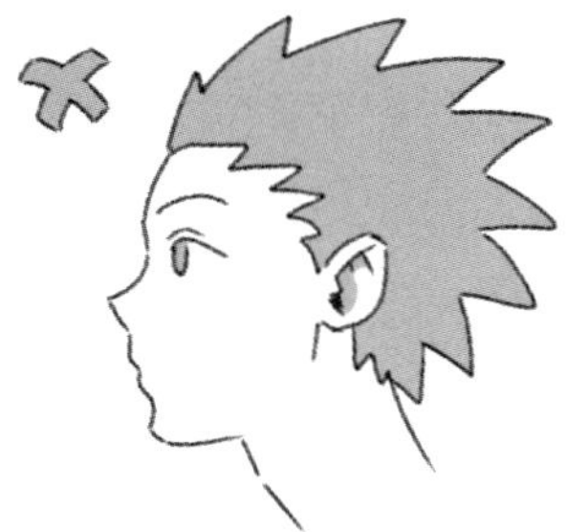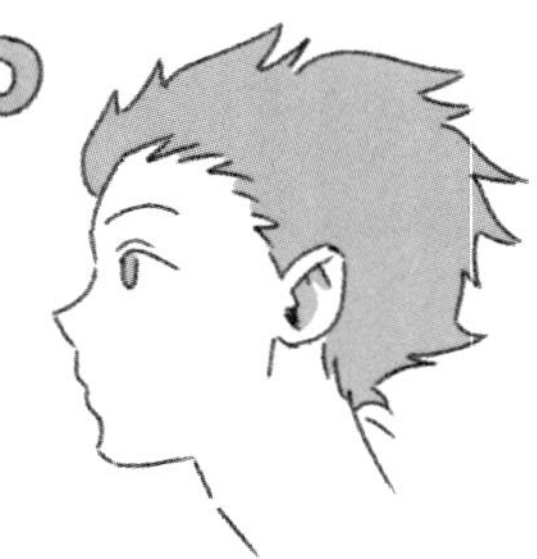

To create an interesting shape for the hair, play with the size of the different tufts. Instead of showing them all as being the same size, draw a small one, then a medium one, then a large one. This will give you a much more dynamic hairdo!

Play with the shapes and the position of the root of the hair to create all kinds of different haircuts: curly, smooth, short, long ... etc.

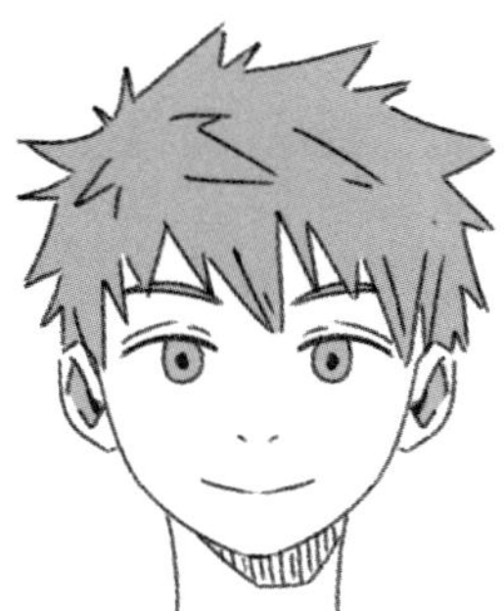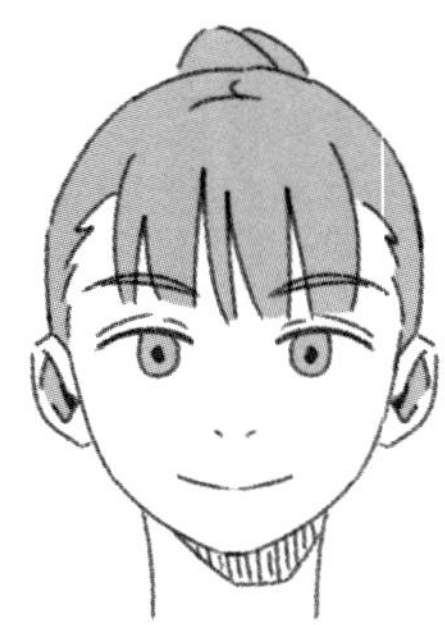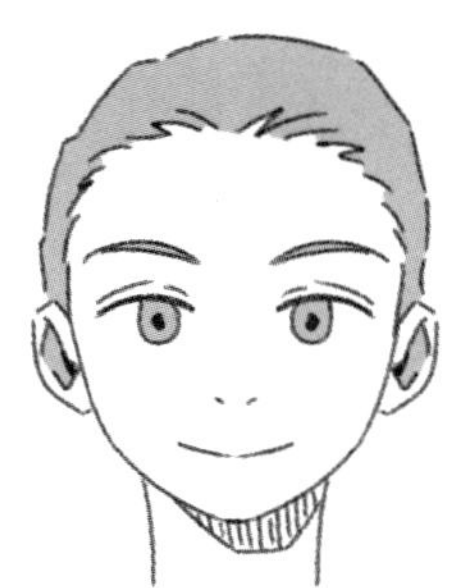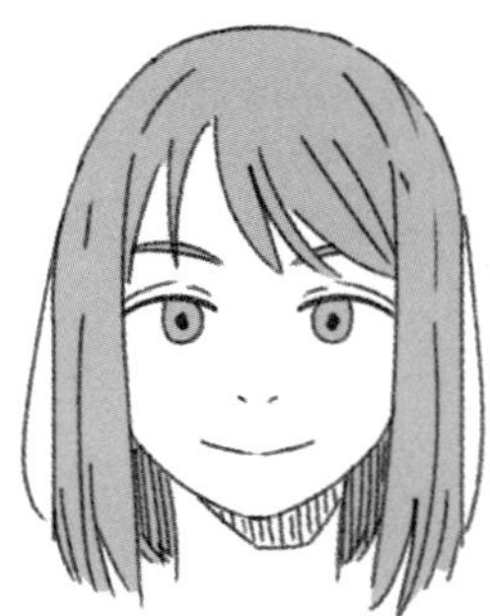

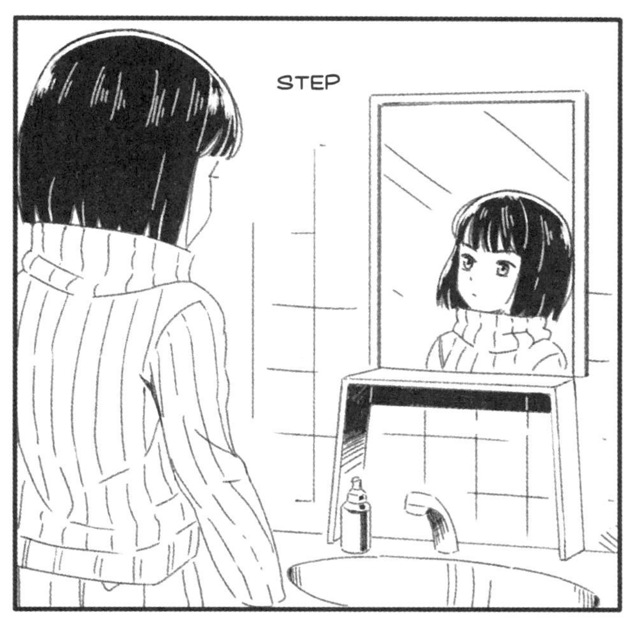

STEP

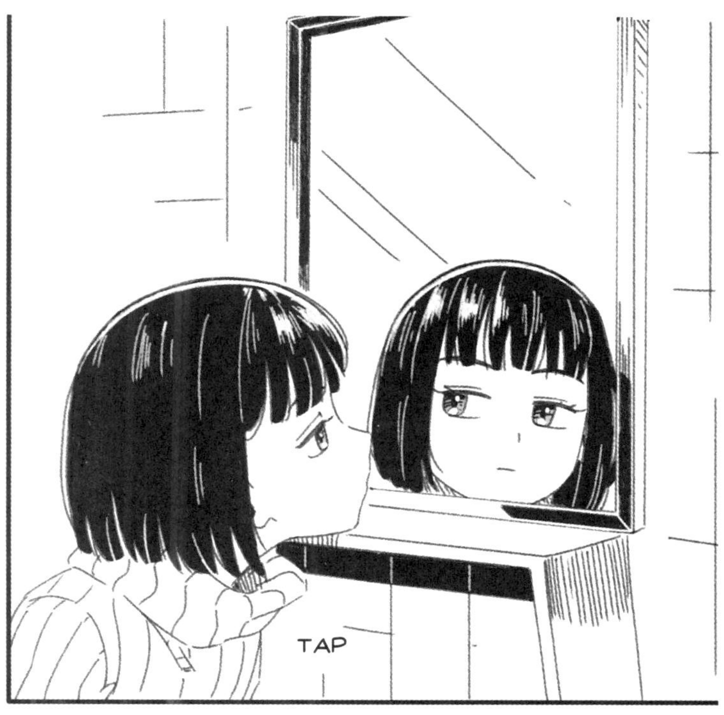

TAP

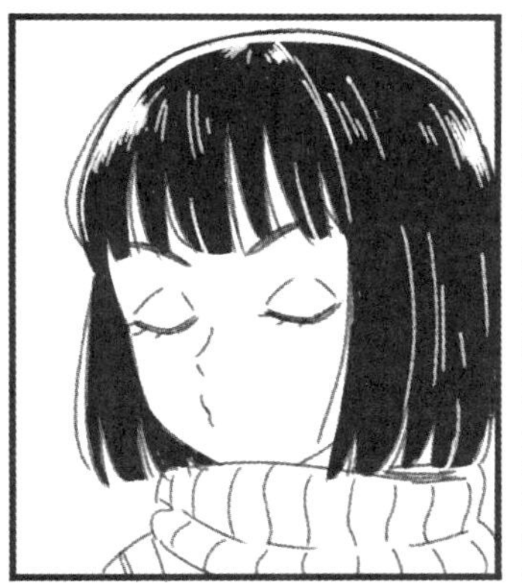

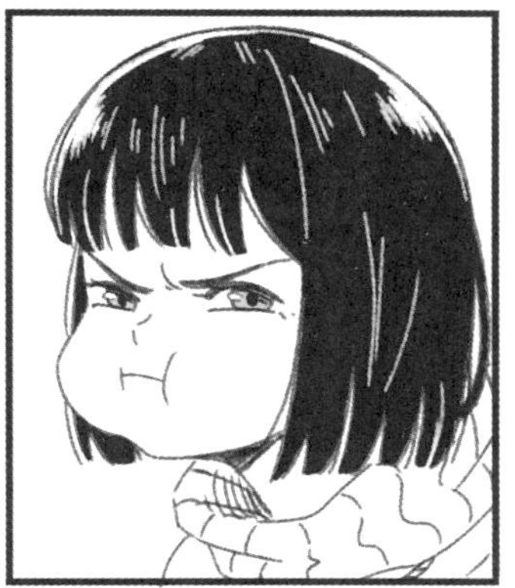

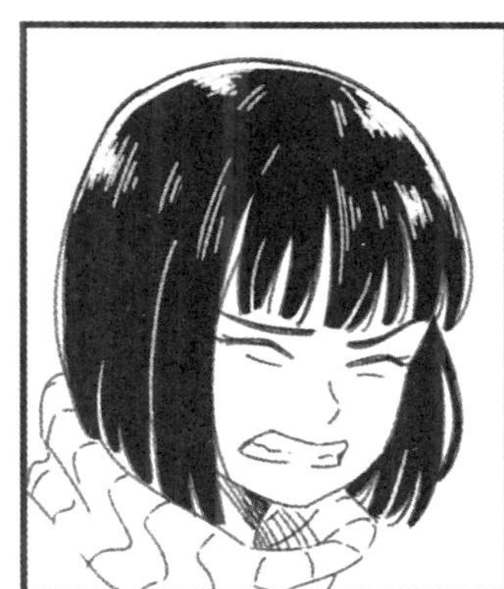

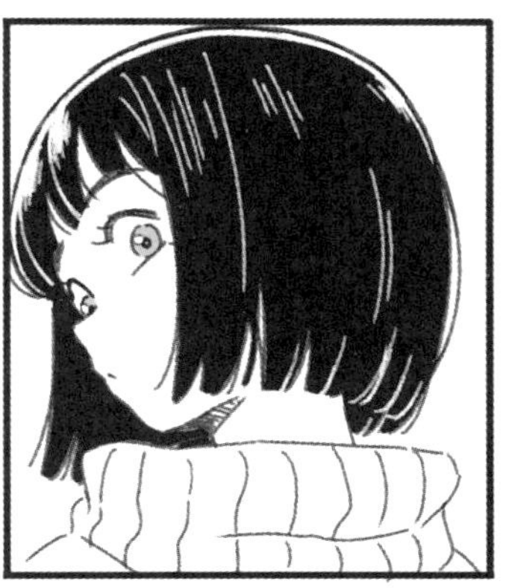

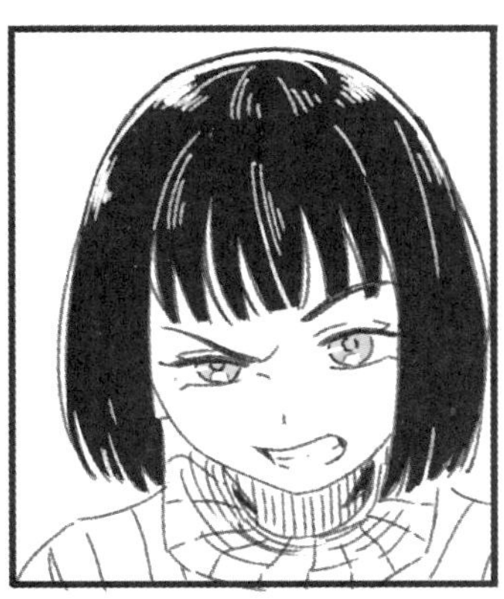

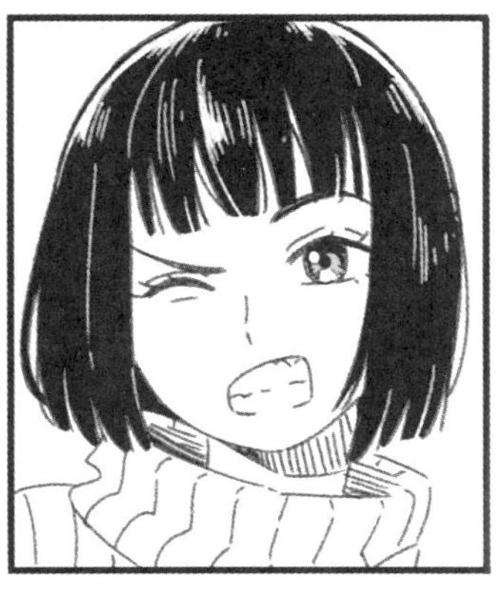

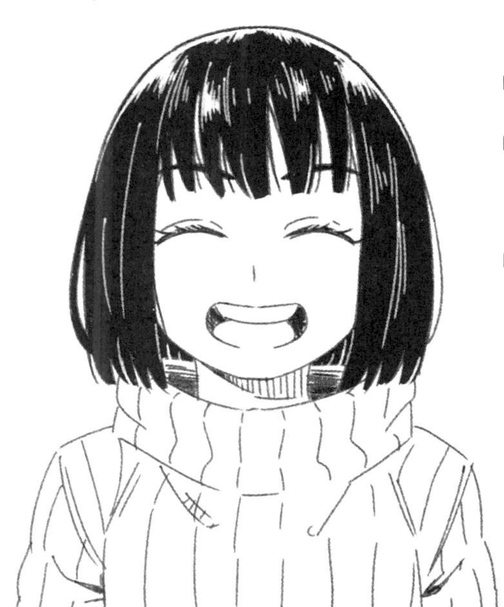

HA!
HA!
HA!
HA!
HA!

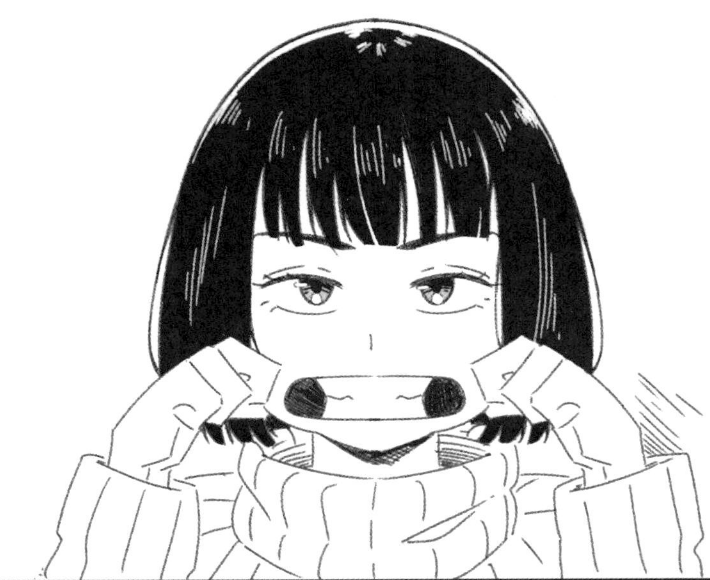

In a story, it's sometimes a good idea to just drop the words and let the drawing express the message.

"Show, don't tell."

Facial expressions let us show our emotions and thus communicate with other people.

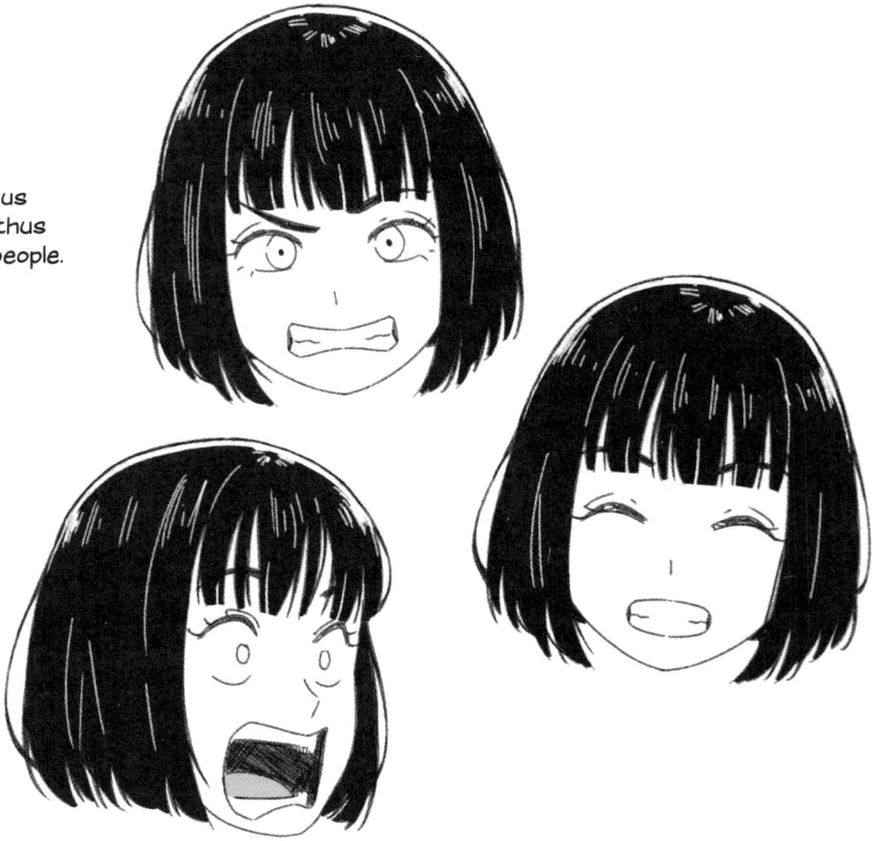

They will bring your characters to life and give them energy and personality.

The eyes are placed inside the reference
squares that were created when we
established the structure for the face.
The distance between the two eyes is usually
the same as the width of an eye.

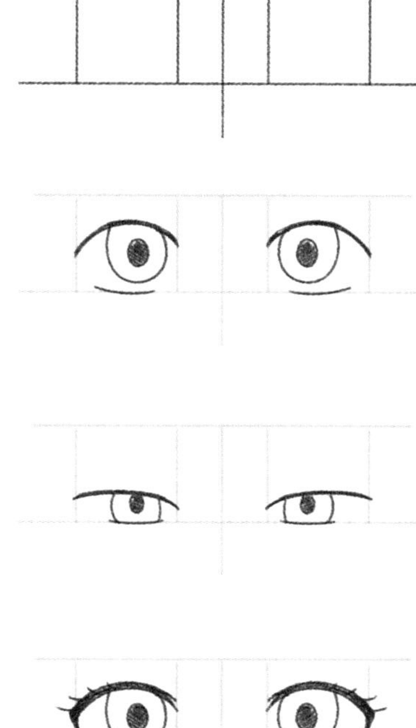

Draw a curve at the top and then one at the
bottom. The bottom of the eye is positioned
along the bottom line of the reference square.
The iris is a simple circle, with a smaller black
circle inside it for the pupil.

The top of the eye is defined by
the bottom of the upper eyelid.

To represent a female character, you usually
draw an eyeliner line and eyelashes on the
upper eyelid. The iris is generally larger.

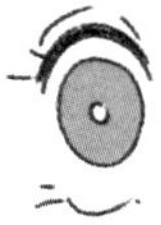 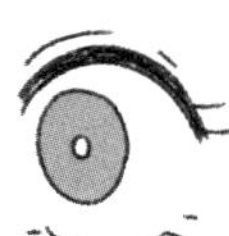 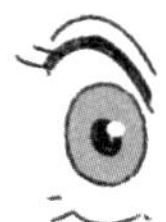 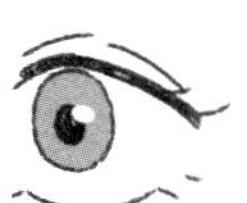

Change how wide the eyelids are open and the
shape of the eye to create different expressions.

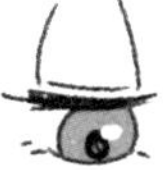 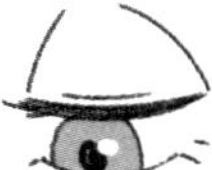 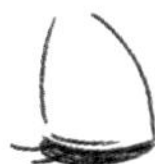 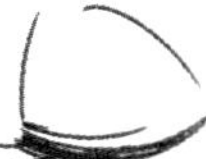

Eyes are the window to the soul.
You can change the size and shape of the iris
and the pupil to show the emotion that you want.

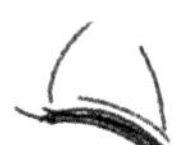 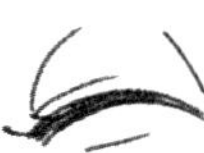 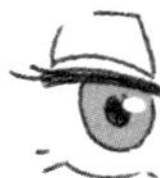 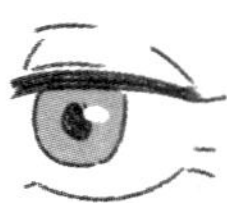

The shape of the eyebrows has a significant impact on the facial expression.

They can indicate anger or nervousness if they are puckered into a frown; or surprise or excitement if they are arched upward.

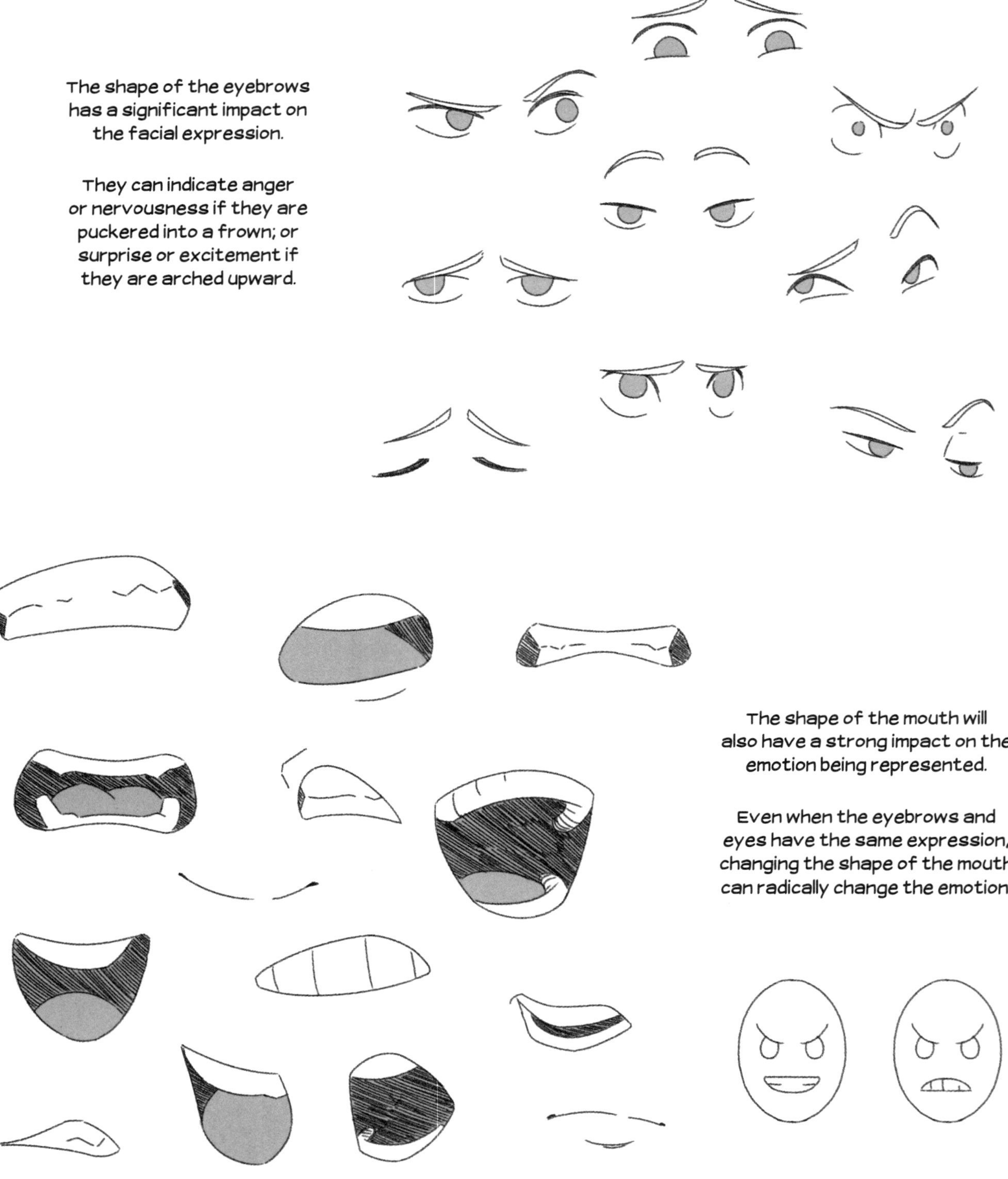

The shape of the mouth will also have a strong impact on the emotion being represented.

Even when the eyebrows and eyes have the same expression, changing the shape of the mouth can radically change the emotion.

By putting together the expressions of the eyes, the eyebrows,
and the mouth, you can show a wide range of emotions.

Some examples of common facial expressions:

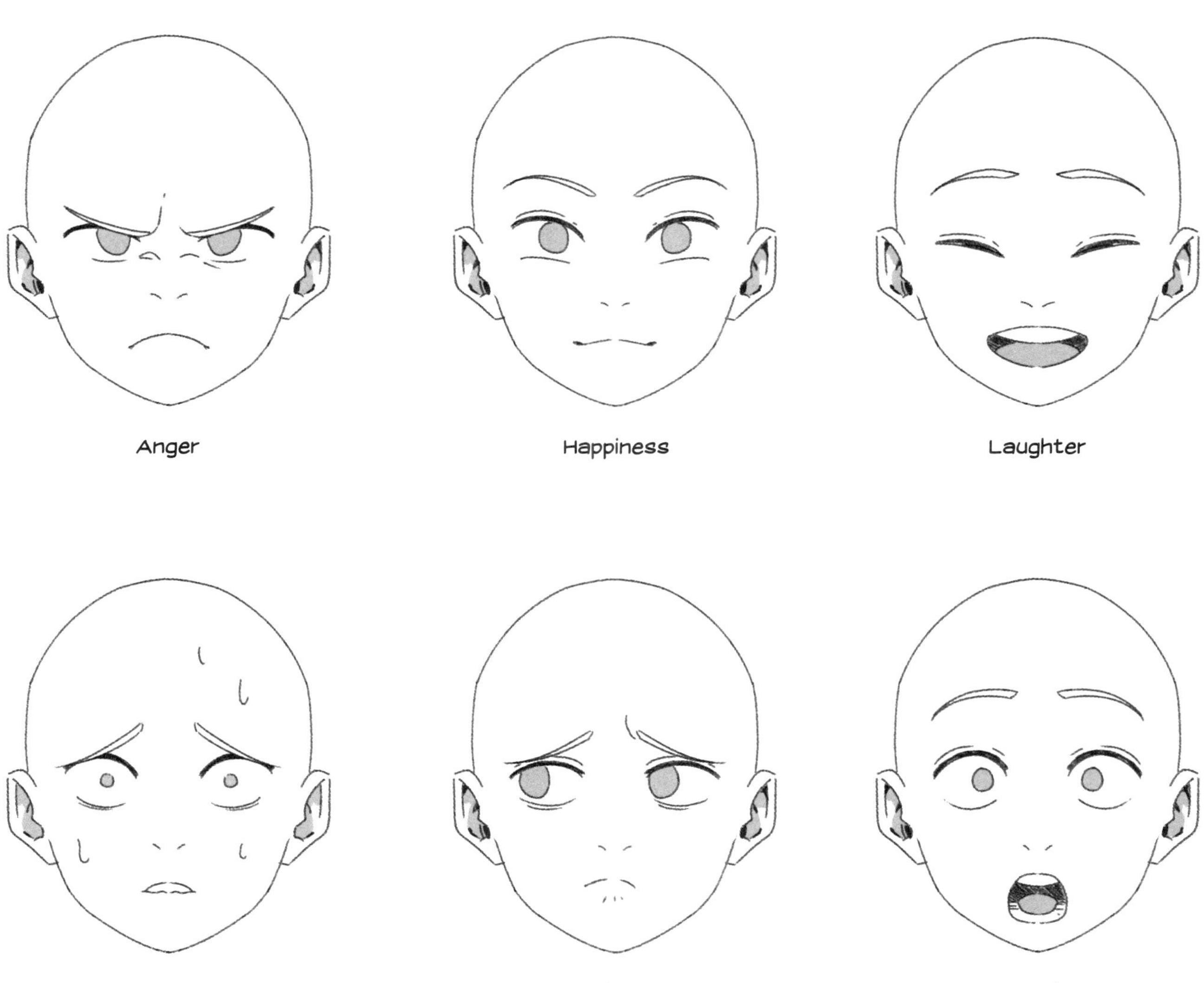

Anger

Happiness

Laughter

Fear

Sadness

Surprise

You can have fun making the expressions more extreme by
emphasizing the facial features we have just looked at and,
to make it harder, by changing the position of the face:

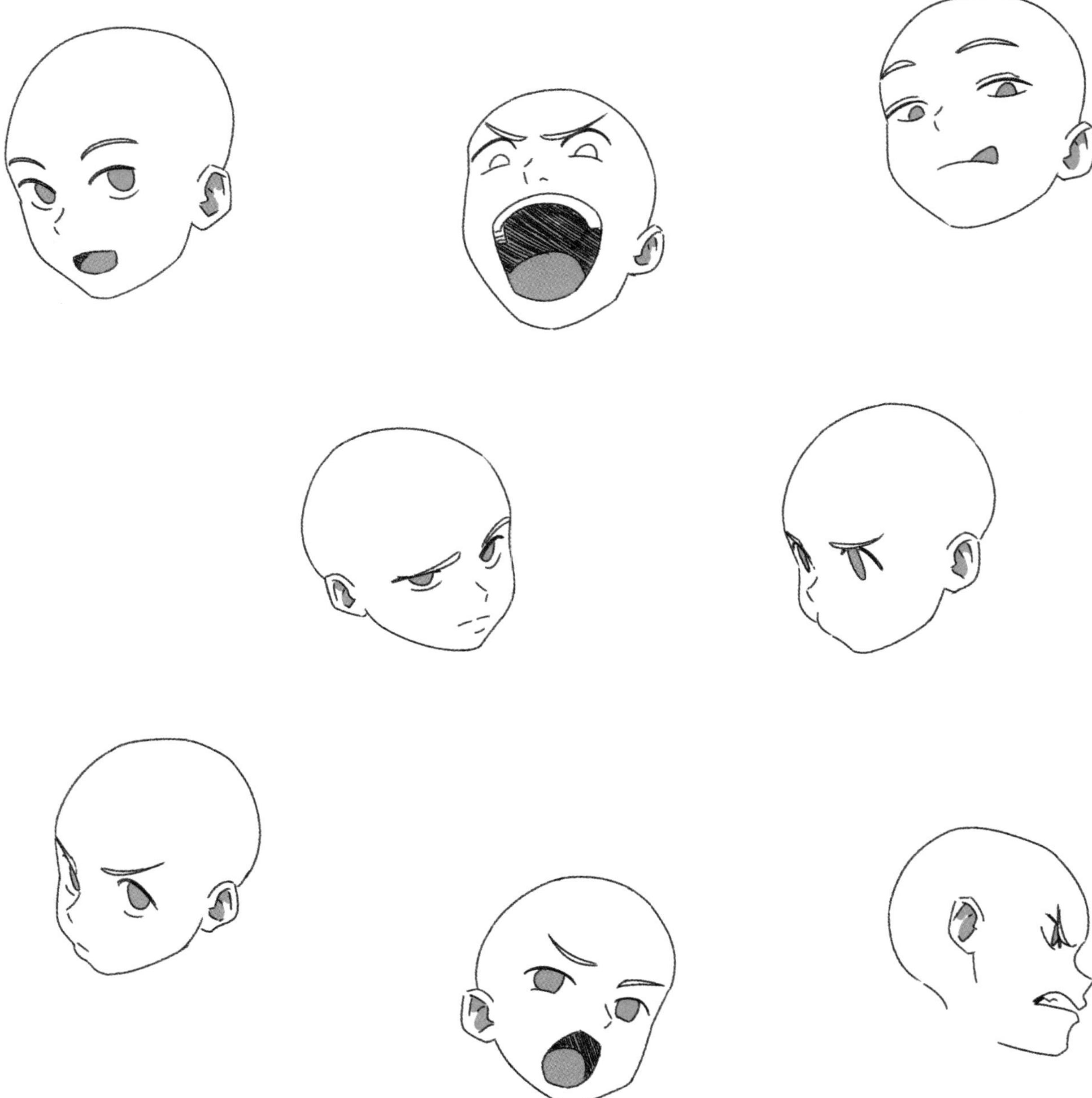

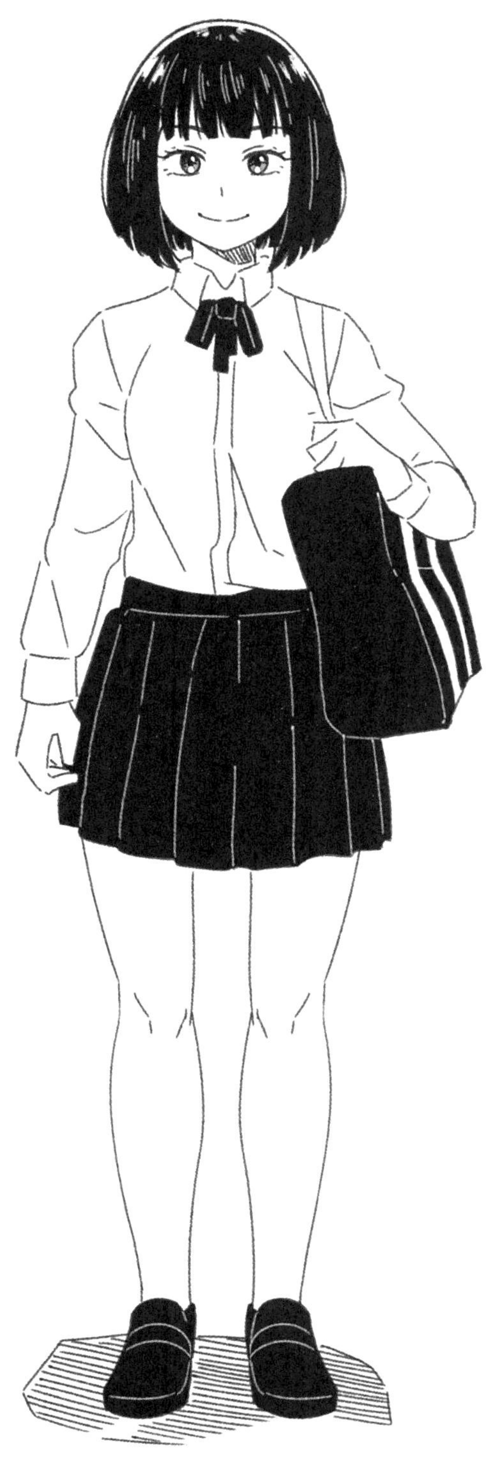

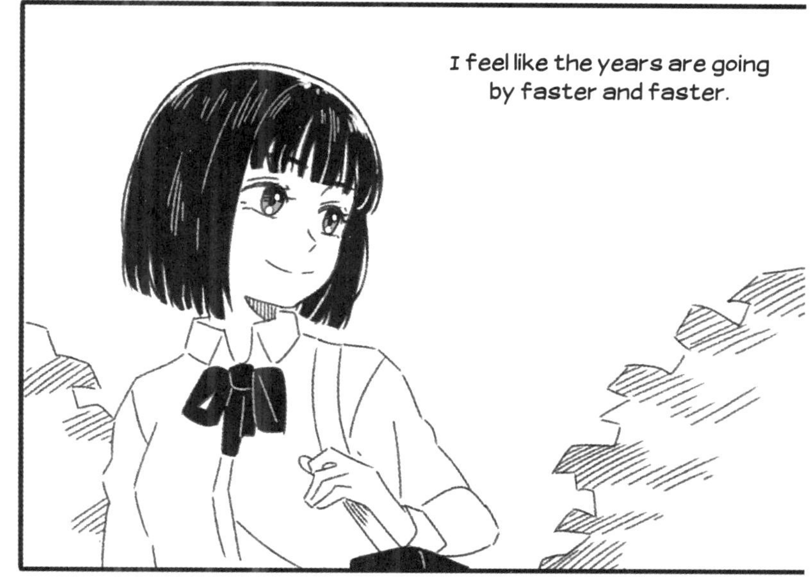

I just started back to school after the summer and I'm realizing that my body has changed, and so have the bodies of the people around me.

That makes it all harder to draw ...

The anatomy of the human body is very complex. To make it easier to draw, condense the main muscle groups into simple shapes.

The model you drew earlier will serve as a basic framework. Now cover this framework with more shapes to make it look like a real body.

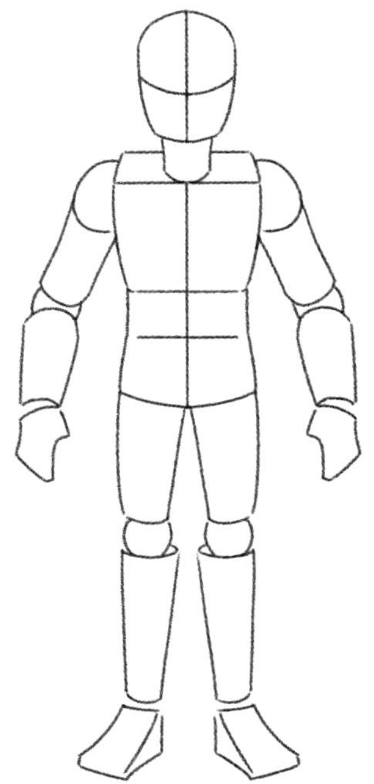

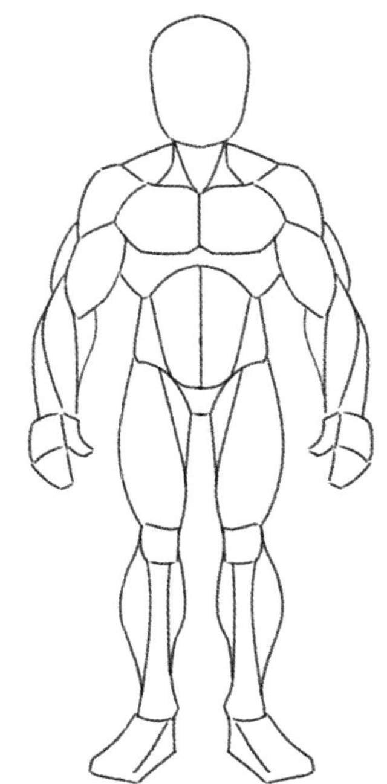

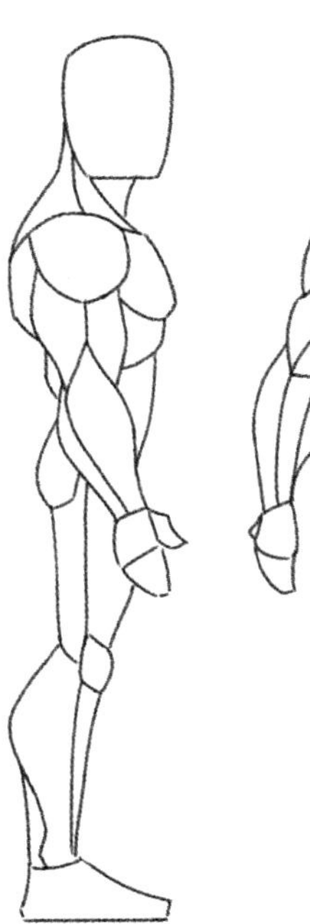

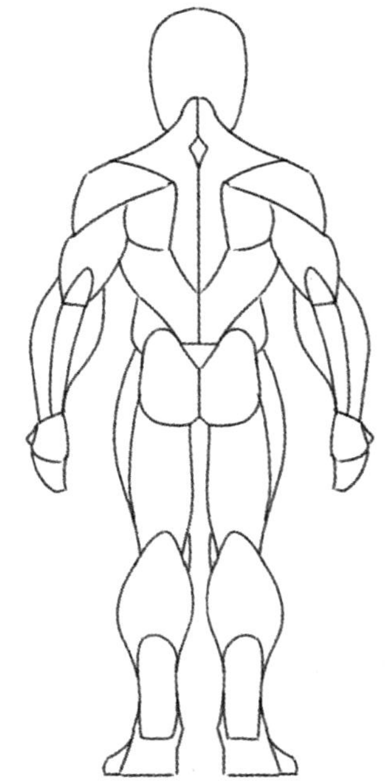

The sternocleidomastoid muscle connects the back of the ears with the hollow of the neck, making a triangle. It is often shown in drawings.

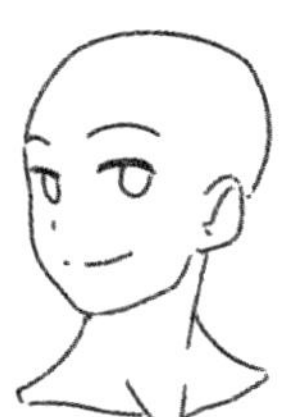

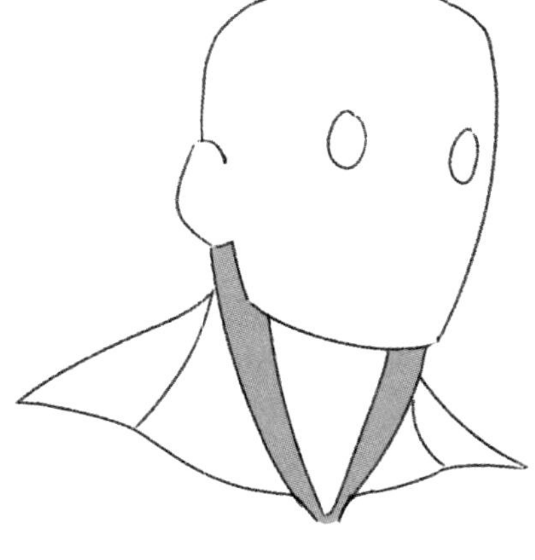

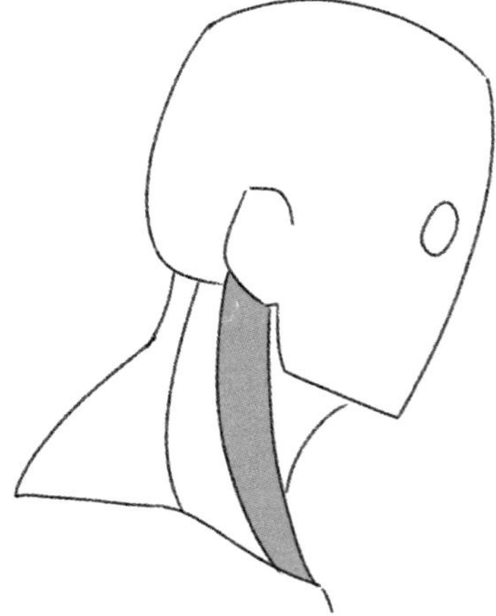

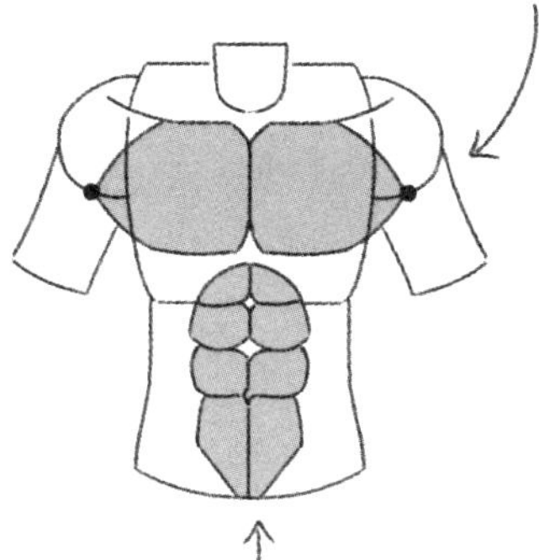

The pectoral muscles are connected to the deltoids (the shoulder muscles).

Abdominal line

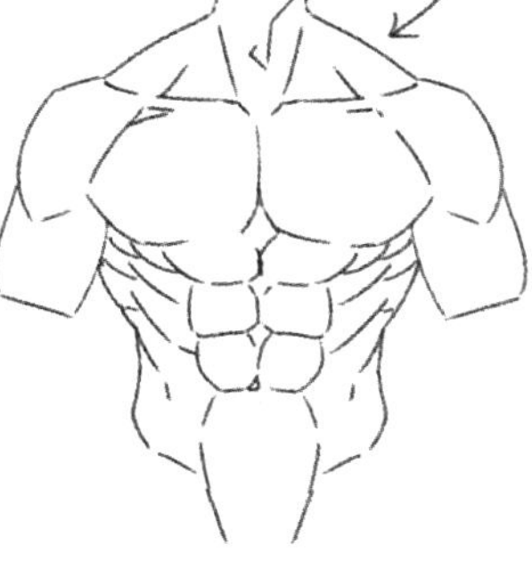

Arched shape of the trapezoids

The bottom of the pectorals are positioned in the middle of the rib cage.

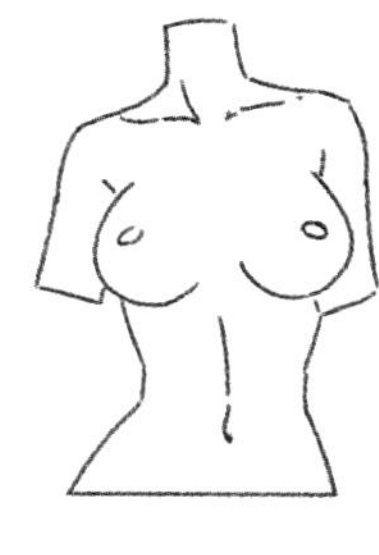

For women, we add two rounded shapes (of variable size) on top of the pectorals to show the breasts.

The collarbones are a very important reference point for the torso. They connect the hollow of the neck with the top of the deltoids.

When the shoulders are raised or lowered, the collarbones follow their motion!

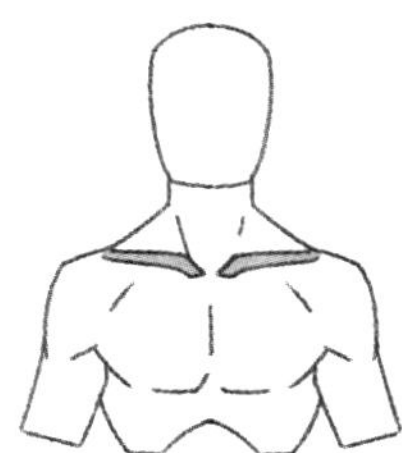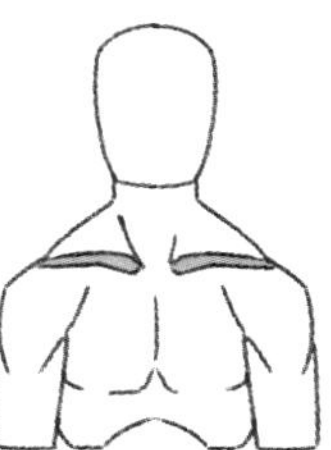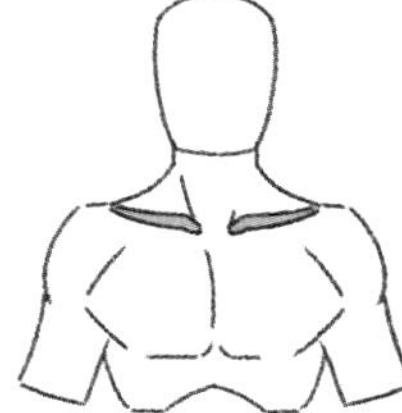

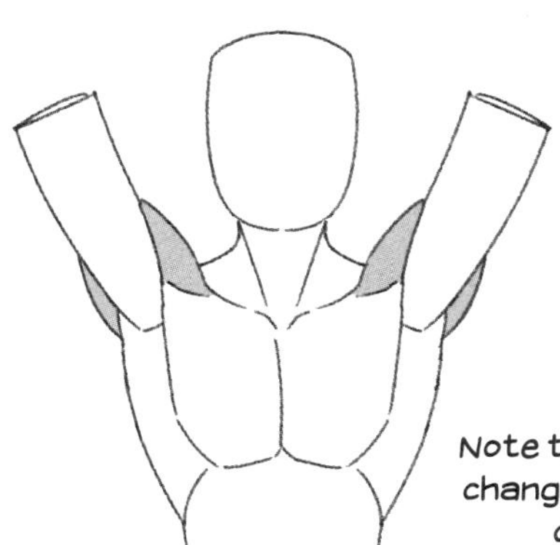

When the arms are raised, the shoulders are partially hidden and the back muscles become visible.

Note that the shape of the pectorals changes because they continue to be connected to the deltoids.

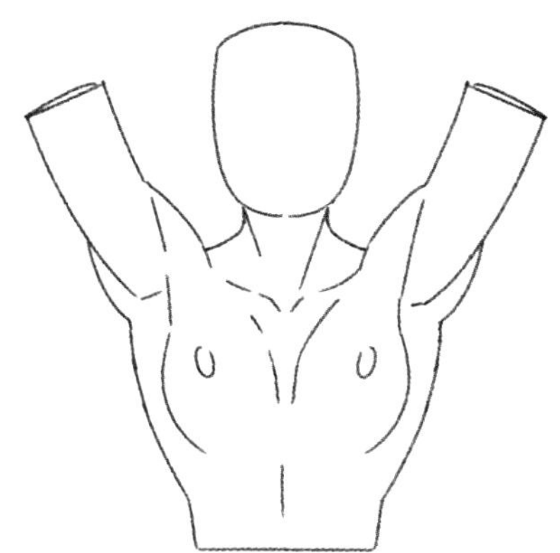

On a woman, the breasts are elongated.

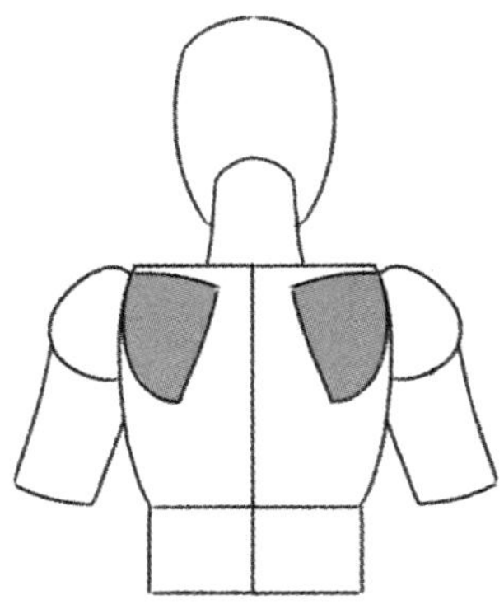

The shoulder blades, shaped like triangles, are a good indicator for where to place the back muscles.

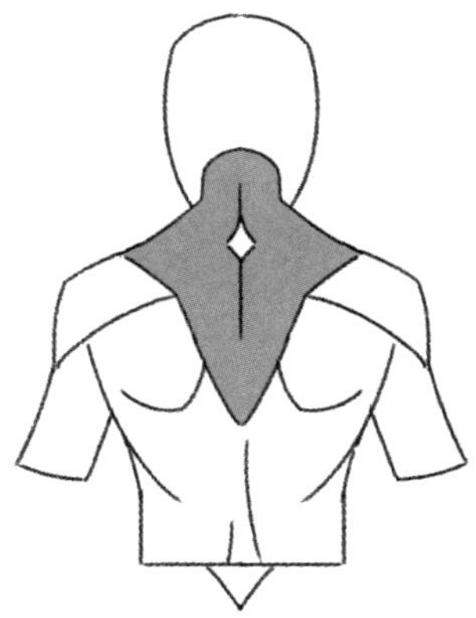

The trapezoid is connected to the base of the skull and descends onto the back in a triangle shape.

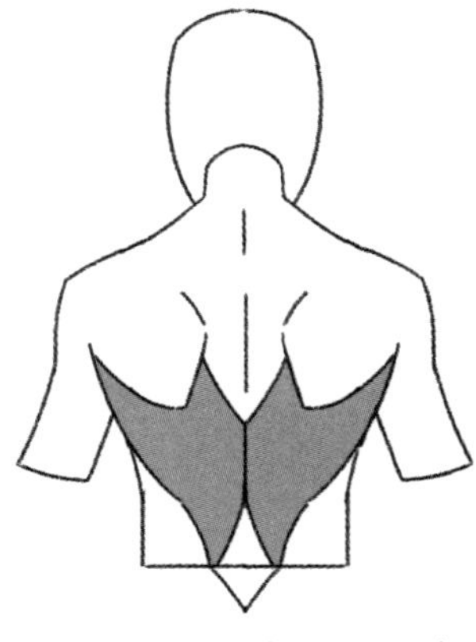

The latissimus dorsi muscles are connected from the inside of the shoulders down to the pelvis.

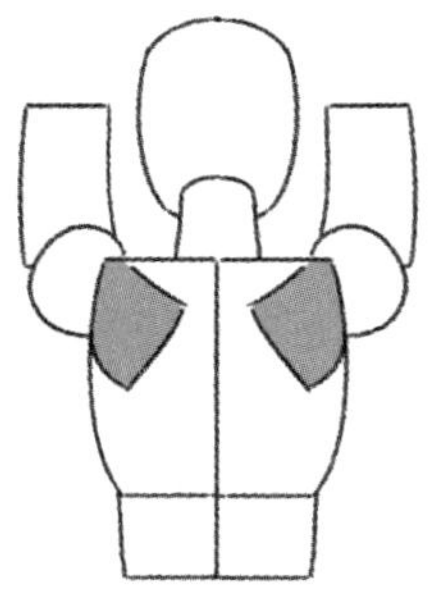 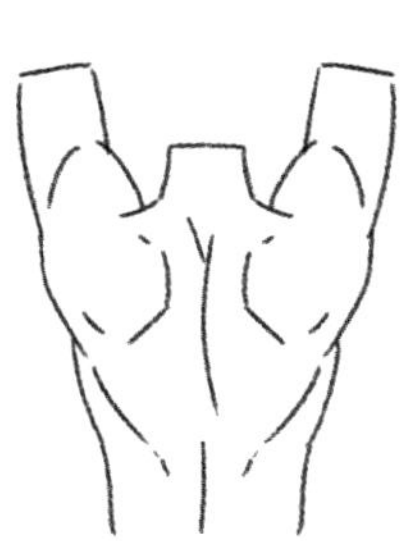 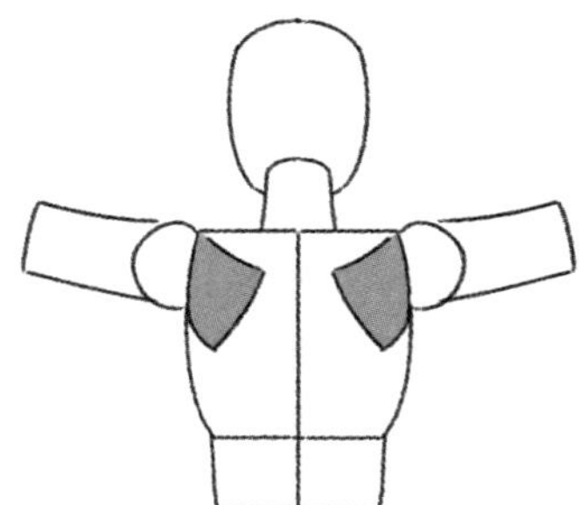 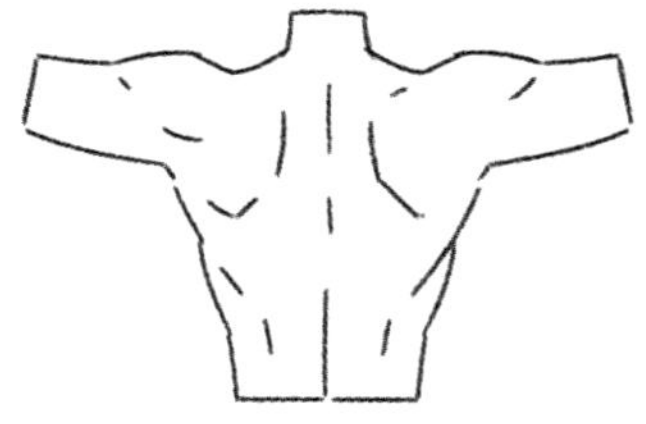

When the arms are raised, the shoulder blades accompany the motion and pivot, which helps us in positioning the muscles.

In a ¾ view, the proportions change, of course.

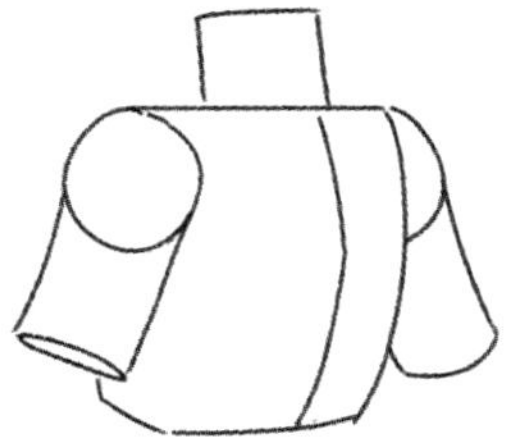 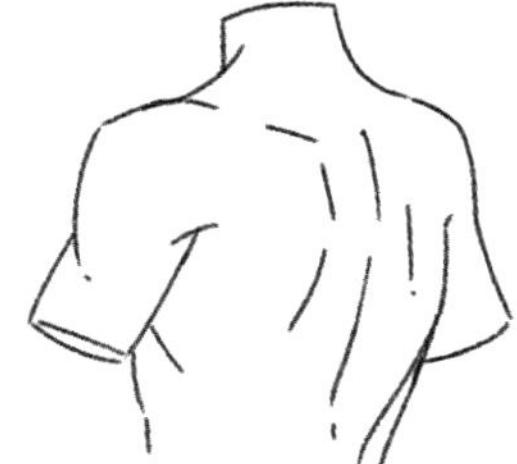 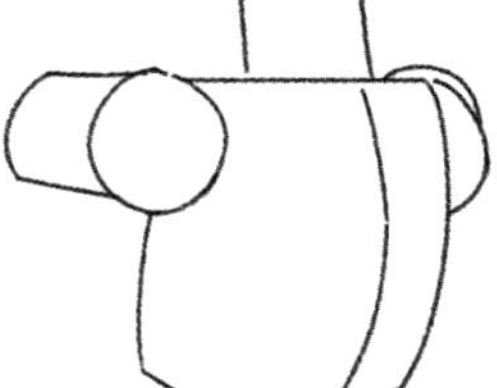 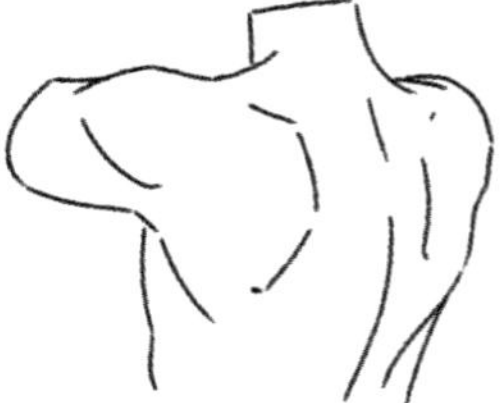

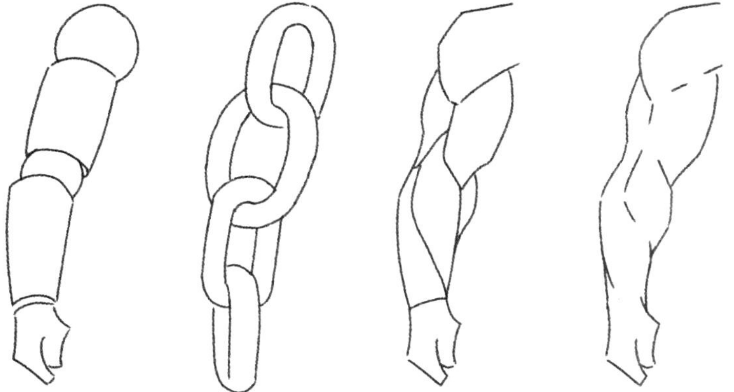

The arm muscles are very complicated to draw. It can be useful to look at them like the links of a chain.

Notice that the biceps and the triceps are almost perfectly separated by the deltoid.

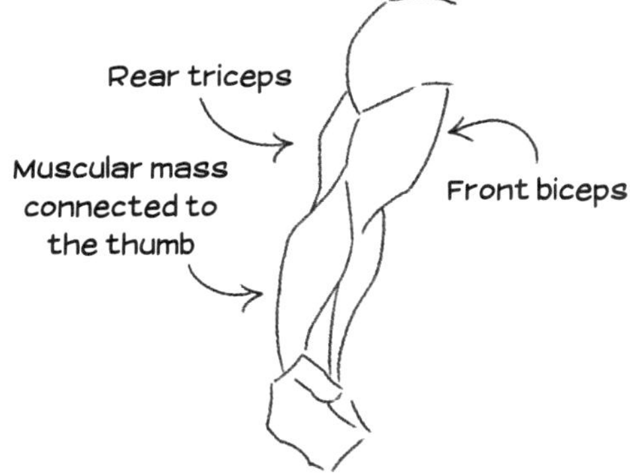

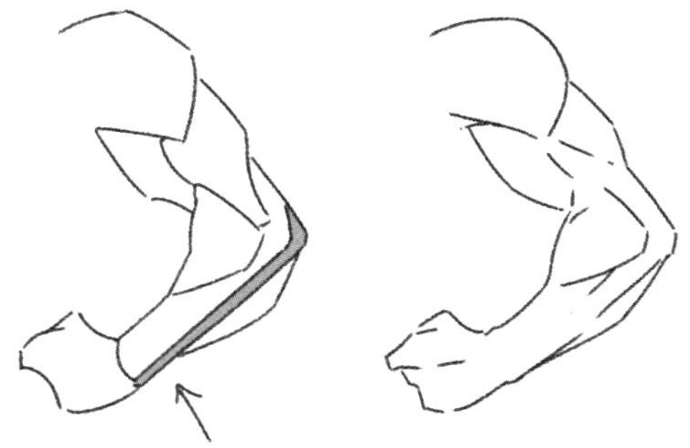

The elbow is connected to the little finger by a bone. This is a very useful reference point.

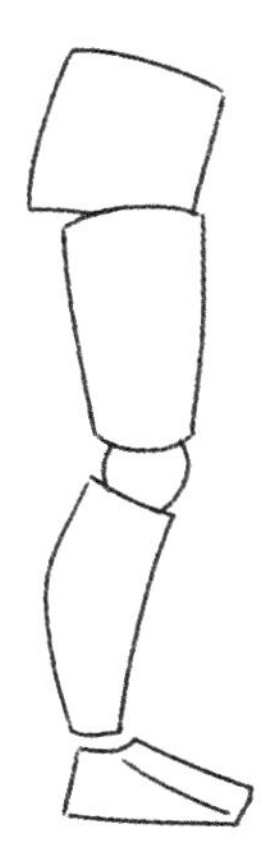

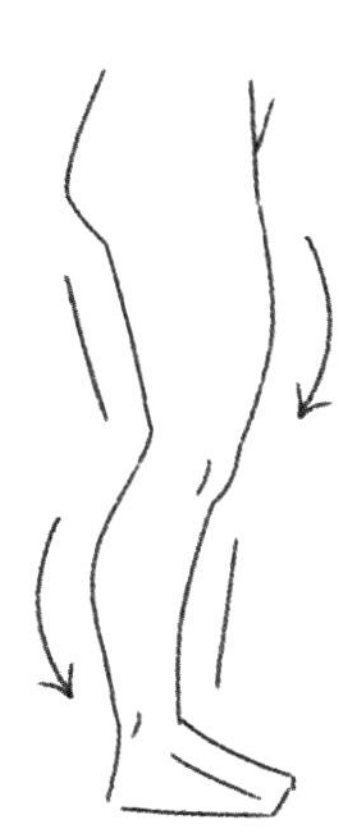

The leg, seen in profile, has a very visible line of thrust.

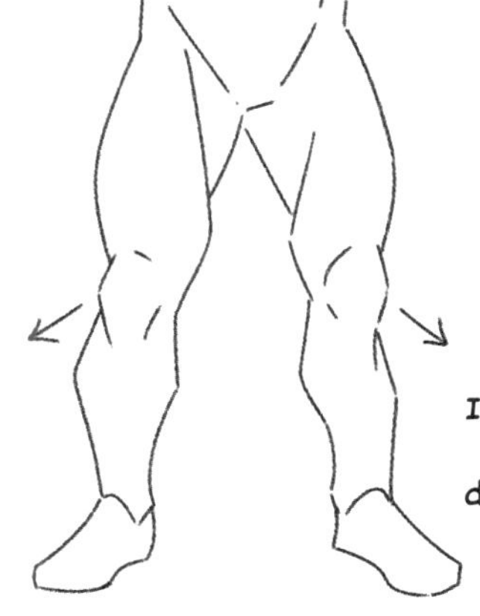

In general, the knees point in the same direction as the feet.

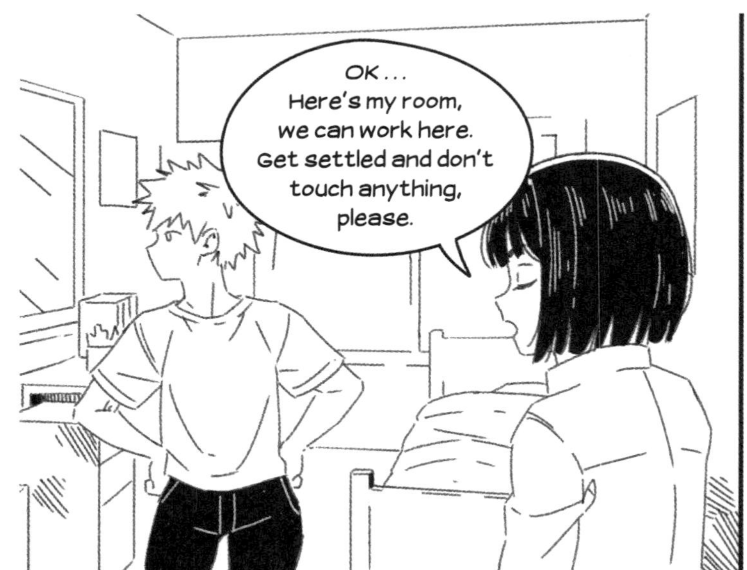

OK...
Here's my room, we can work here. Get settled and don't touch anything, please.

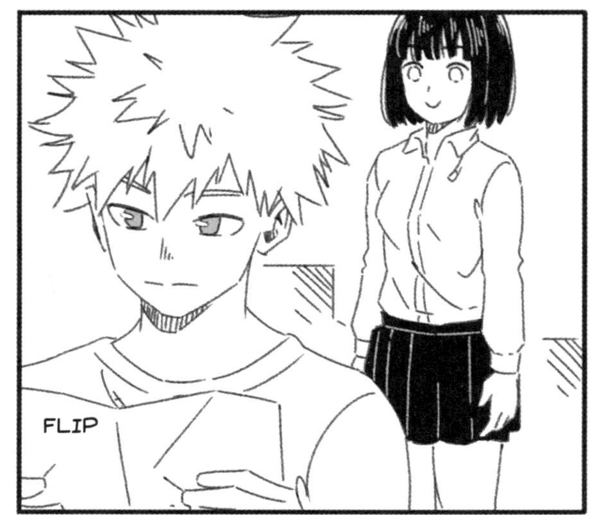

FLIP

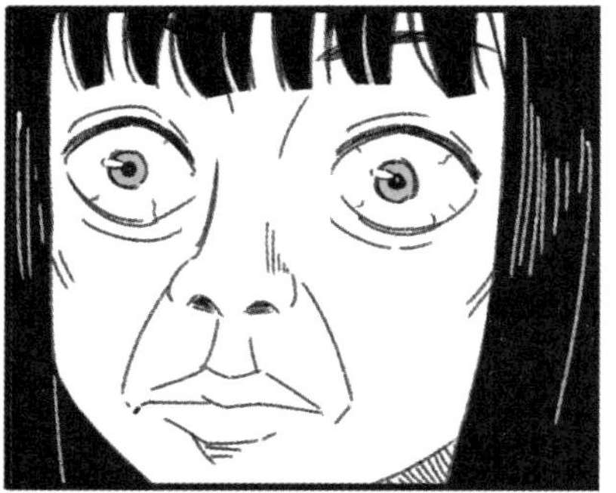

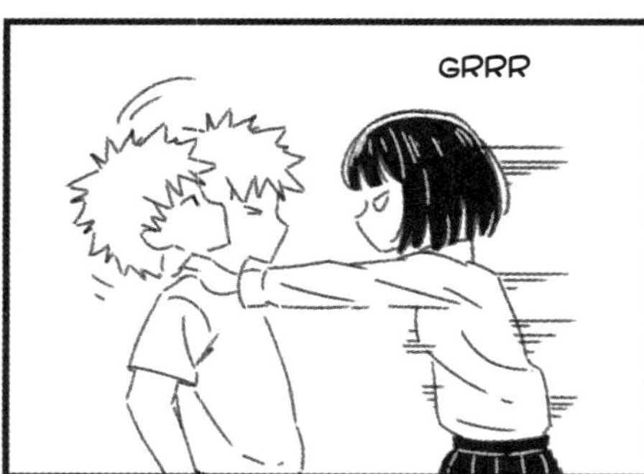

GRRR

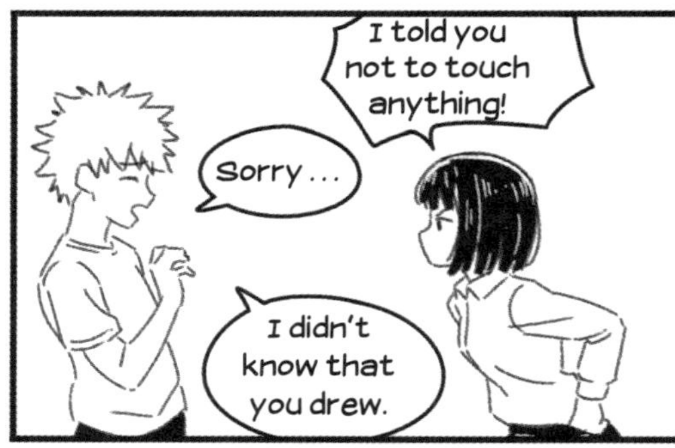

I told you not to touch anything!
Sorry...
I didn't know that you drew.

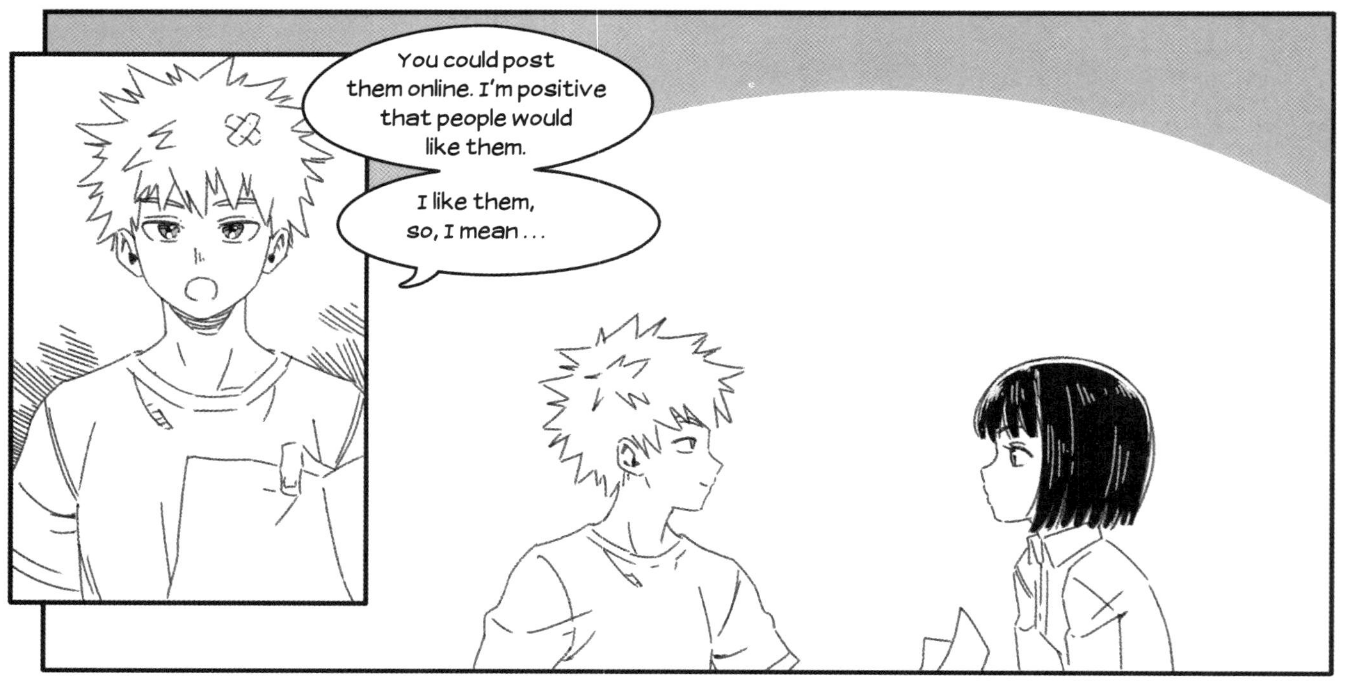

You could post them online. I'm positive that people would like them.
I like them, so, I mean...

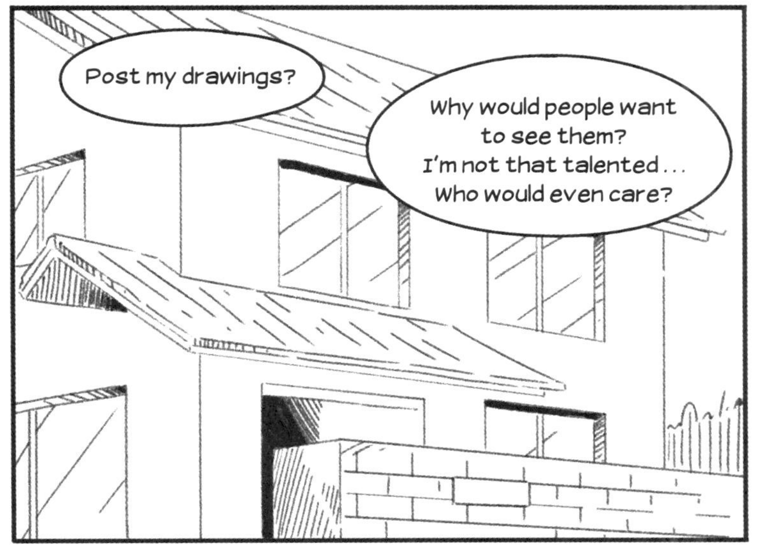
Post my drawings?
Why would people want to see them?
I'm not that talented...
Who would even care?

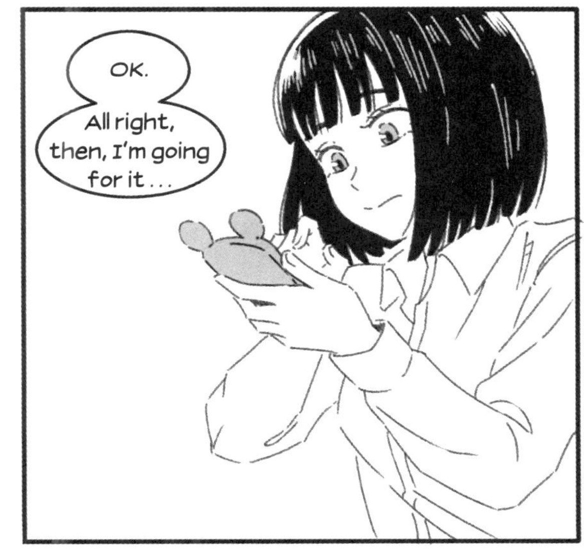
OK.
All right, then, I'm going for it...

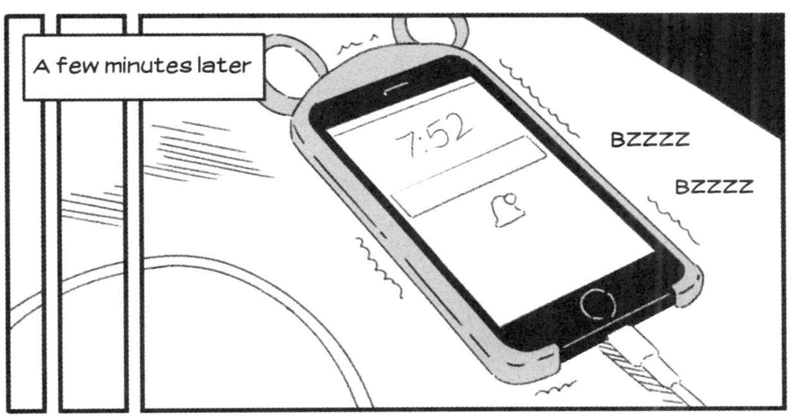
A few minutes later
7:52
BZZZZ
BZZZZ

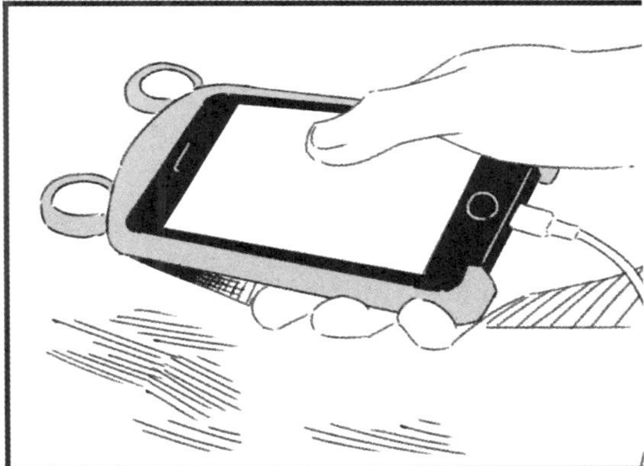

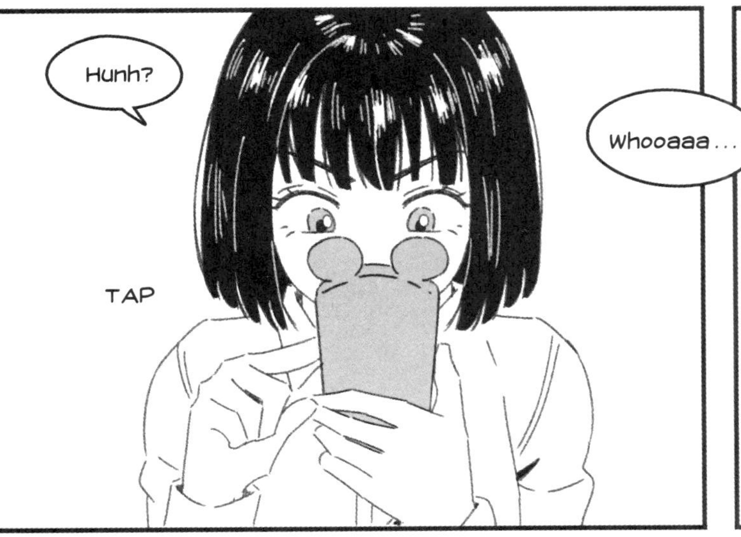
Hunh?
TAP

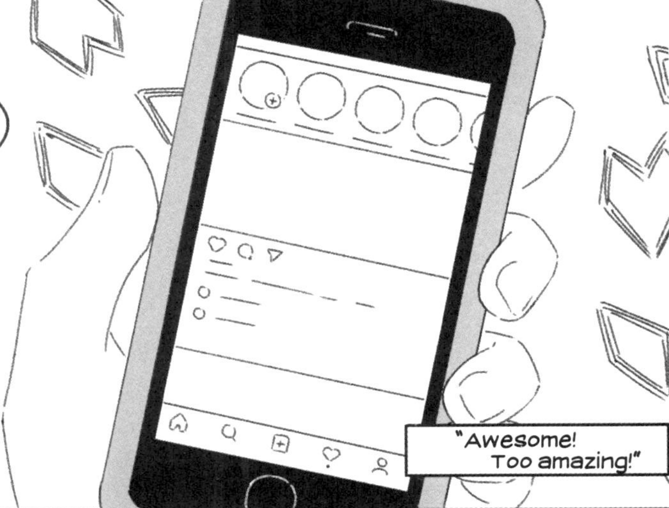
Whooaaa...
"Awesome!
Too amazing!"

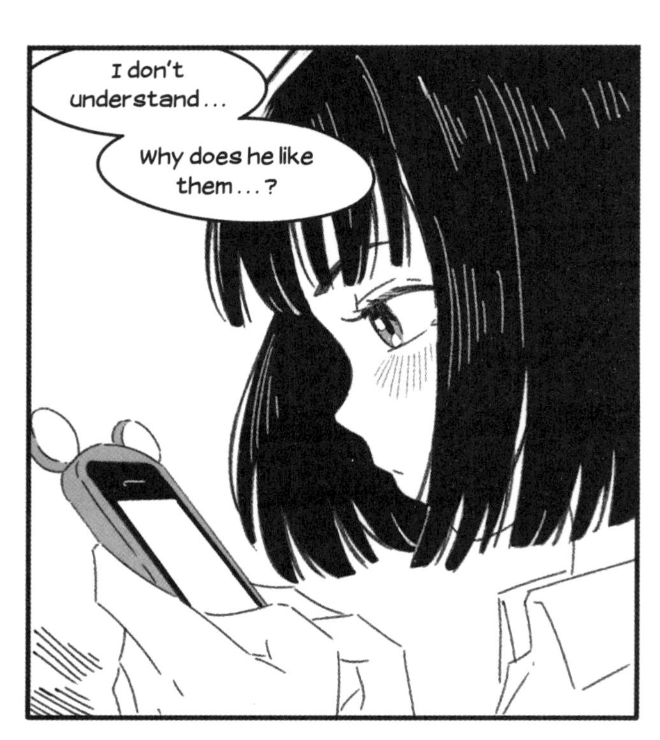

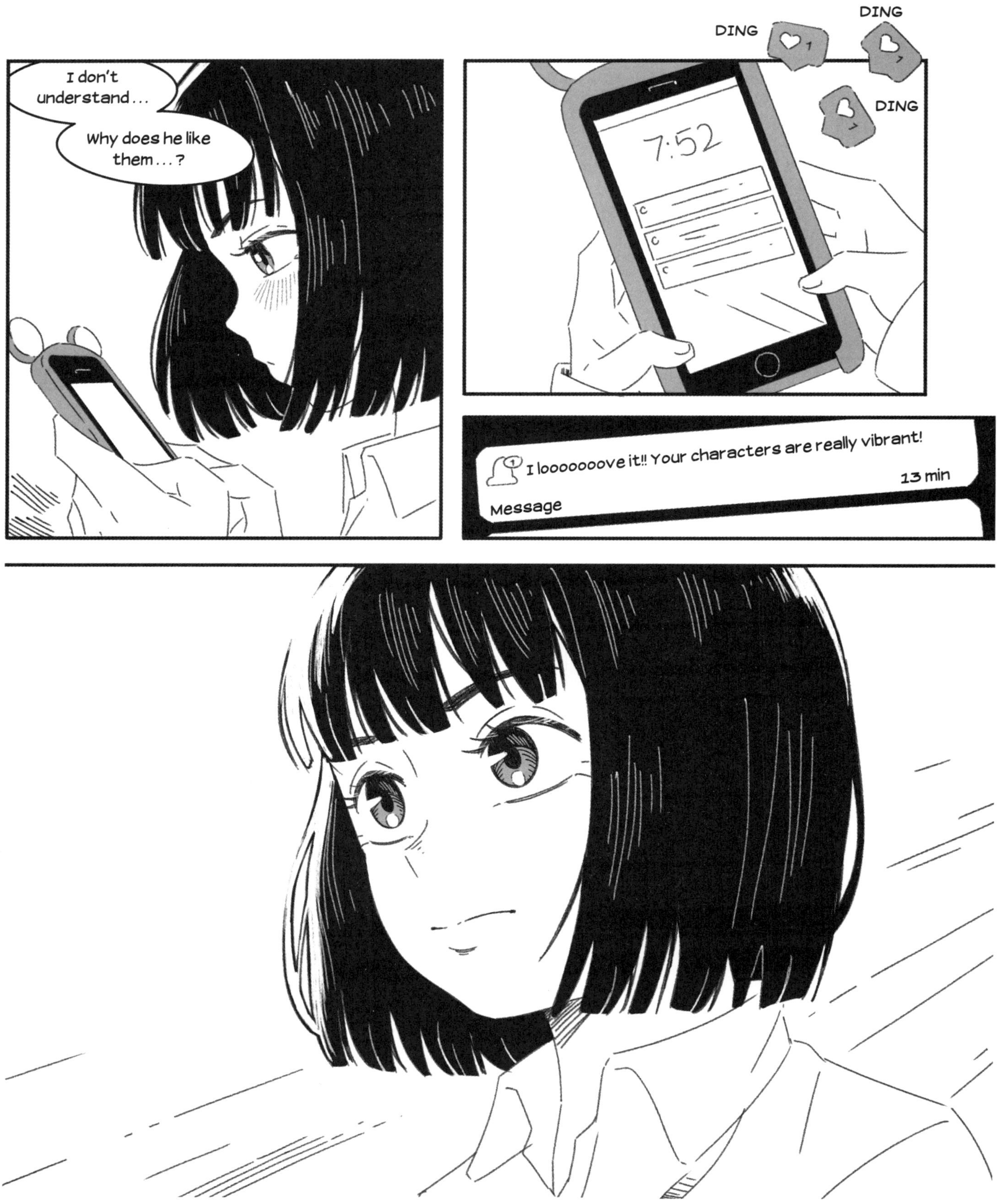

I don't understand...
Why does he like them...?

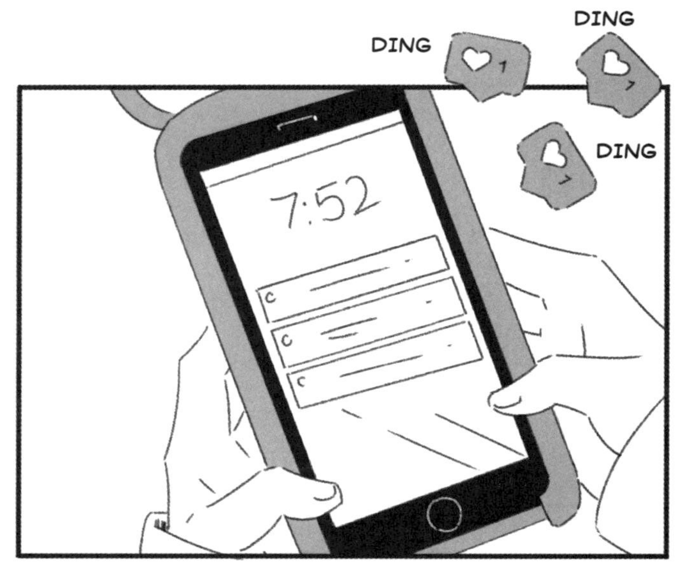

DING
DING
DING
7:52
I loooooove it!! Your characters are really vibrant!
13 min
Message

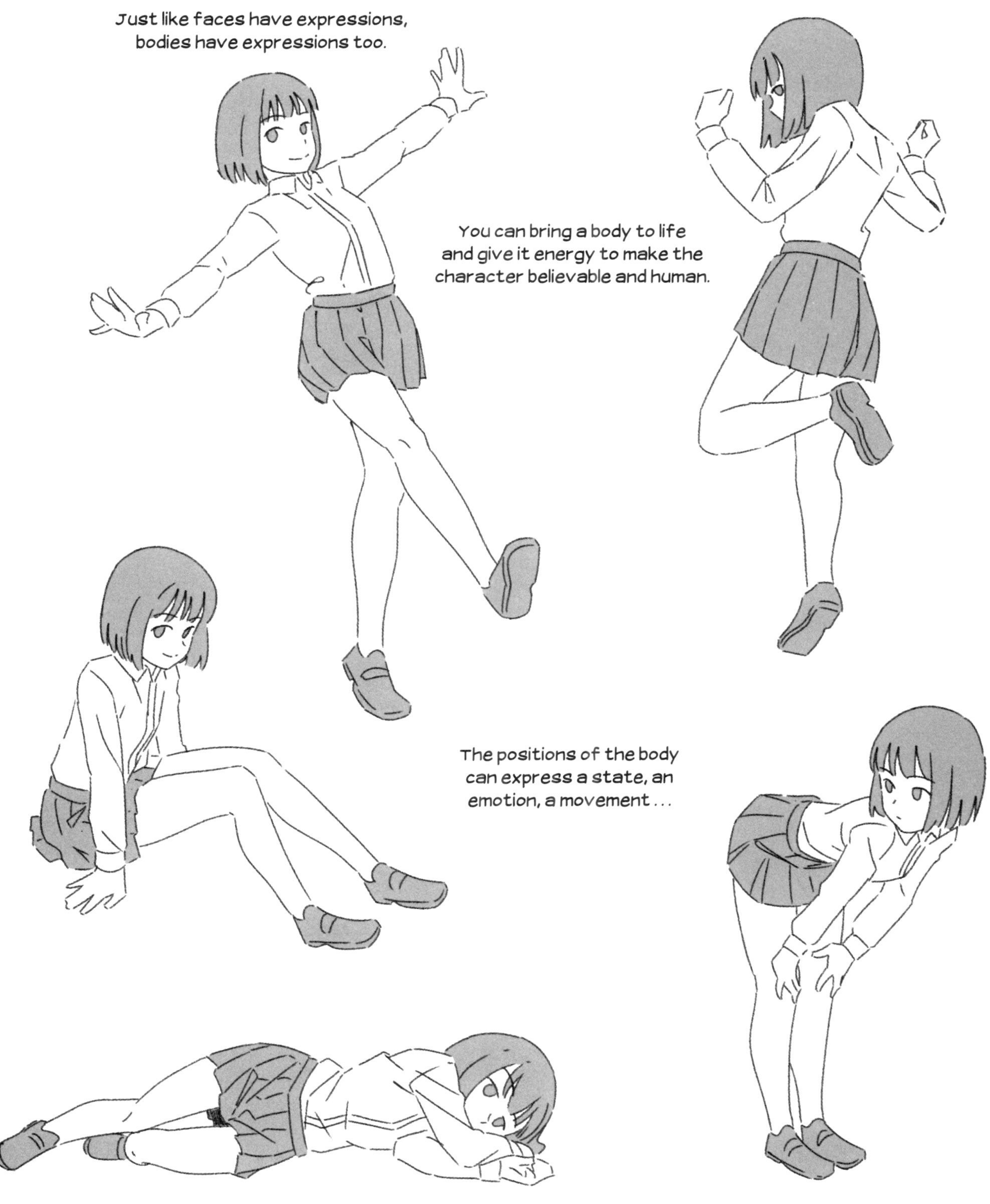

Just like faces have expressions,
bodies have expressions too.

You can bring a body to life
and give it energy to make the
character believable and human.

The positions of the body
can express a state, an
emotion, a movement...

The line of action is an expression of the figure's energy. It is a continuous, invisible S- or C-shaped line that runs the length of the body. You could think of it as the spinal column of the pose.

It is generally a continuous line running from one end of the drawing to the other. It describes the character's movement and makes the pose more interesting.

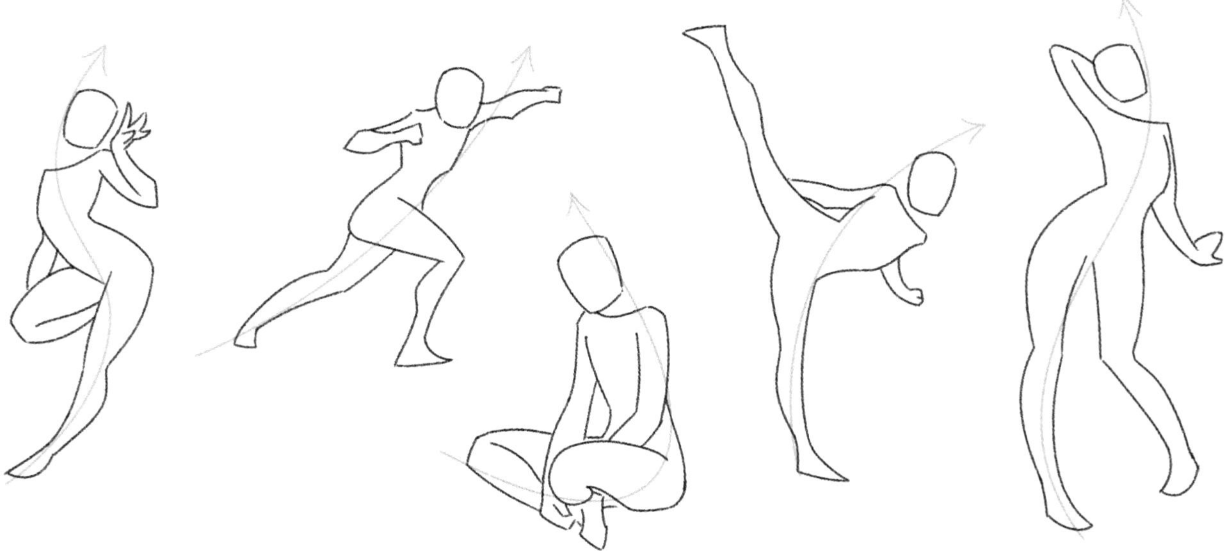

You can exaggerate the pose by exaggerating the line of action. This will accentuate the energy of the pose.

There is one main line of action for the entirety of the body, but you can also draw secondary action lines for each limb.

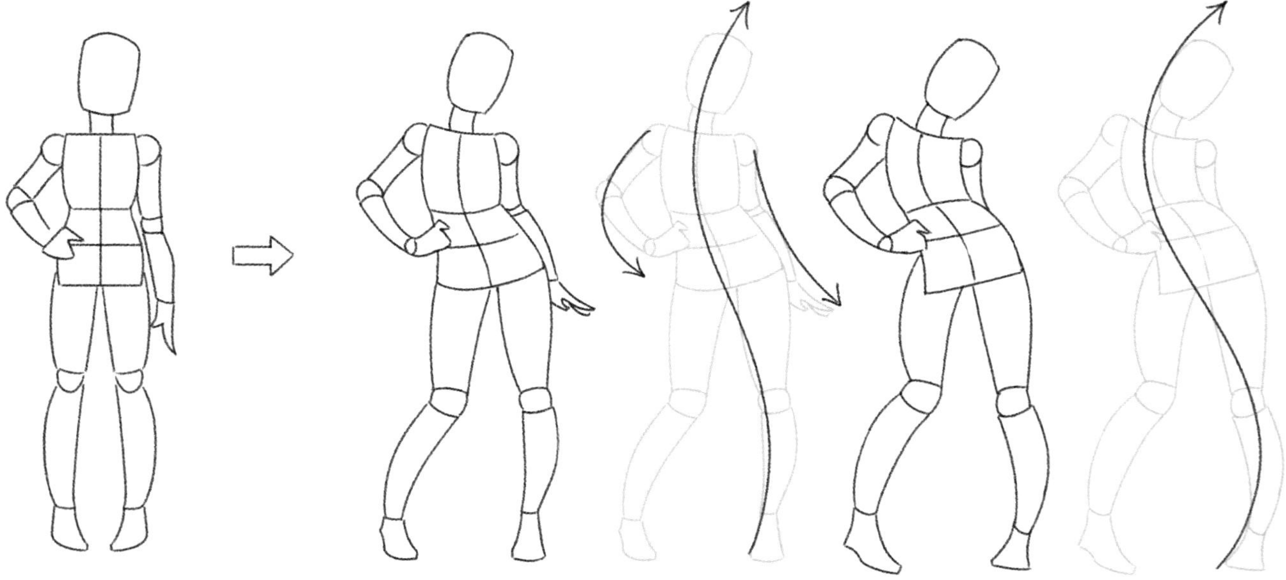

Even if the character is striking a dynamic pose, it still has to answer to a certain balance, otherwise the body would look like it was falling downward.

To find the body's center of gravity, simply draw a straight line from the base of the neck all the way down to the ground. In order for the body to remain balanced, the feet have to be on either side of this point.

When one leg is in the air, all of the body's weight rests on the other foot. In order to maintain balance, that foot has to be placed at the level of the center of gravity.

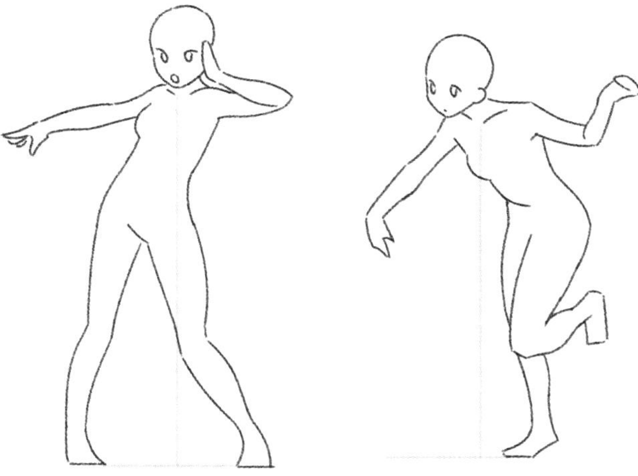

Even a simple pose that does not include any action follows a certain rhythm. This is key so that the character will not look like a soulless puppet and will appear more natural.

The human body is constantly adapting its position to maintain its balance.

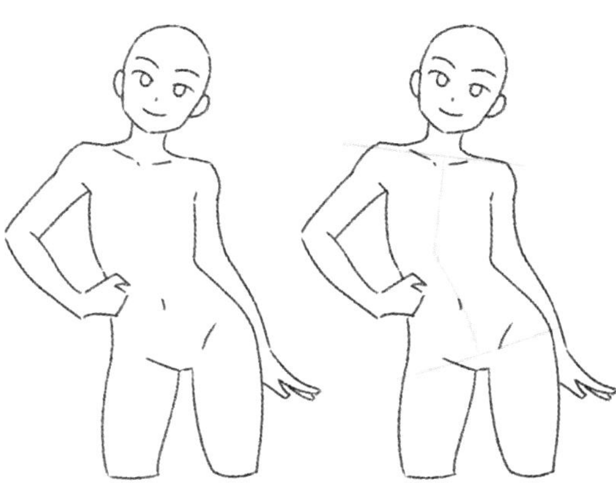

In this kind of pose, one side of the torso is compressed, while the other is elongated.

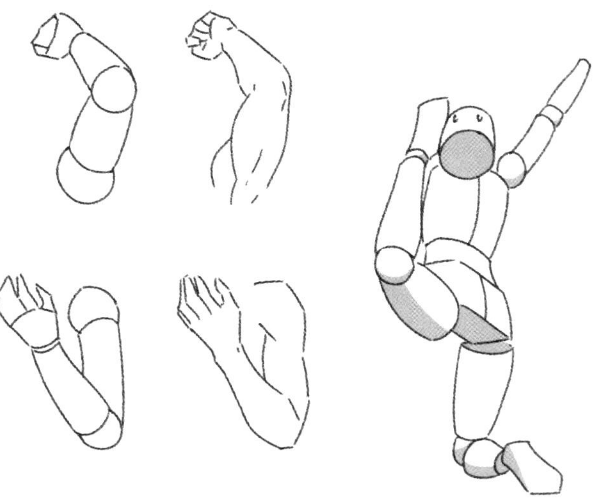

In a dynamic pose, some parts of the body can approach or recede from us. To give a sense of depth to the drawing, use what we call foreshortening!

Remember that we simplified the body into geometric shapes, such as boxes and cylinders. All you have to do to create the illusion of depth is draw these shapes in perspective.

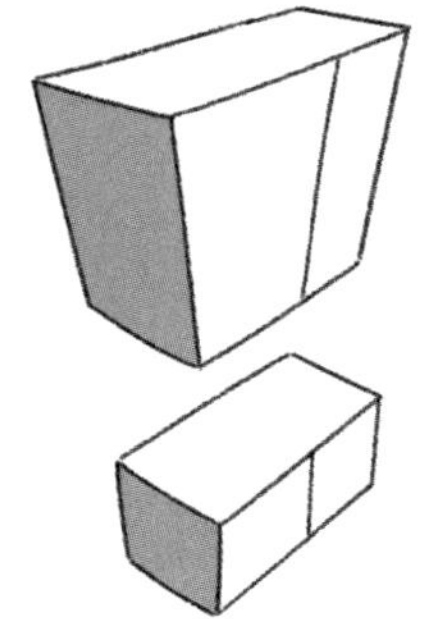
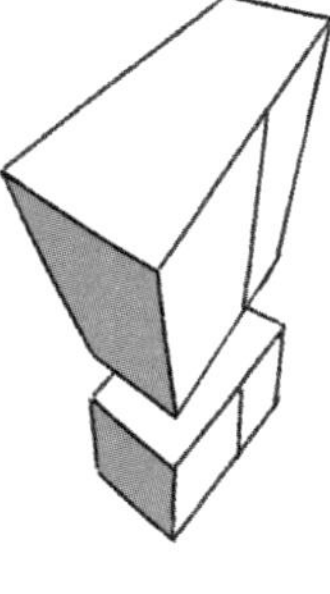
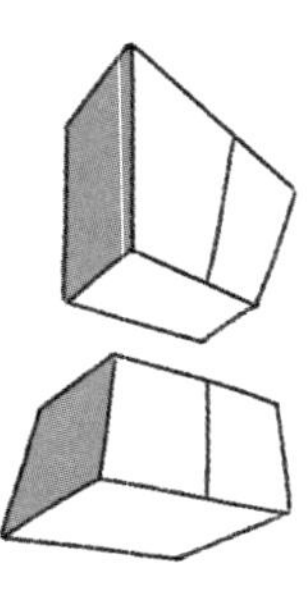

The foreshortenings that the body creates are particularly visible in bird's-eye views and views from below.

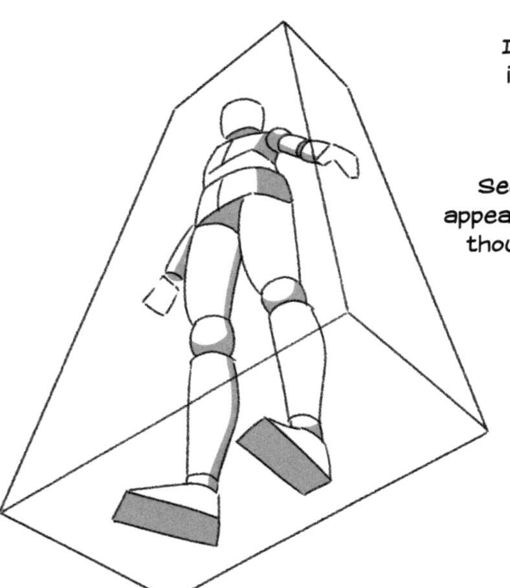

It can help to draw a box in perspective and then draw the body inside it.

Seen from below, the legs will appear larger than the torso, even though they are the same size.

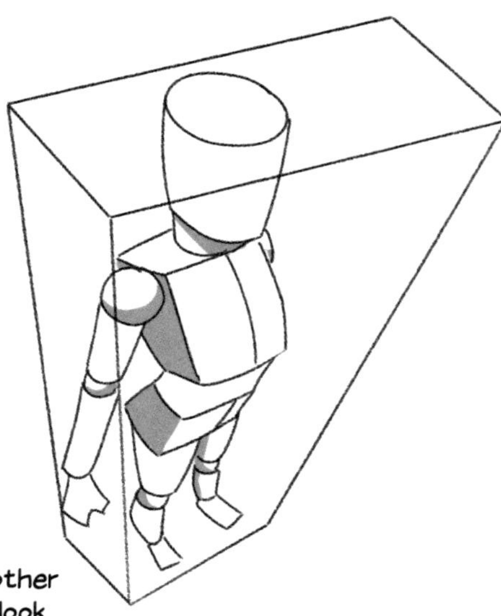

Seen from above, it's the other way around: the torso will look larger than the legs.

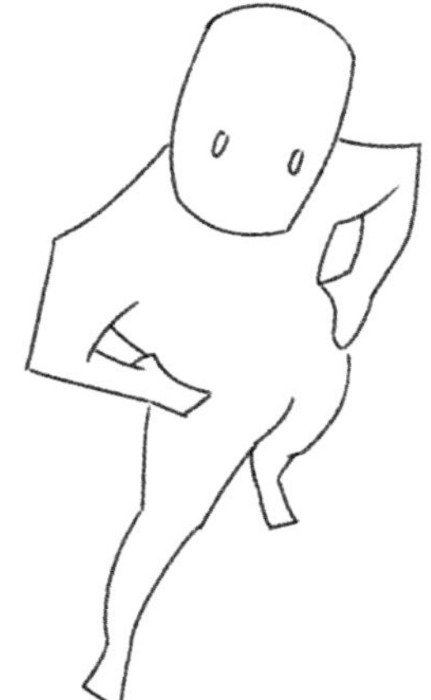
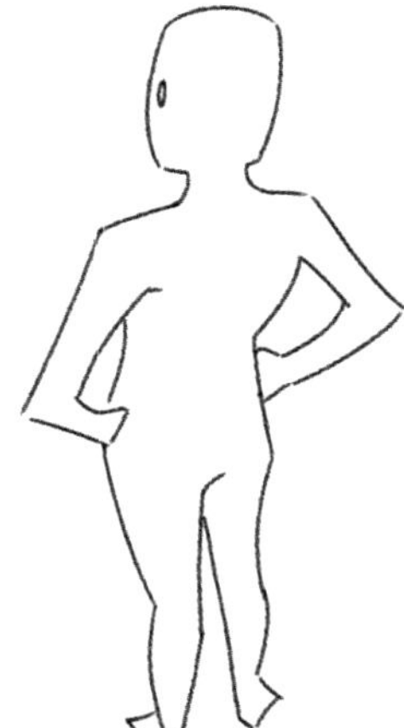
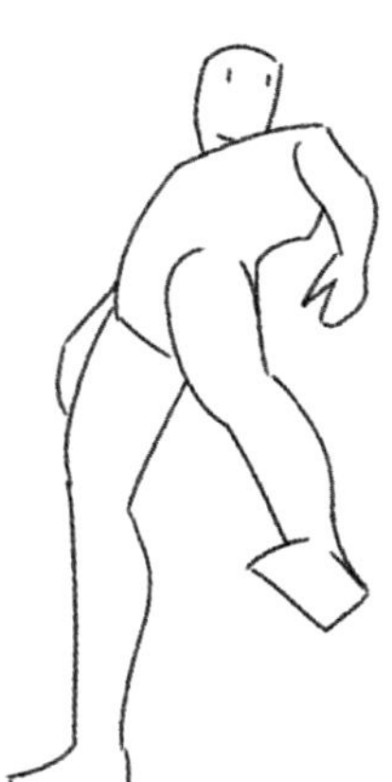

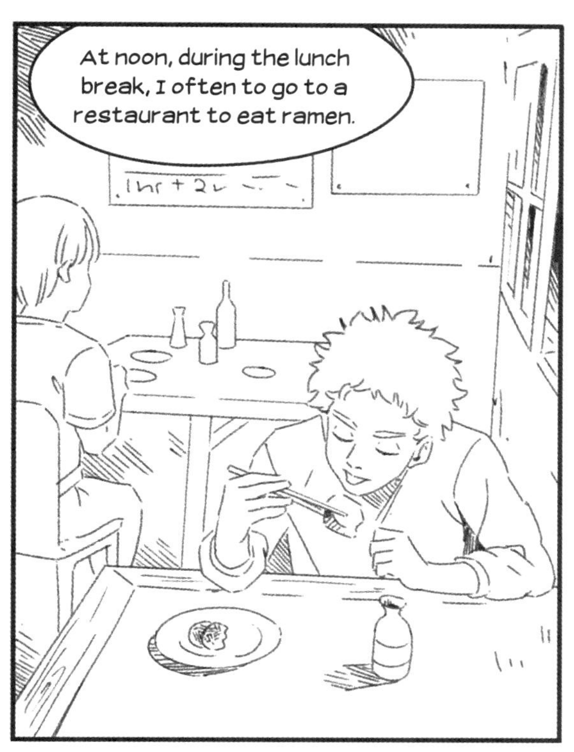
At noon, during the lunch break, I often to go to a restaurant to eat ramen.

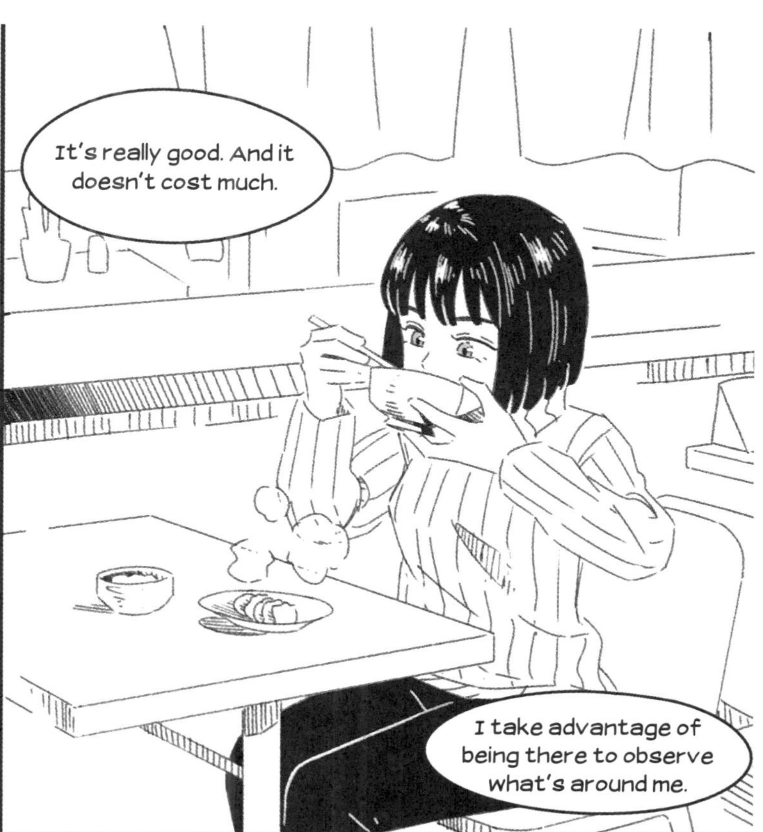
It's really good. And it doesn't cost much.
I take advantage of being there to observe what's around me.

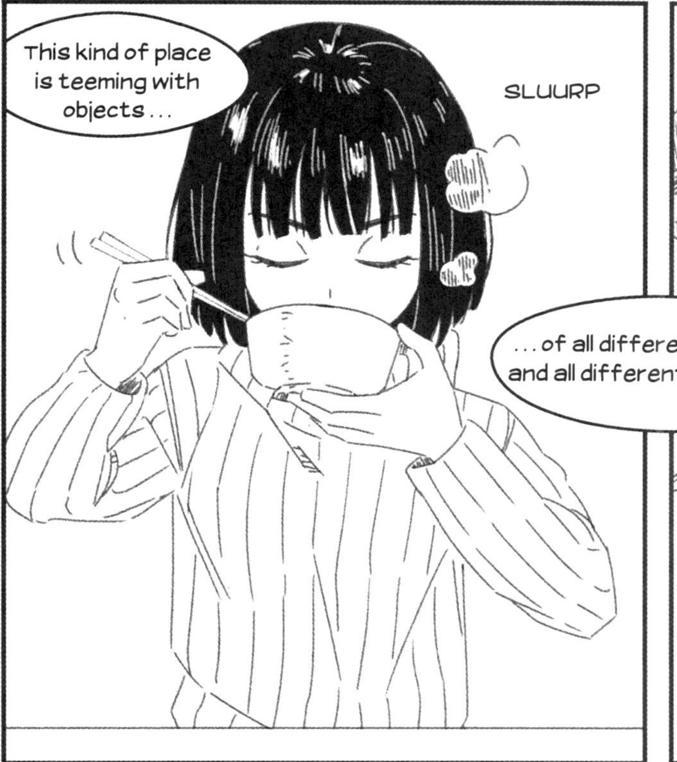
This kind of place is teeming with objects...
SLUURP
...of all different shapes and all different textures.

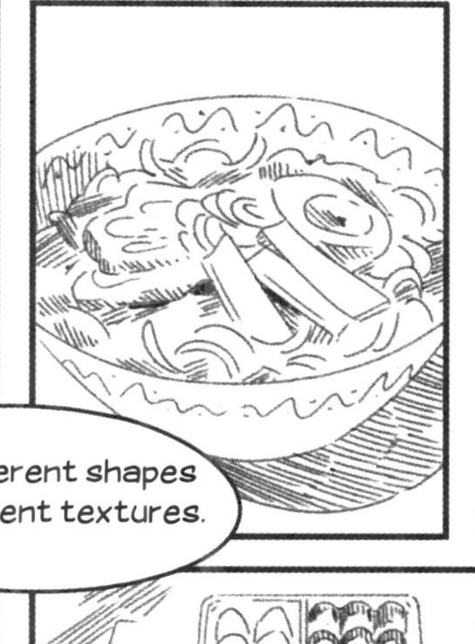

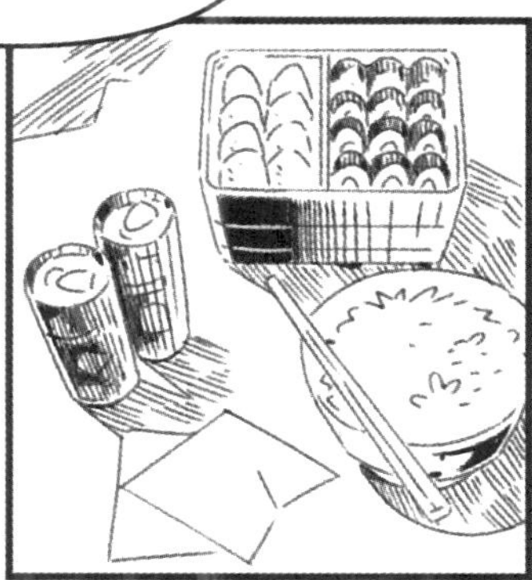

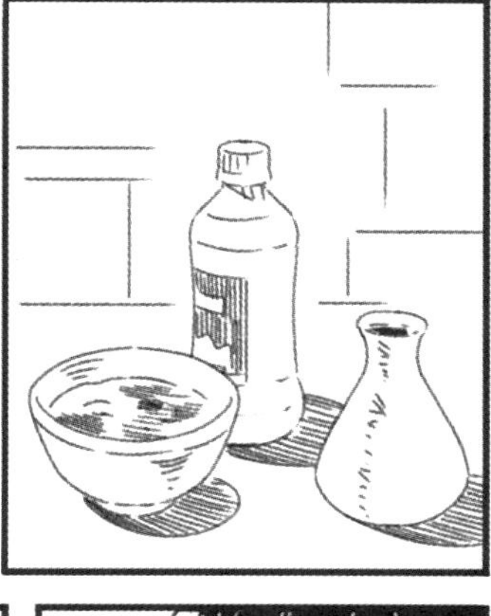

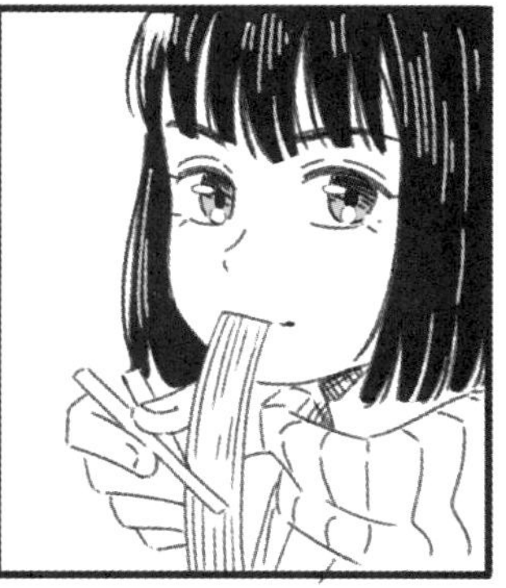

To make a world believable, it's
not enough to just draw people.

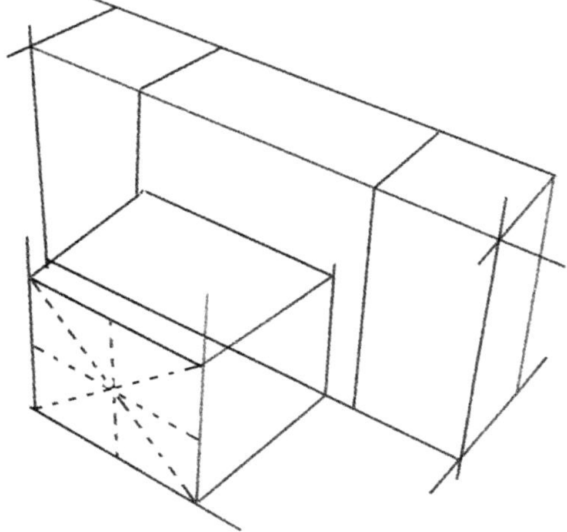

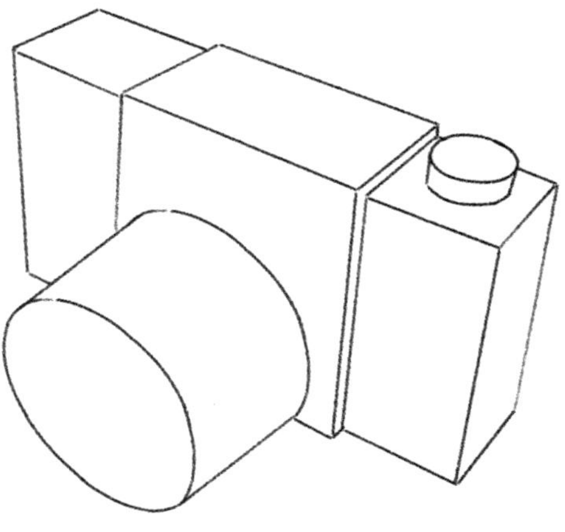

Because we are always interacting with our
environment and the things around us, you also
need to be able to draw inanimate objects.

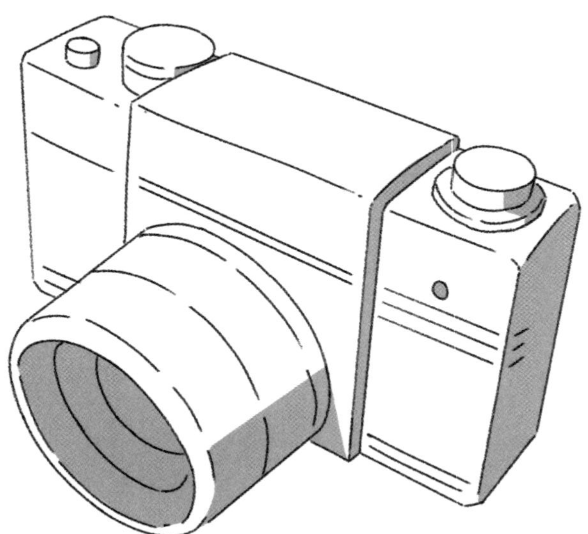

Fortunately, we don't have to learn
how to draw each object perfectly.

Once you have mastered perspective,
the task is greatly simplified.

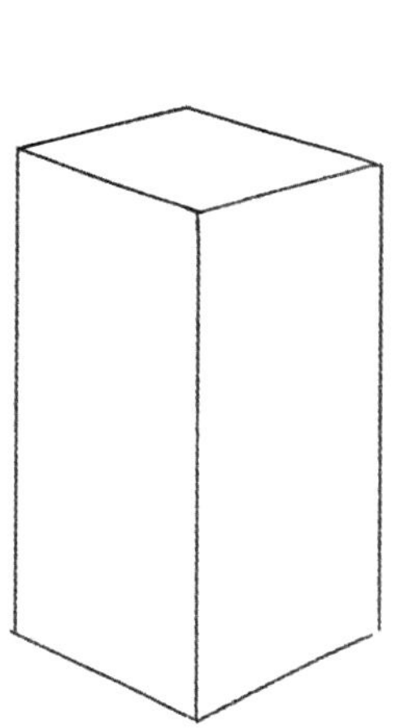 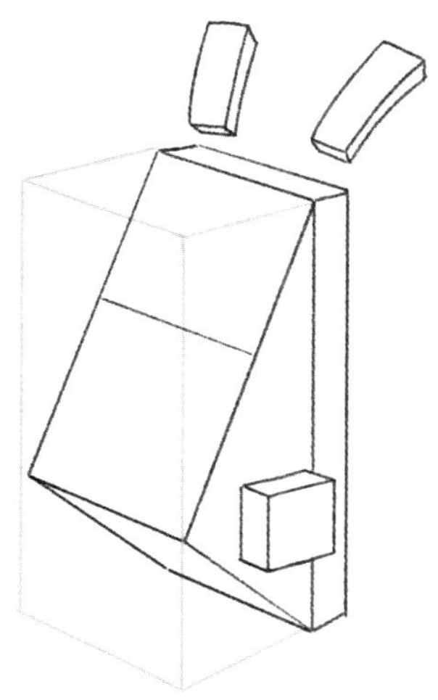 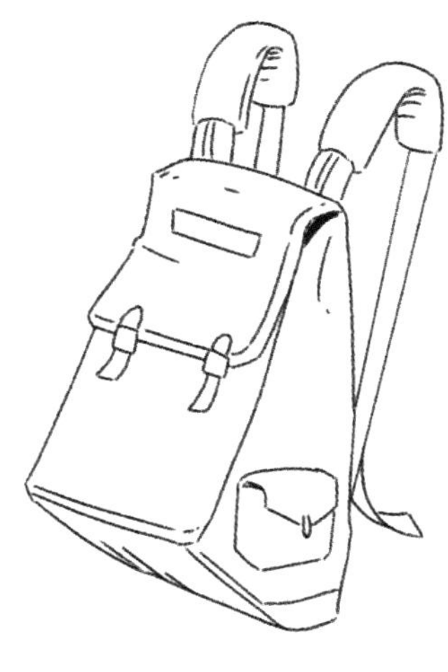

As with everything else, to draw objects, start with simple shapes.
Then add the details.

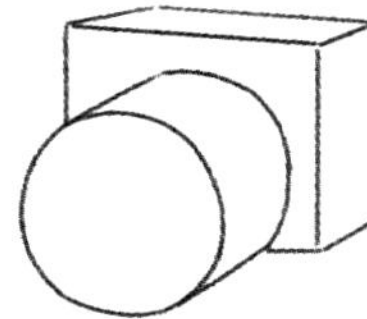 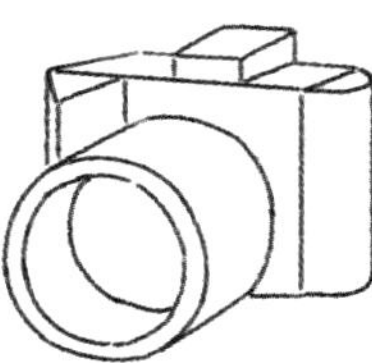 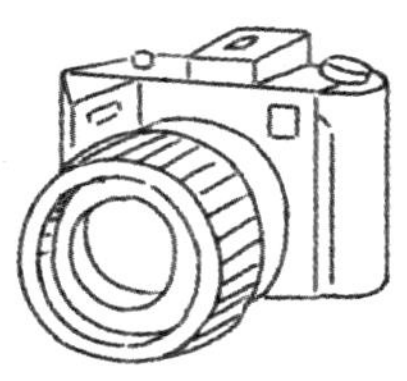

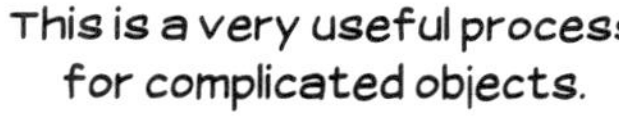

This is a very useful process
for complicated objects.

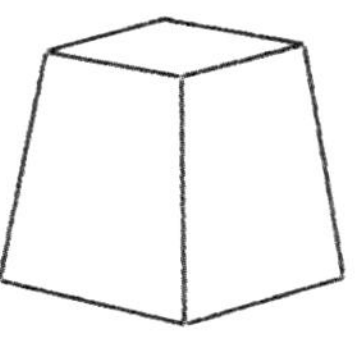 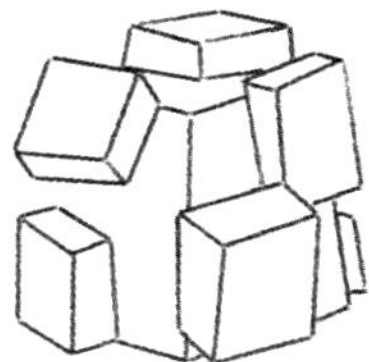 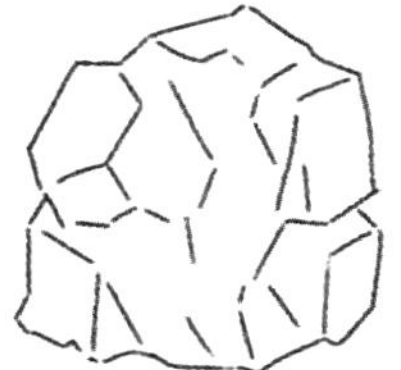

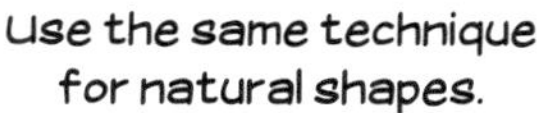

Use the same technique
for natural shapes.

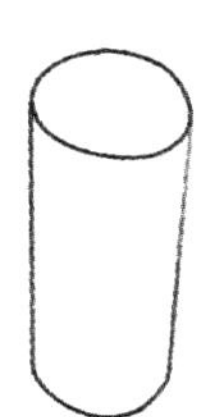 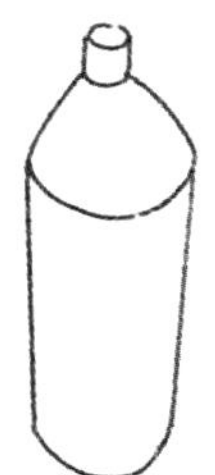 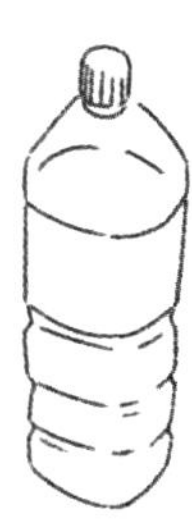

You can change the nature of an
object by changing its texture.

Here are some examples of textures:

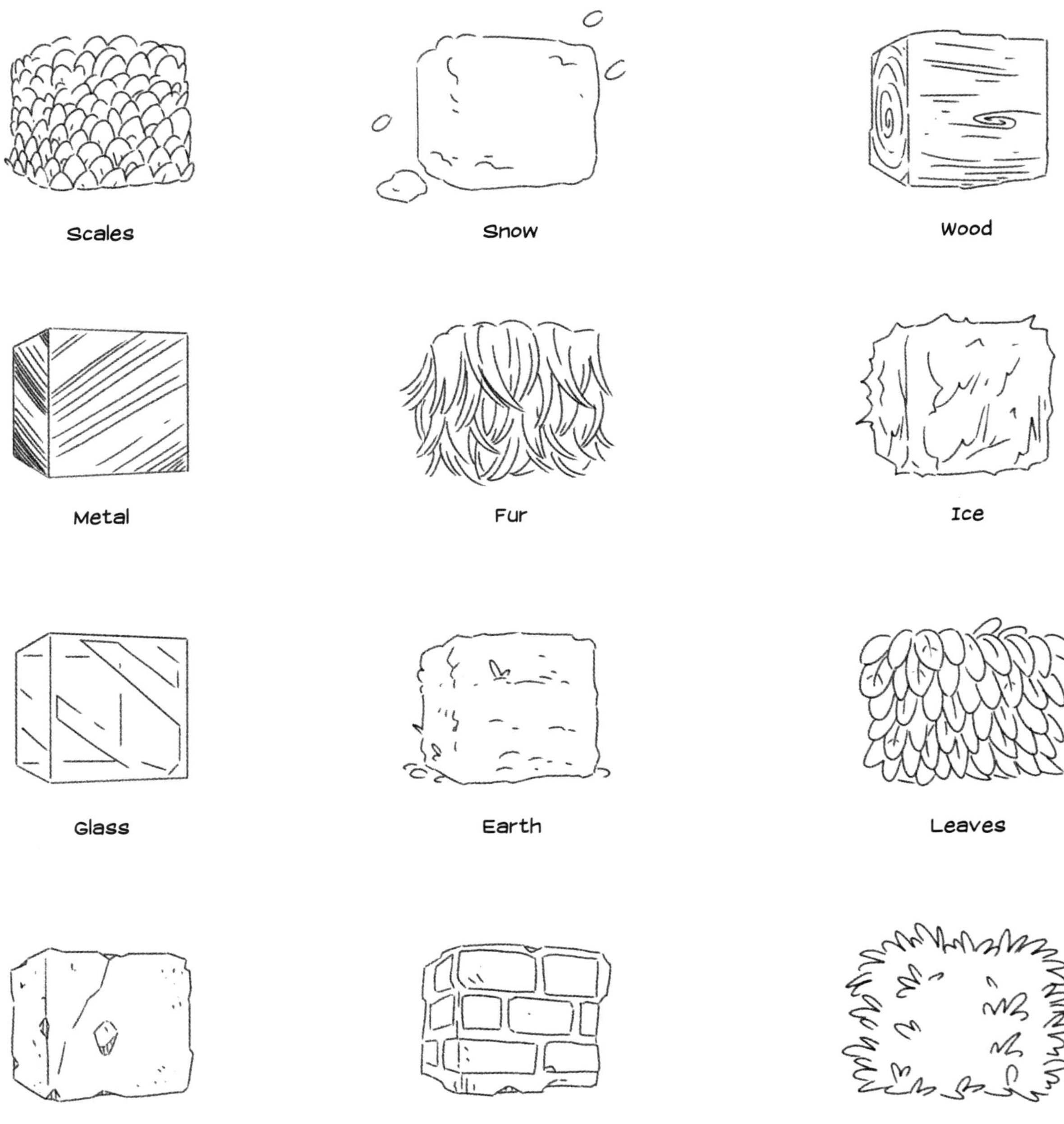

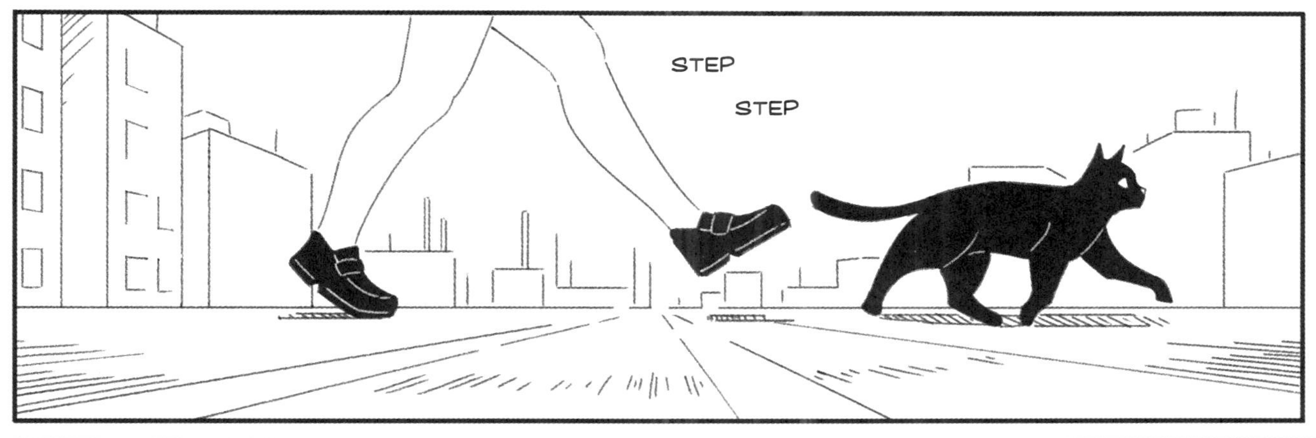

STEP
STEP

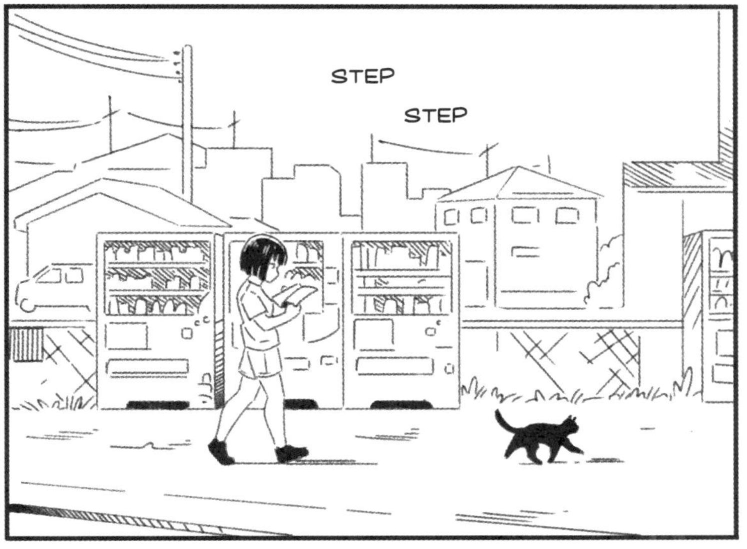

STEP
STEP

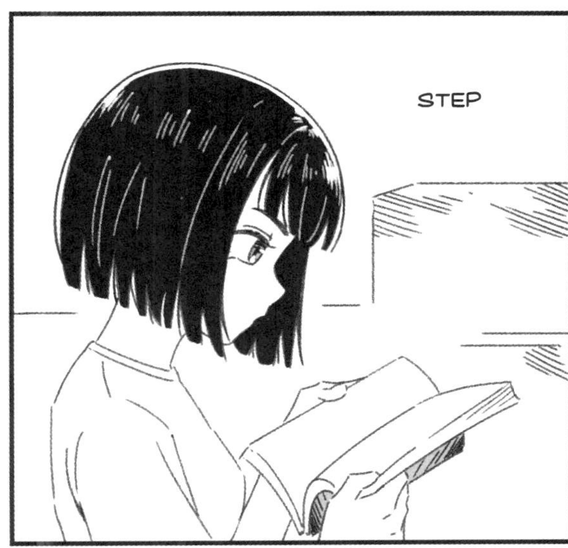

STEP

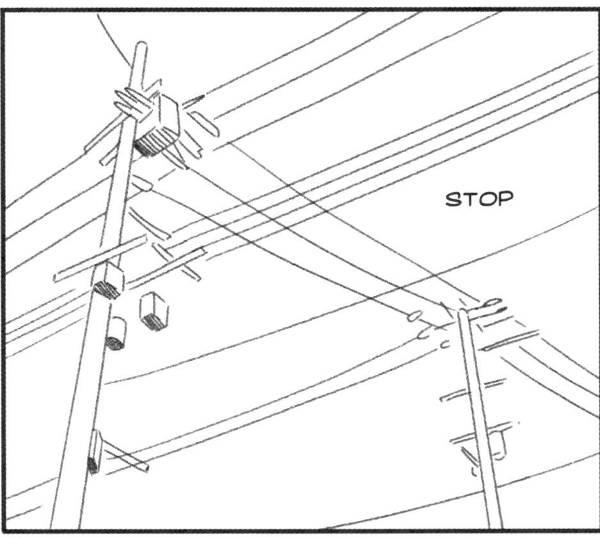

STOP

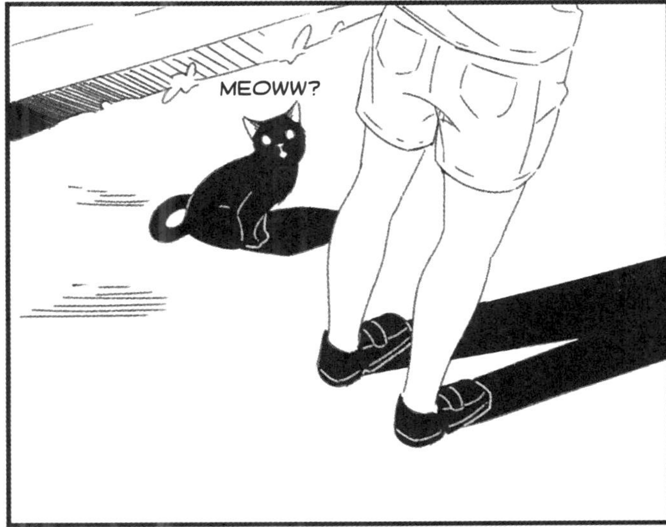

MEOWW?

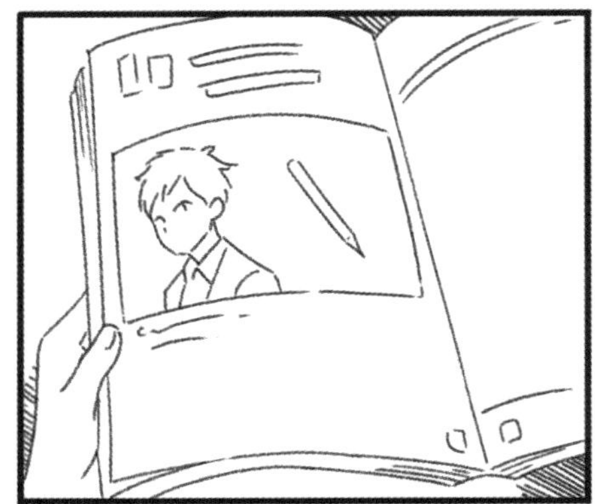
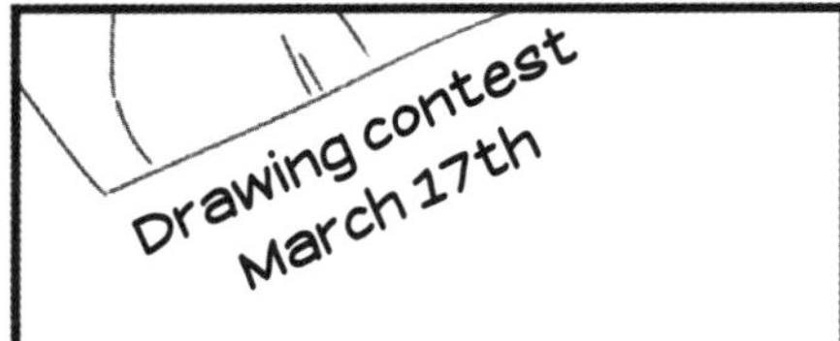

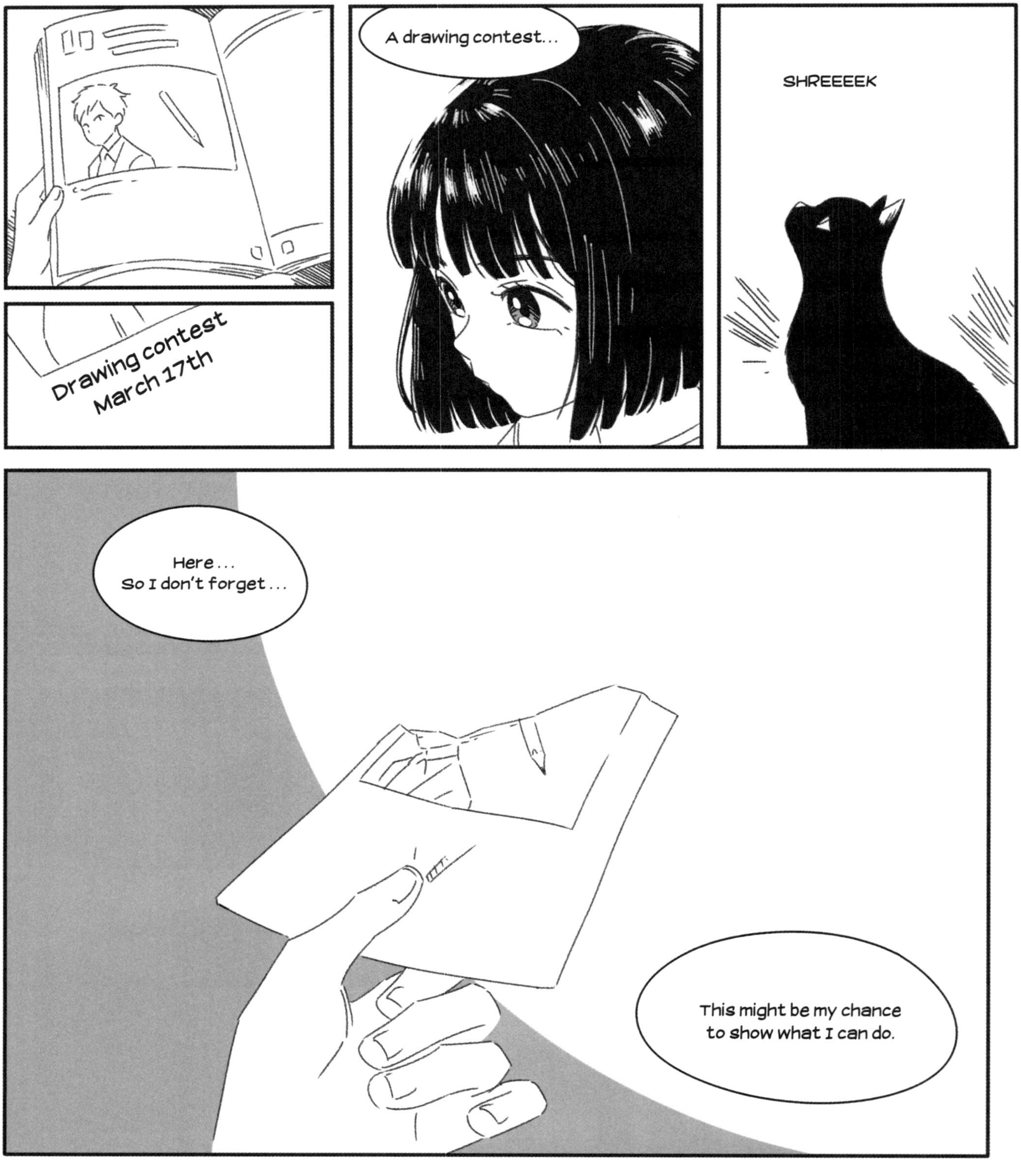

Drawing contest
March 17th

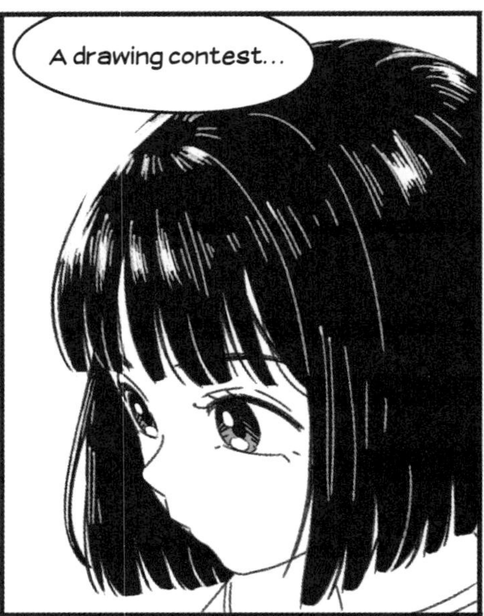

A drawing contest...

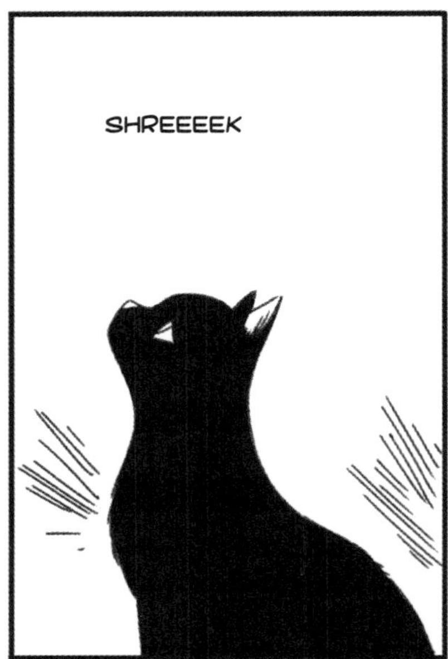

SHREEEEK

Here...
So I don't forget...

This might be my chance
to show what I can do.

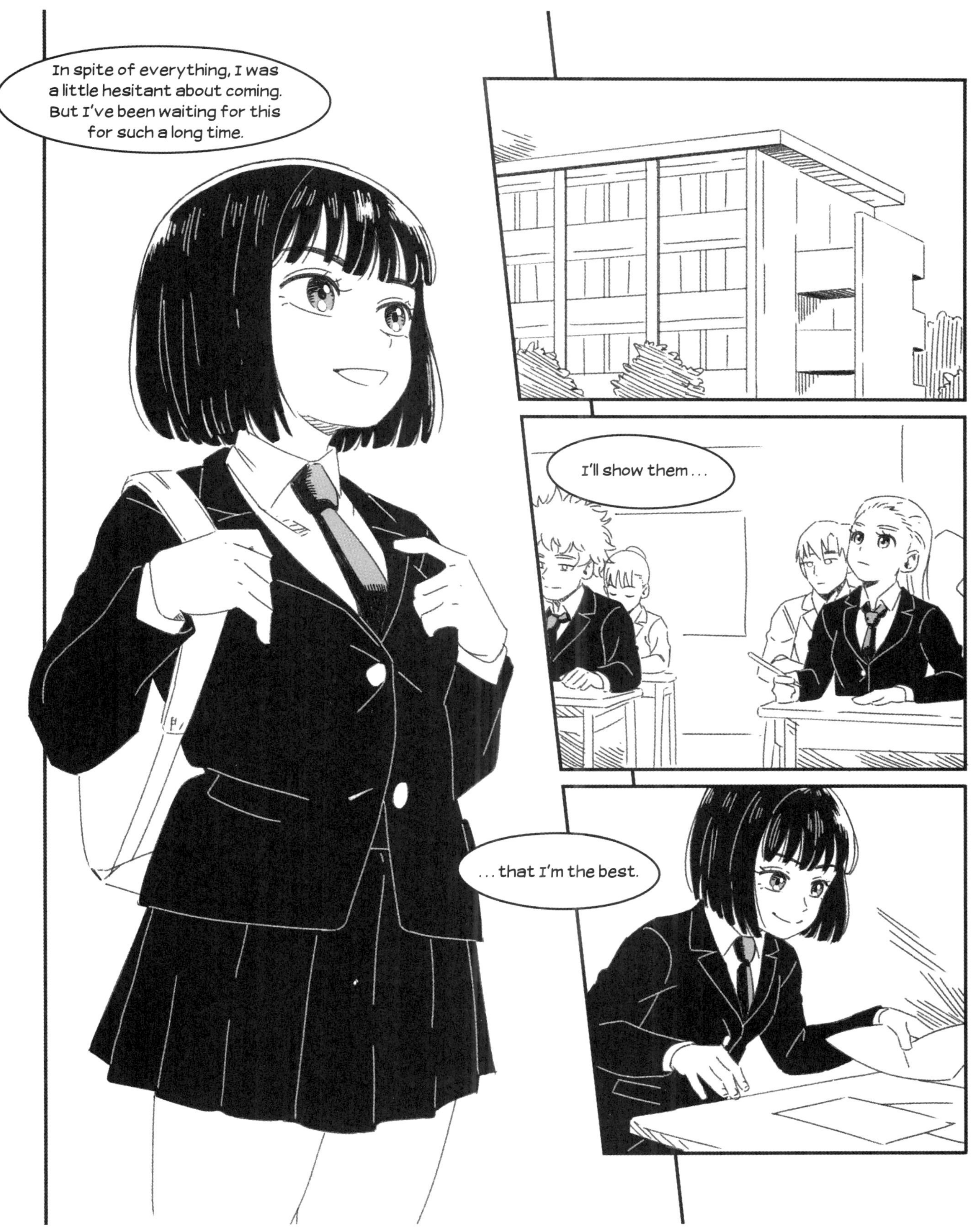

In spite of everything, I was a little hesitant about coming. But I've been waiting for this for such a long time.
I'll show them...
...that I'm the best.

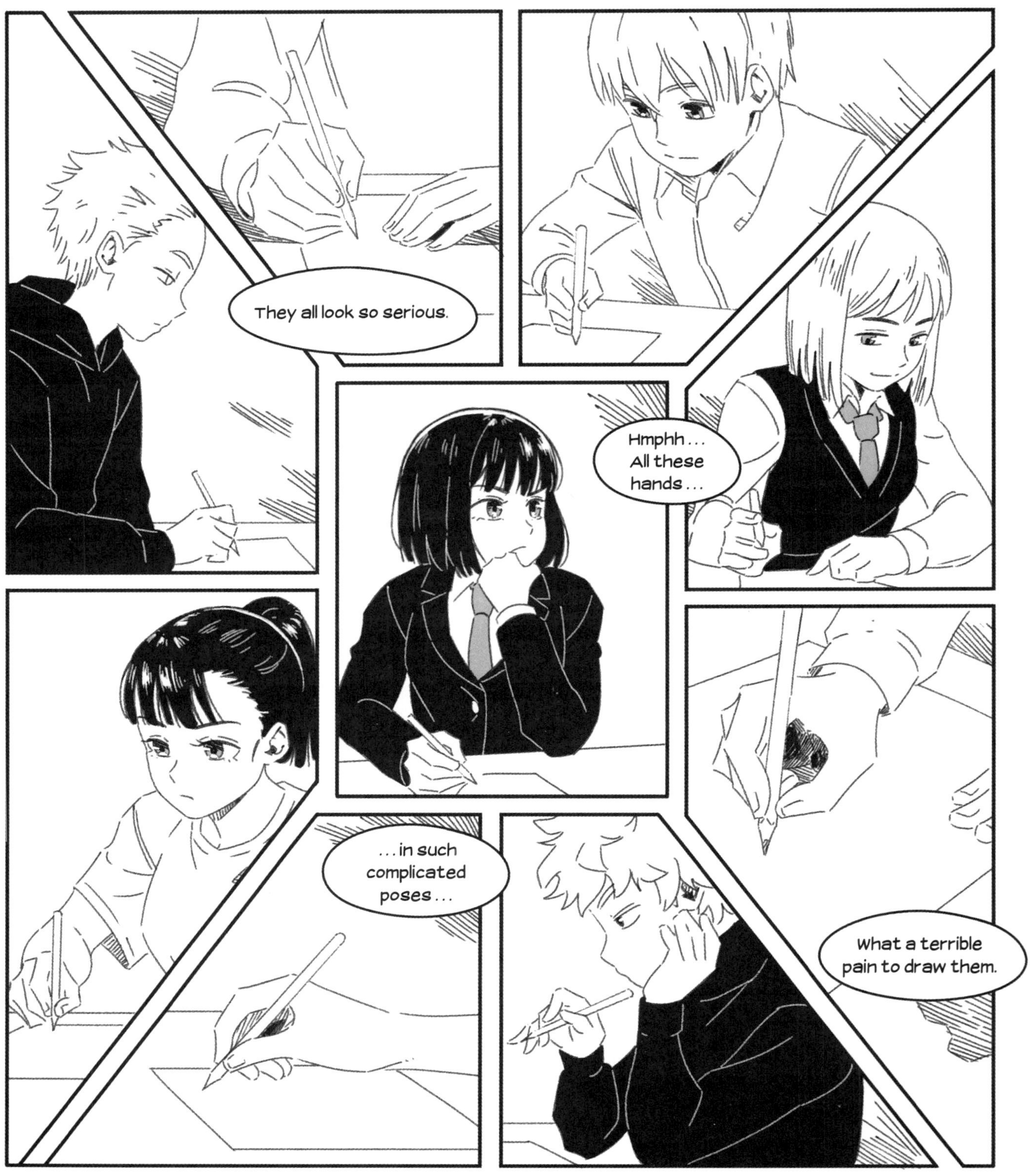

They all look so serious.
Hmphh... All these hands...
...in such complicated poses...
What a terrible pain to draw them.

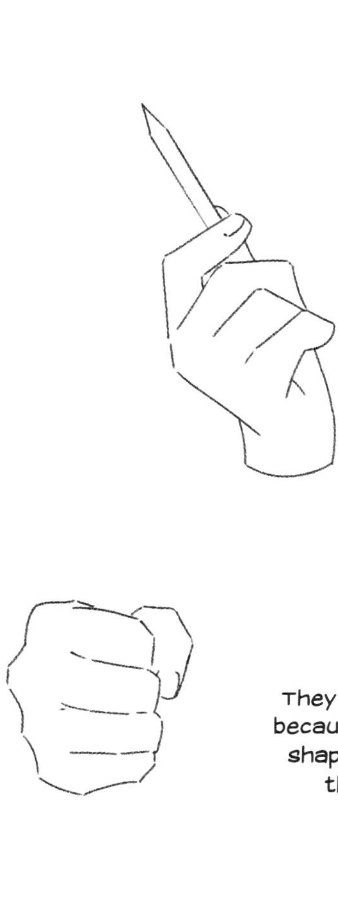
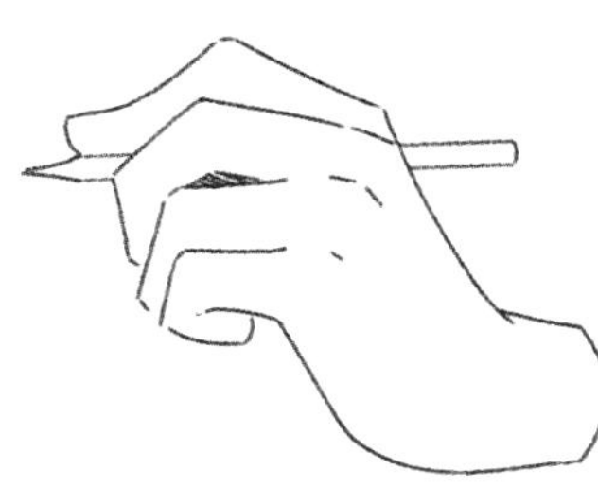

The hands are every
illustrator's nightmare.

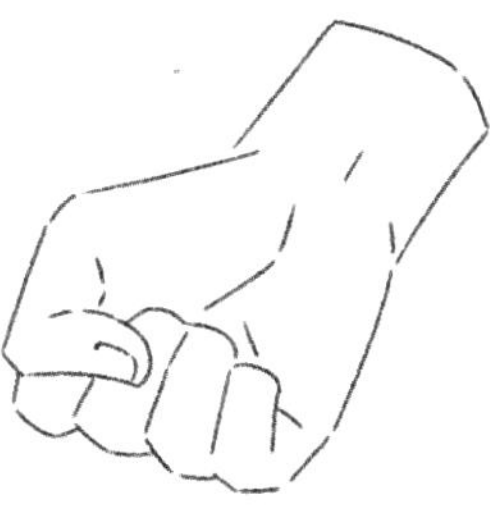

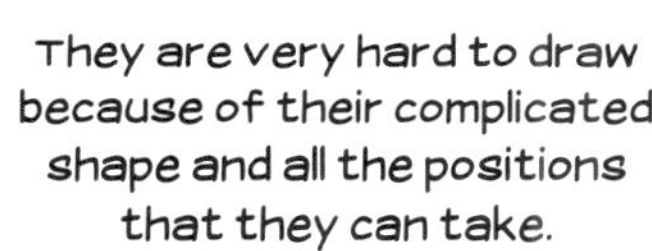

They are very hard to draw
because of their complicated
shape and all the positions
that they can take.

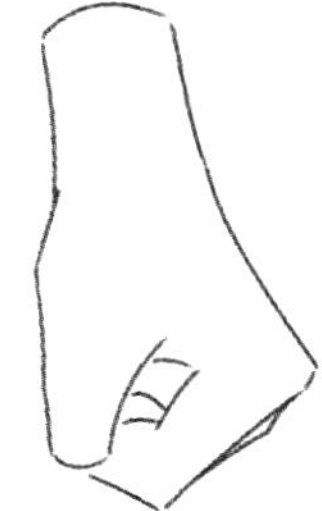

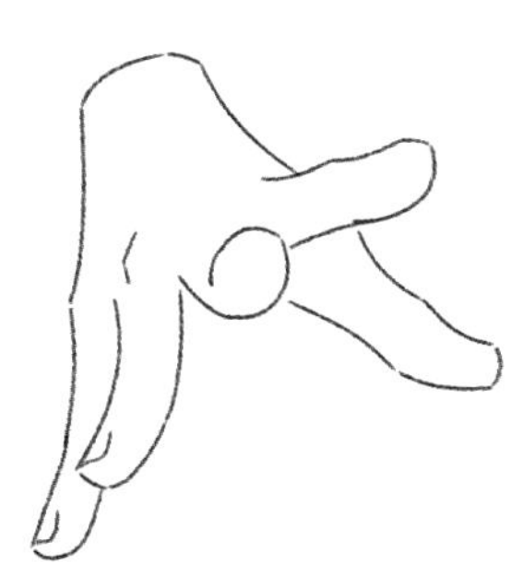

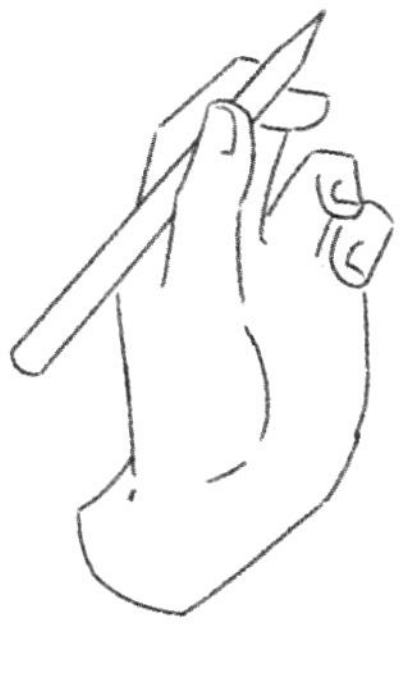

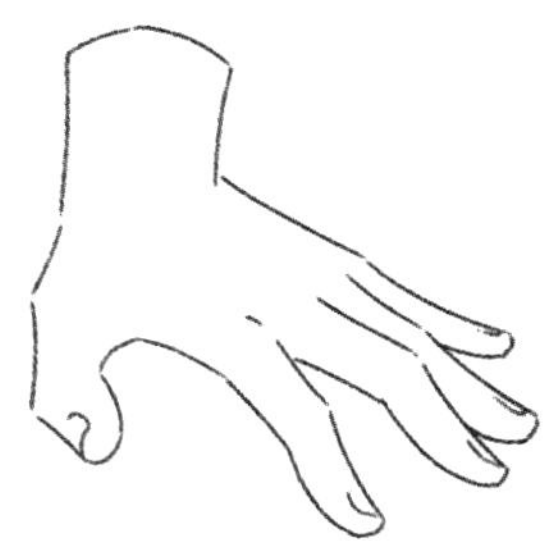

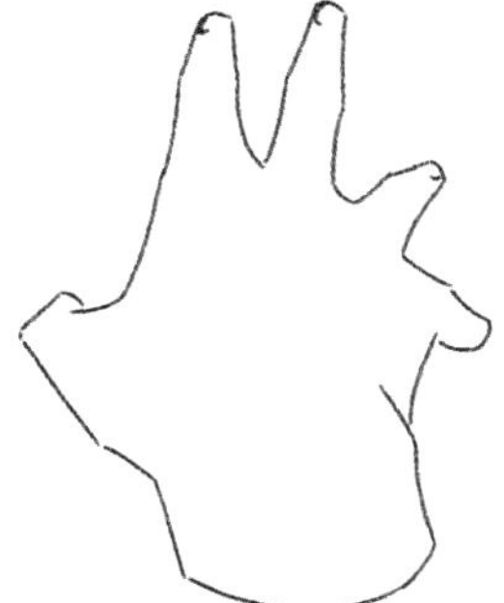

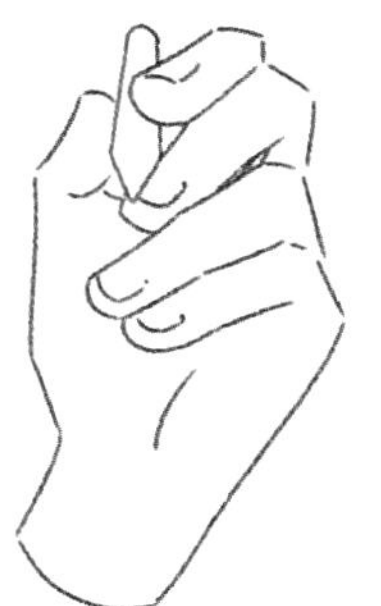

One trick is to learn
the most common hand
positions by heart.

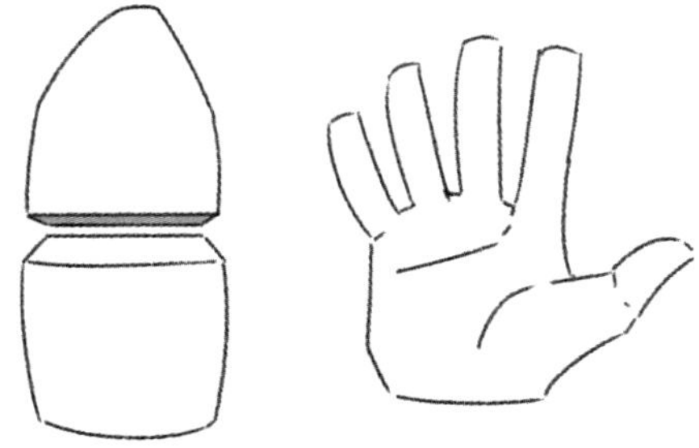

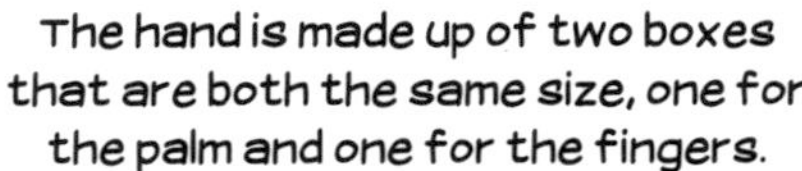

The hand is made up of two boxes
that are both the same size, one for
the palm and one for the fingers.

Start by drawing the palm, which is
a box that is curved slightly upward,
before adding the fingers.

The thumb is attached to
the palm by a triangular box.

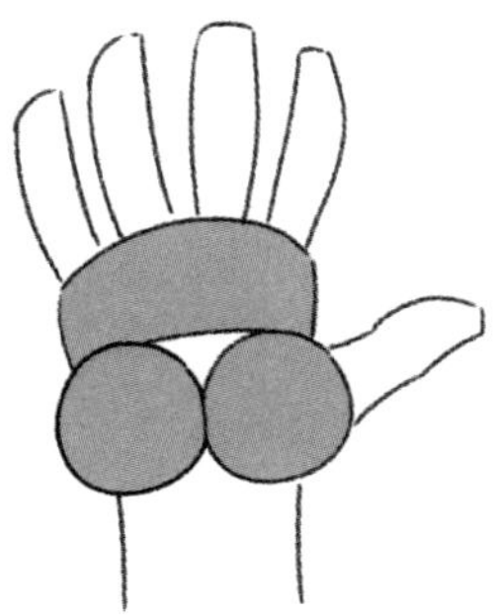

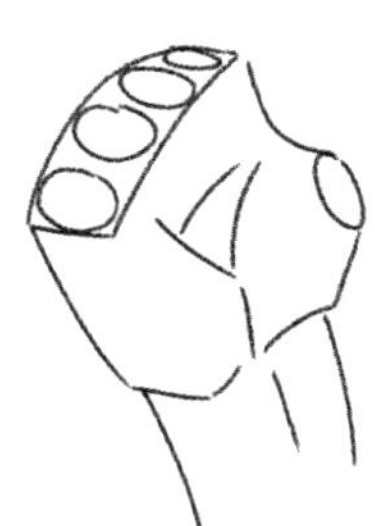

You can get more into the details by
simplifying the palm into three basic
shapes, which give it its volume.

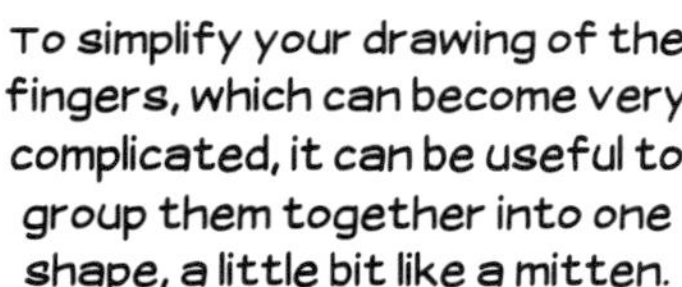

To simplify your drawing of the
fingers, which can become very
complicated, it can be useful to
group them together into one
shape, a little bit like a mitten.

You can also choose to only group
two or three fingers together, to
make the pose more natural.

After that, draw each individual
finger, using the shape you have
drawn as a reference structure.

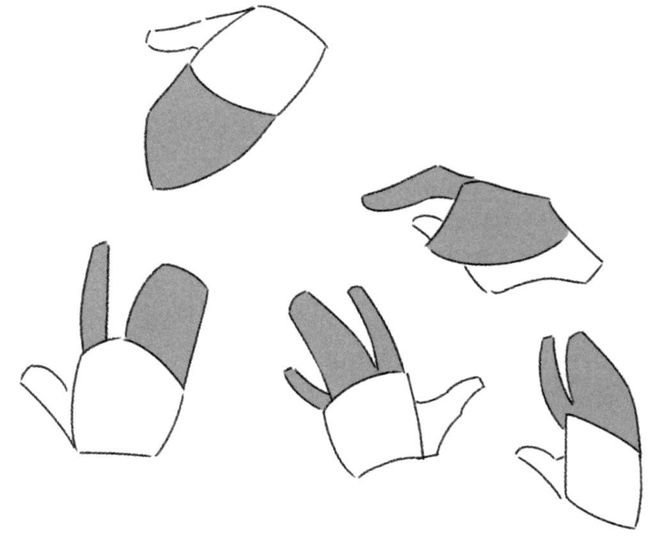

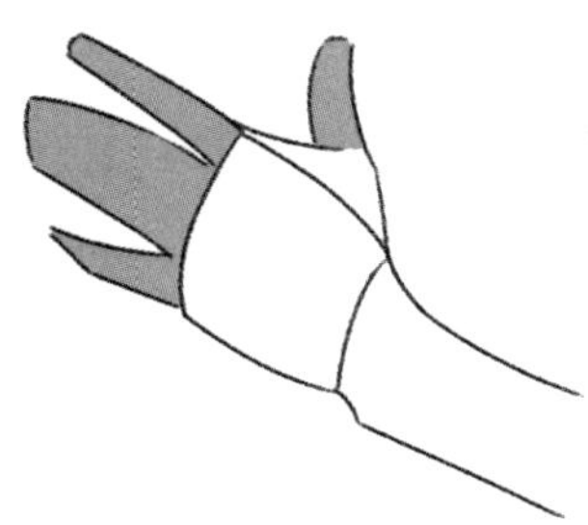

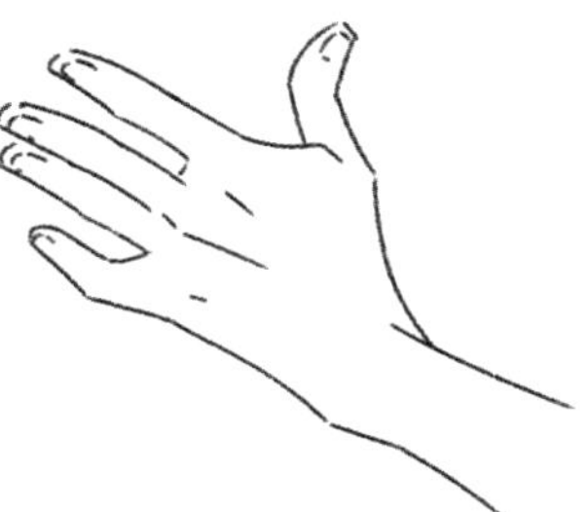

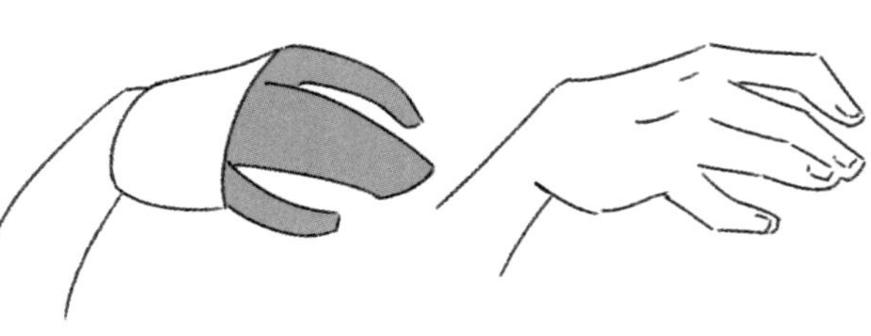

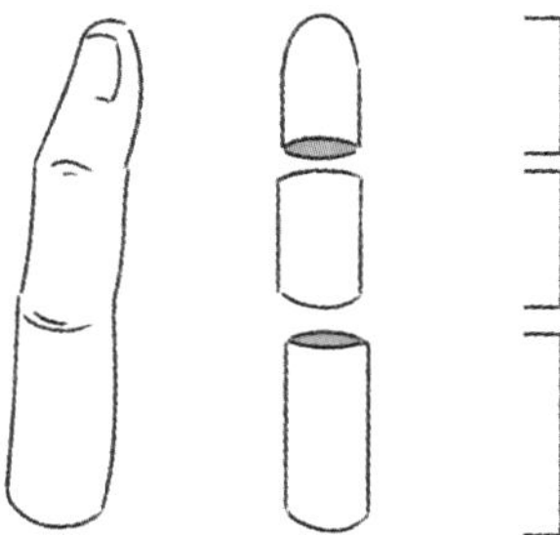

The fingers are made of three cylinders each (the phalanges), of which the bottom one is the largest. The last two are the same size as each other, smaller than the first one.

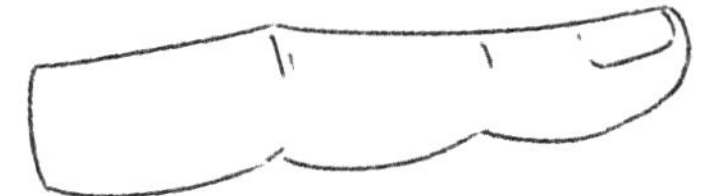

The cylinders are flat on the top side of the finger and rounded on the bottom.

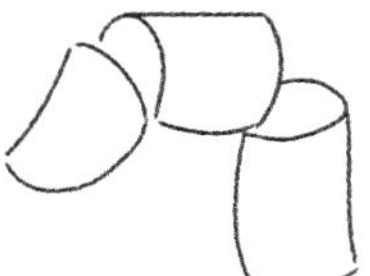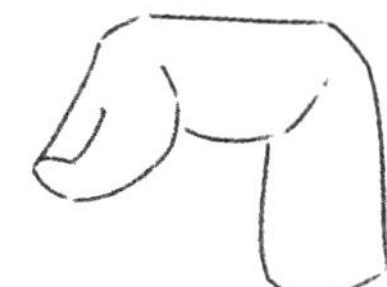

When the finger is bent, the phalanges create folds that converge toward the bulge.

To make a realistic closed fist, it can be useful to break the alignment of the phalanges by raising the index finger a little.

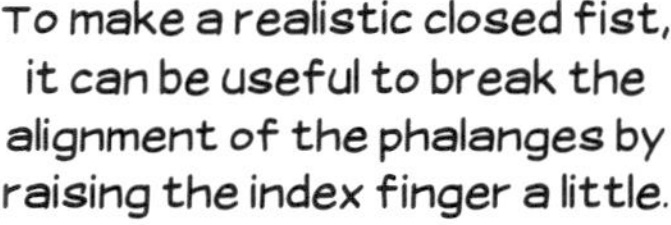

To make it easier to draw the fist, you can first simplify it into a box—like you did with the mitten, but more angular.

In a closed fist, you will also see the bones of the metacarpals pointing upward, like little hills.

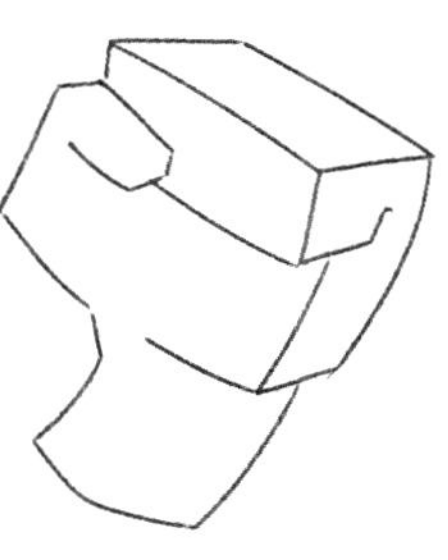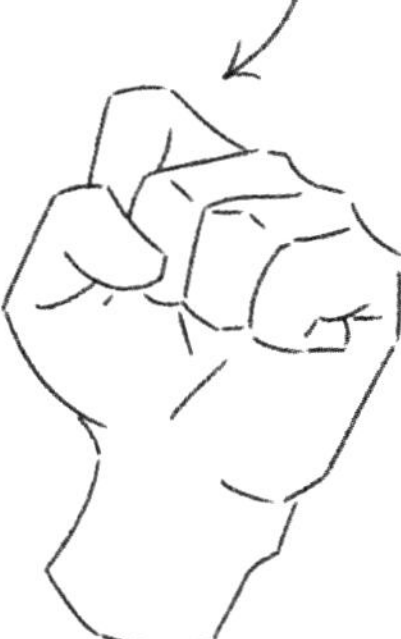

Seen from the side, the closed fingers form a spiral of folds on the skin.

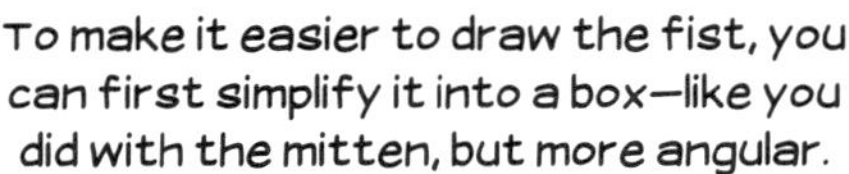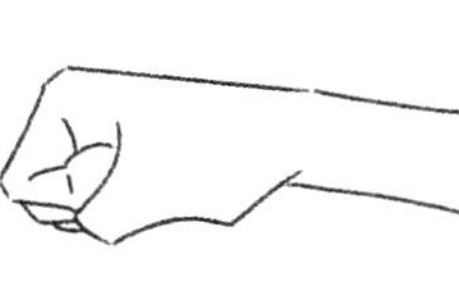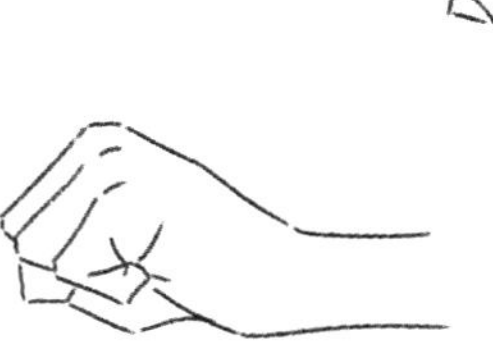

Now you can draw hands in different positions.
As a shortcut, remember that fundamentally,
a hand is nothing but a box and some cylinders.

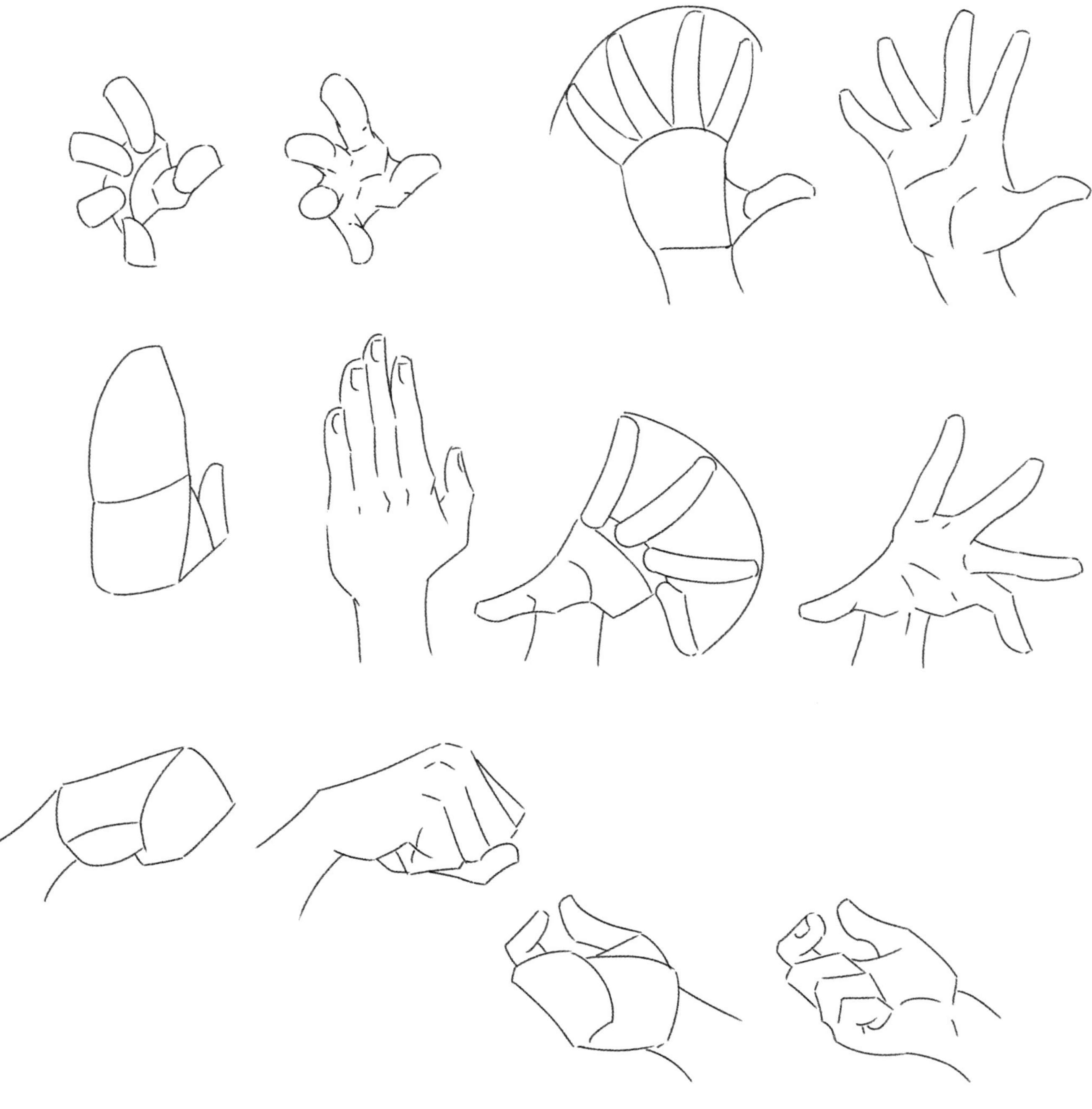

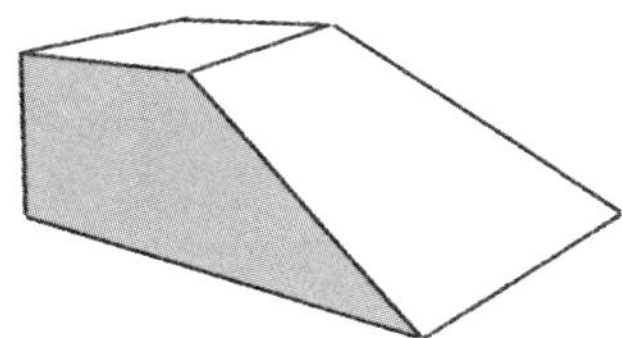 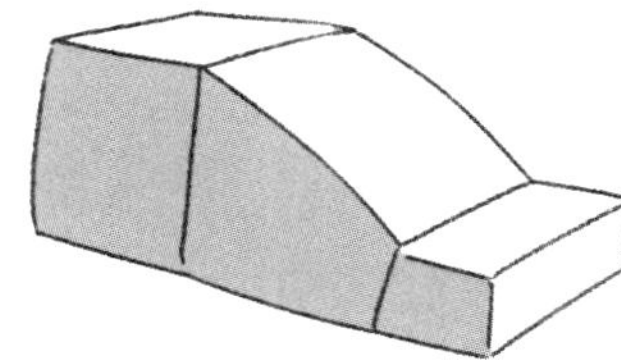 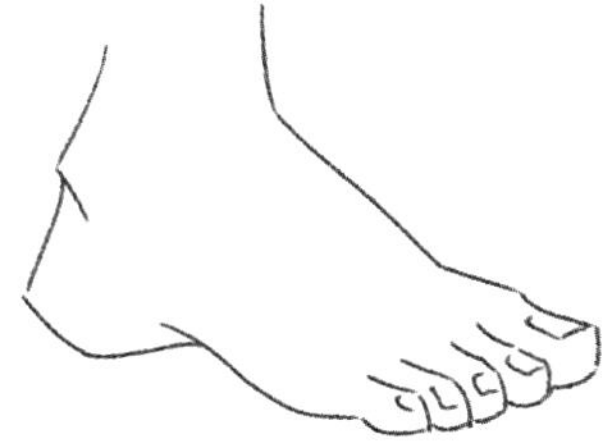

Divide the foot into three parts:
a box for the heel, a tapered box for
the front of the foot, and then one
last rectangular box for the toes.

Indicate the toes using rounded
shapes, making sure that the big toe is
wider and longer than the others.

In a foot seen from the side,
you can see an arched form just
underneath the second box.

In a foot seen from the front,
the boxes are foreshortened
and the foot looks like a triangle.

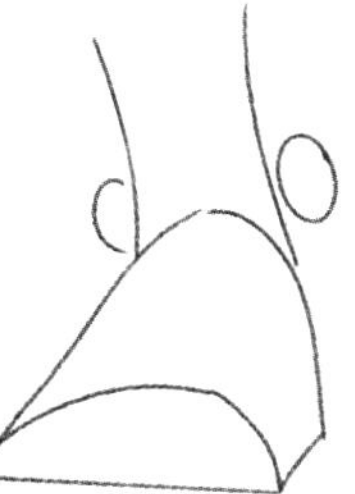 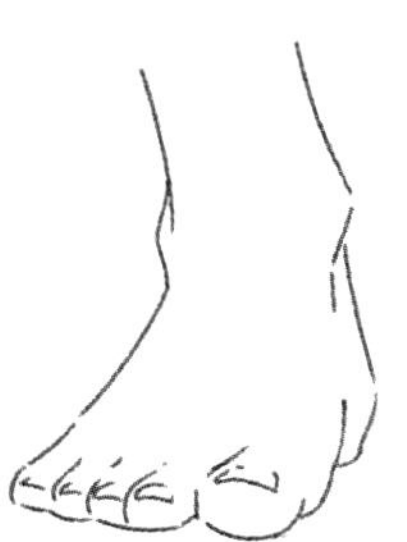

The foot is connected to the ankle by
the anklebones, and these two small
bones are particularly visible when the
foot is seen from the front.

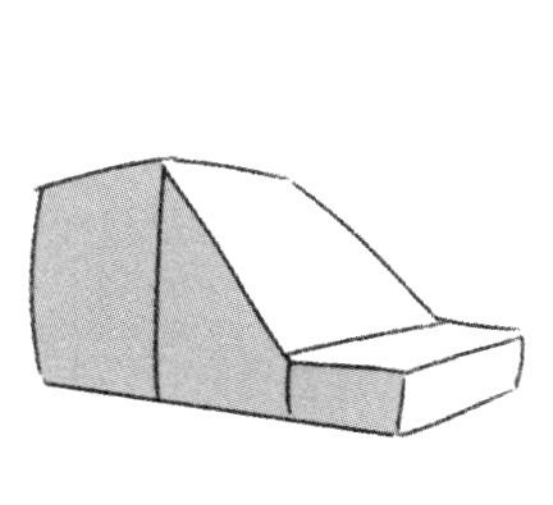 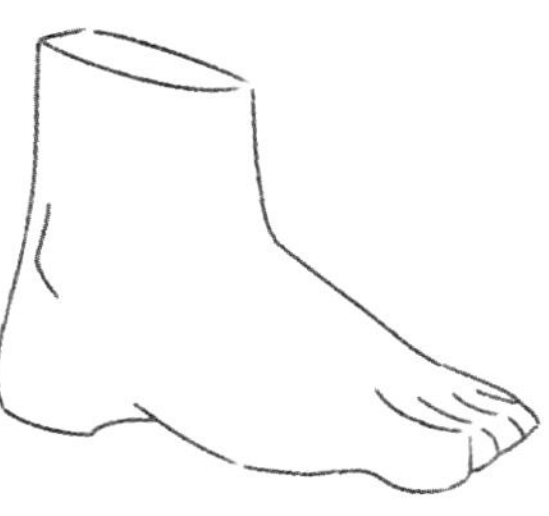

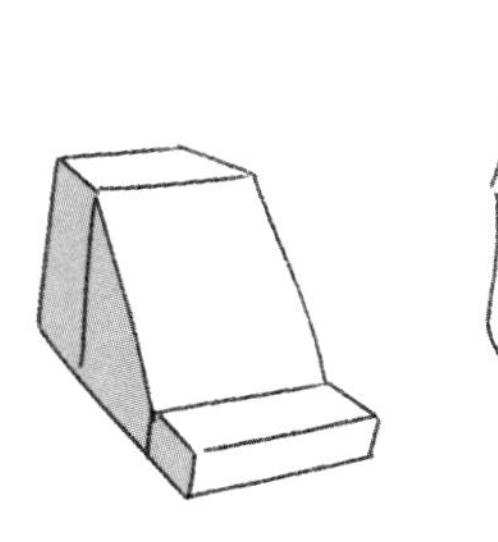 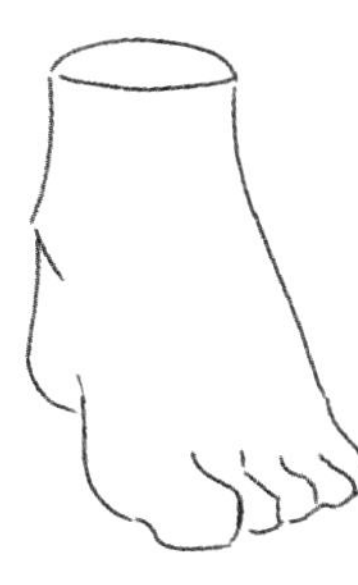

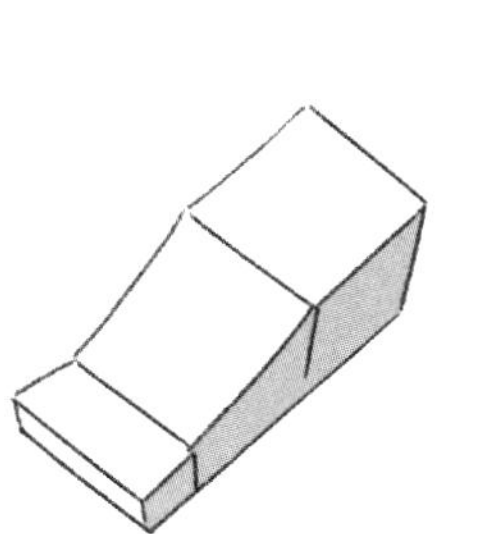 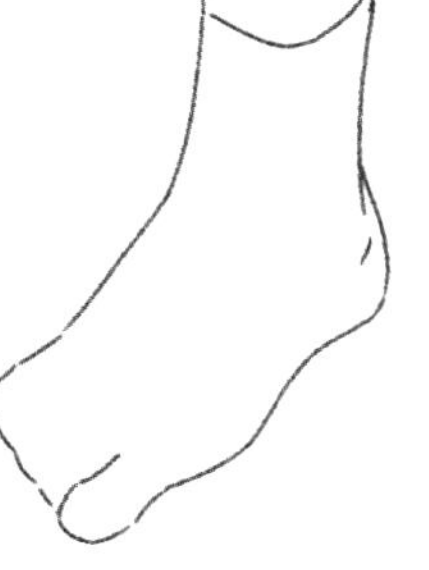

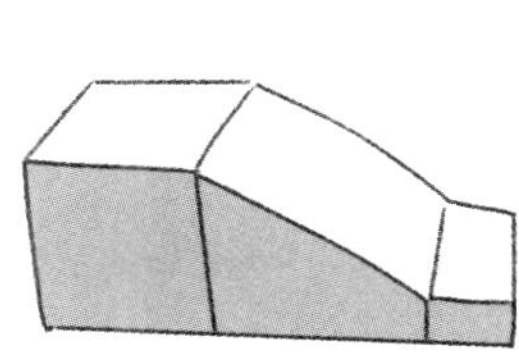 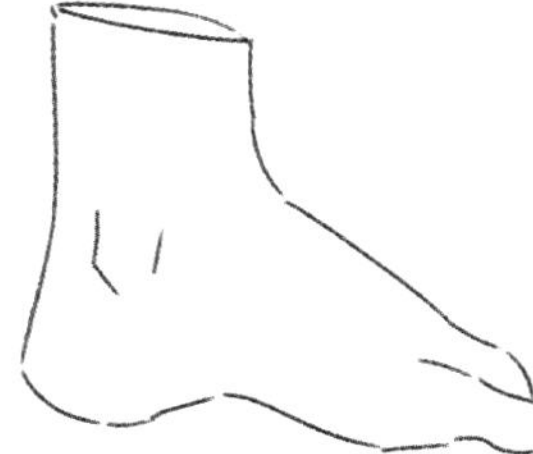

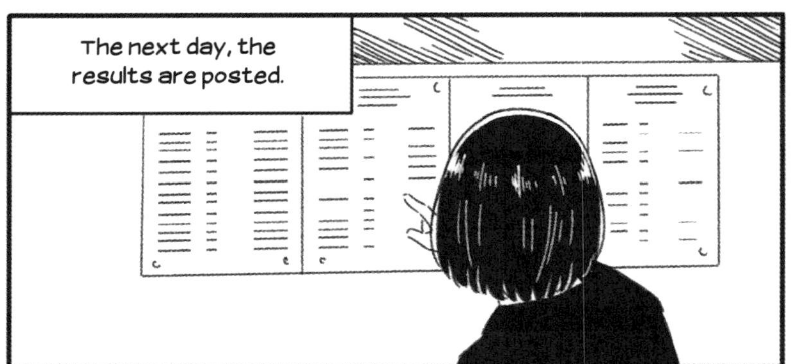

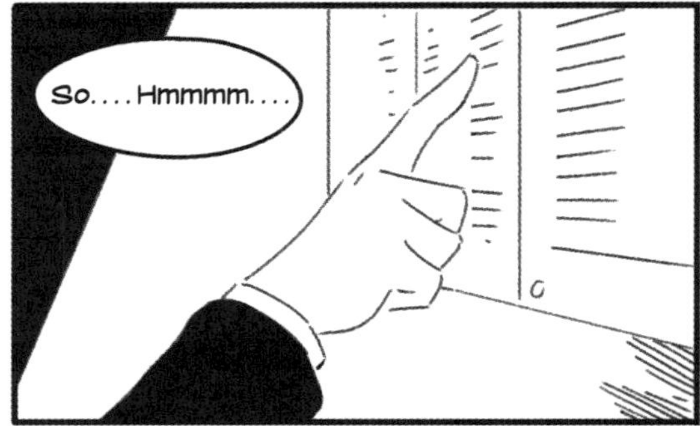

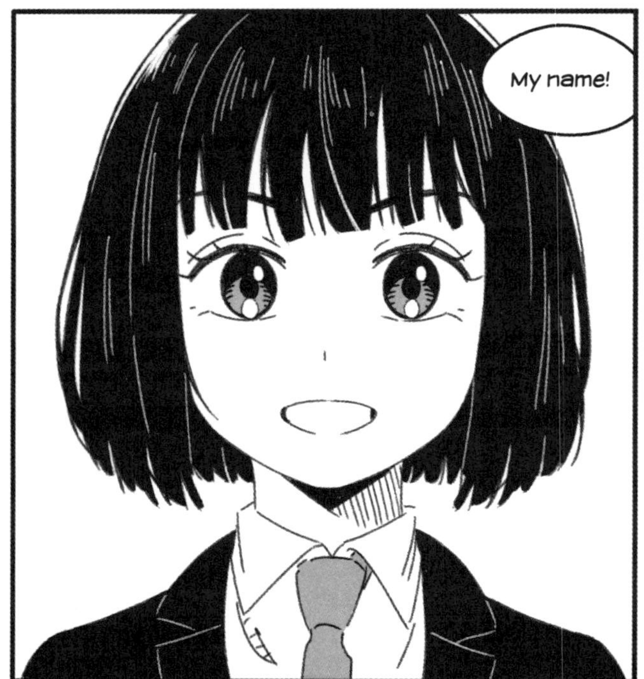

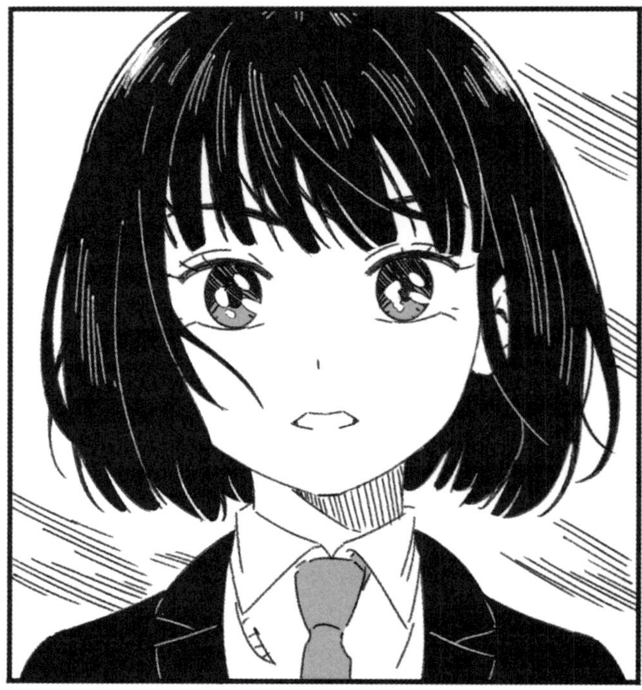

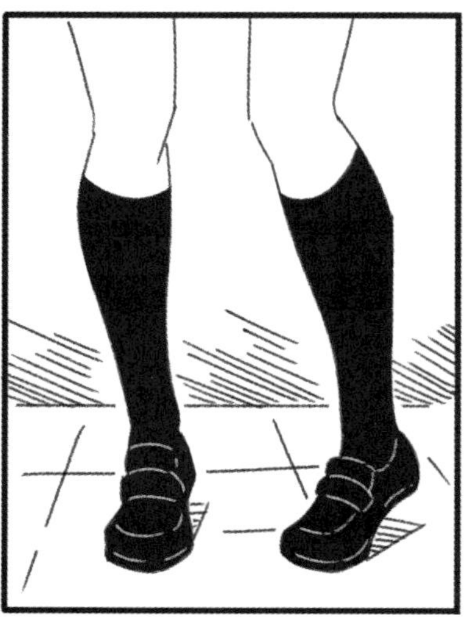

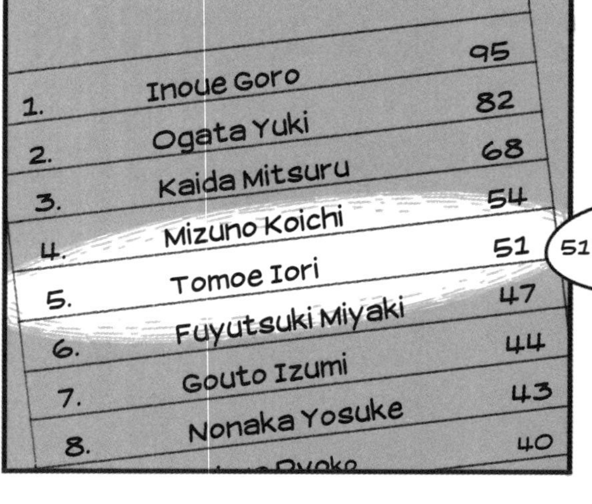

1.	Inoue Goro	95
2.	Ogata Yuki	82
3.	Kaida Mitsuru	68
4.	Mizuno Koichi	54
5.	Tomoe Iori	51
6.	Fuyutsuki Miyaki	47
7.	Gouto Izumi	44
8.	Nonaka Yosuke	43
		40

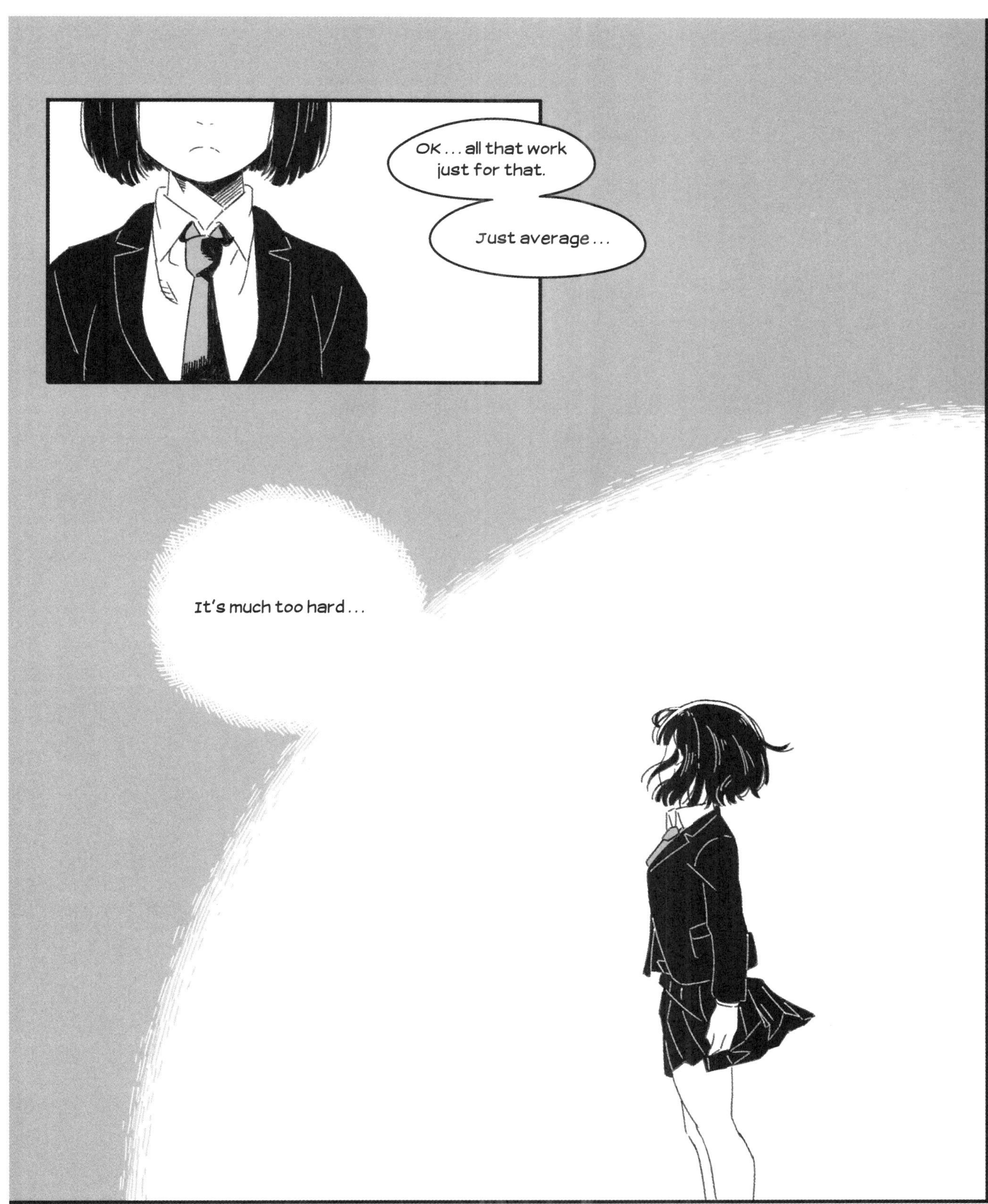
OK ... all that work just for that.
Just average ...
It's much too hard ...

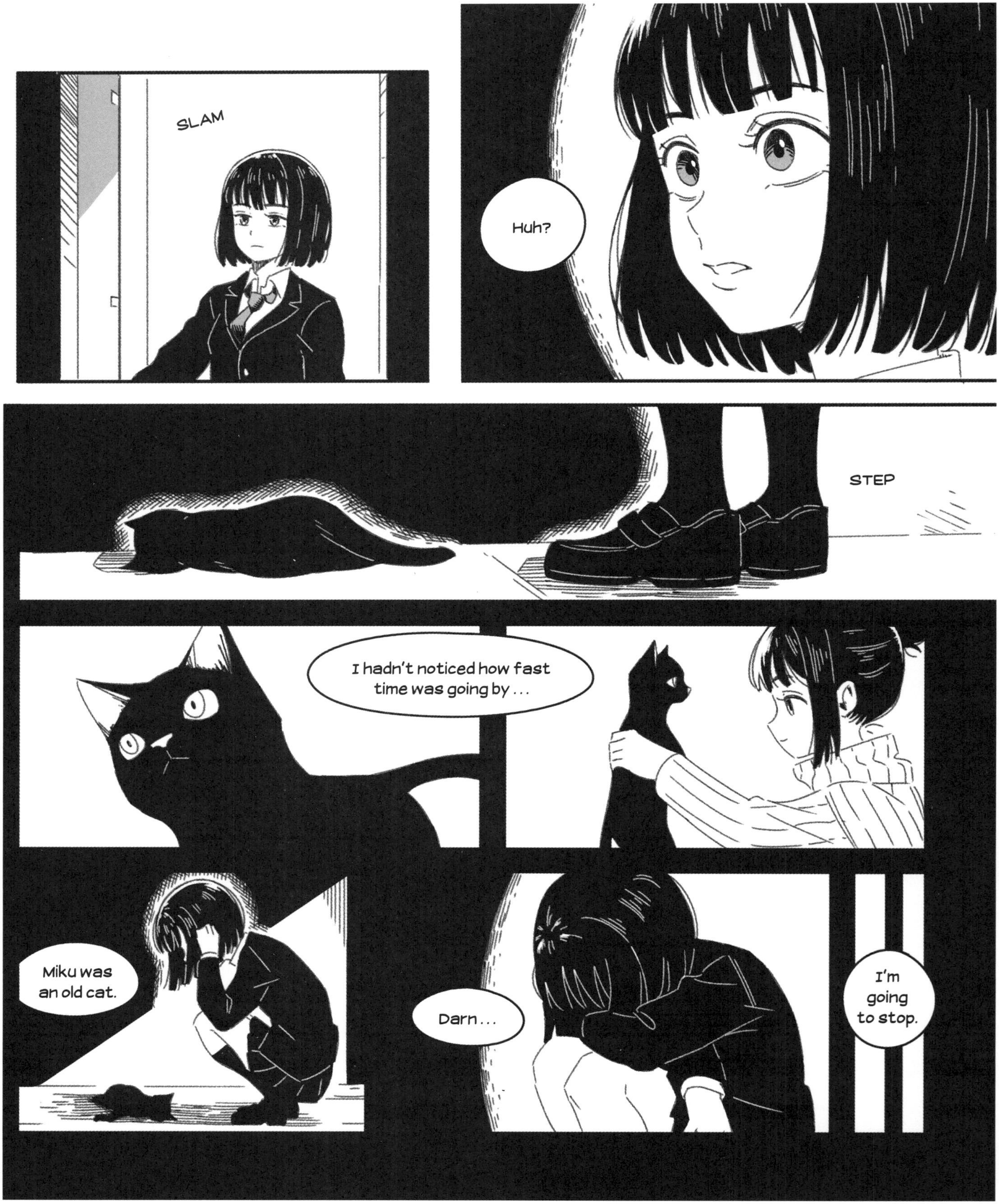

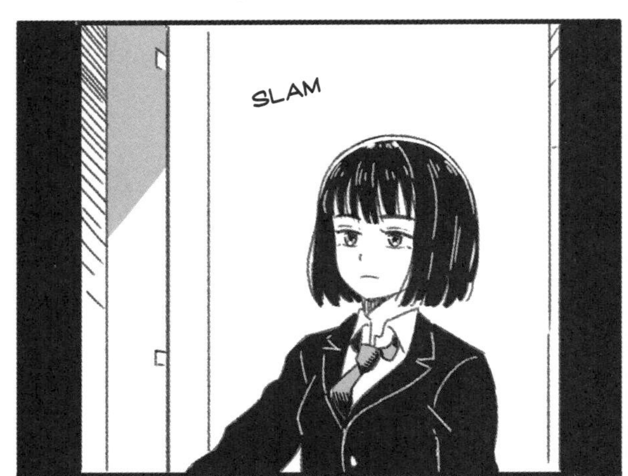

SLAM

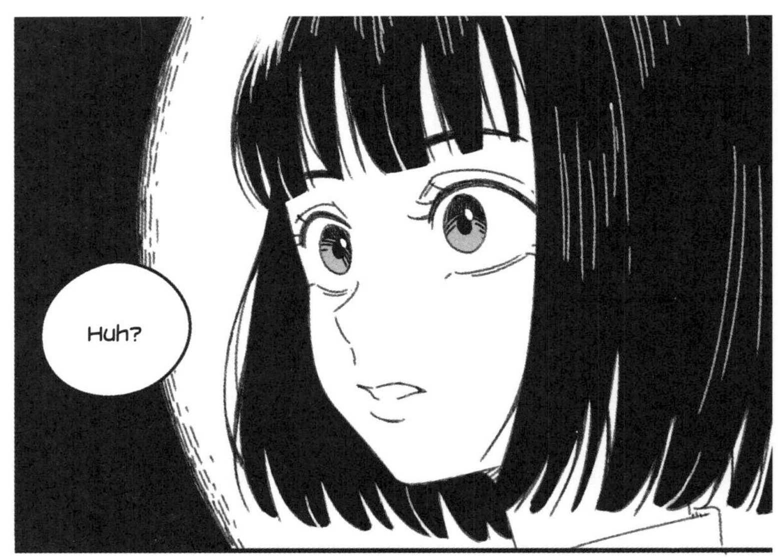

Huh?

STEP

I hadn't noticed how fast time was going by . . .

Miku was an old cat.

Darn . . .

I'm going to stop.

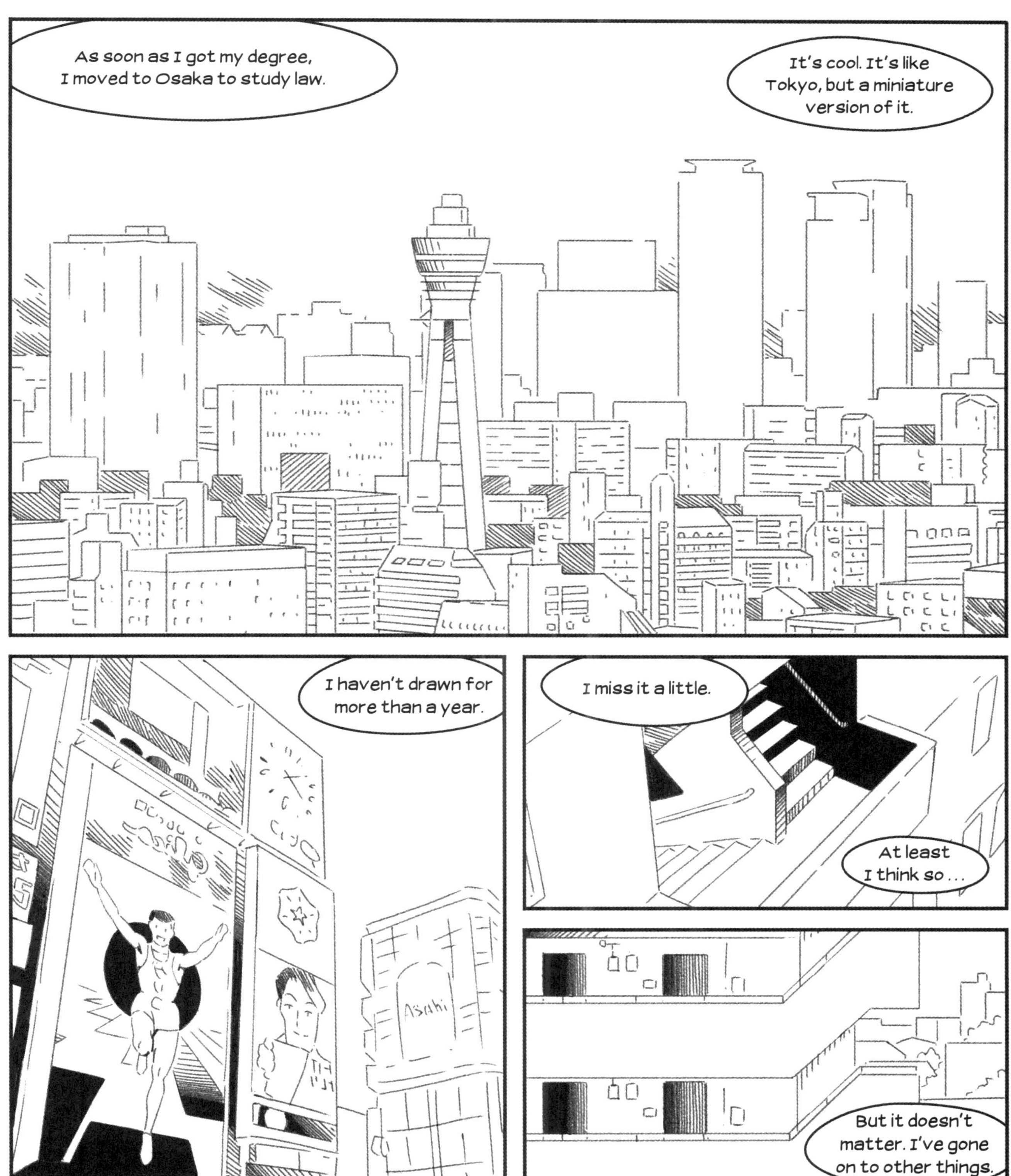

As soon as I got my degree, I moved to Osaka to study law.
It's cool. It's like Tokyo, but a miniature version of it.
I haven't drawn for more than a year.
I miss it a little.
At least I think so ...
But it doesn't matter. I've gone on to other things.
Asahi

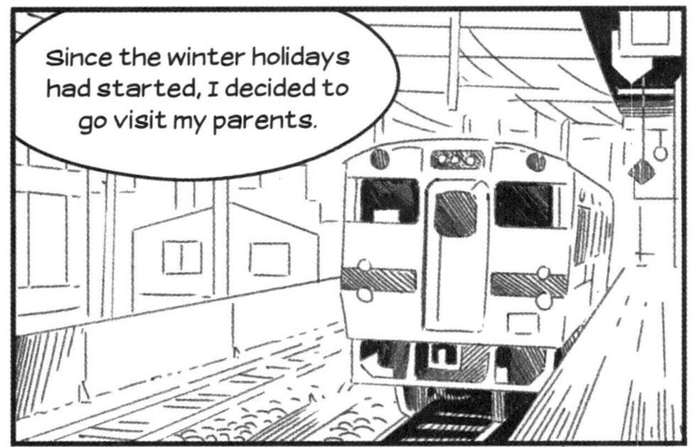

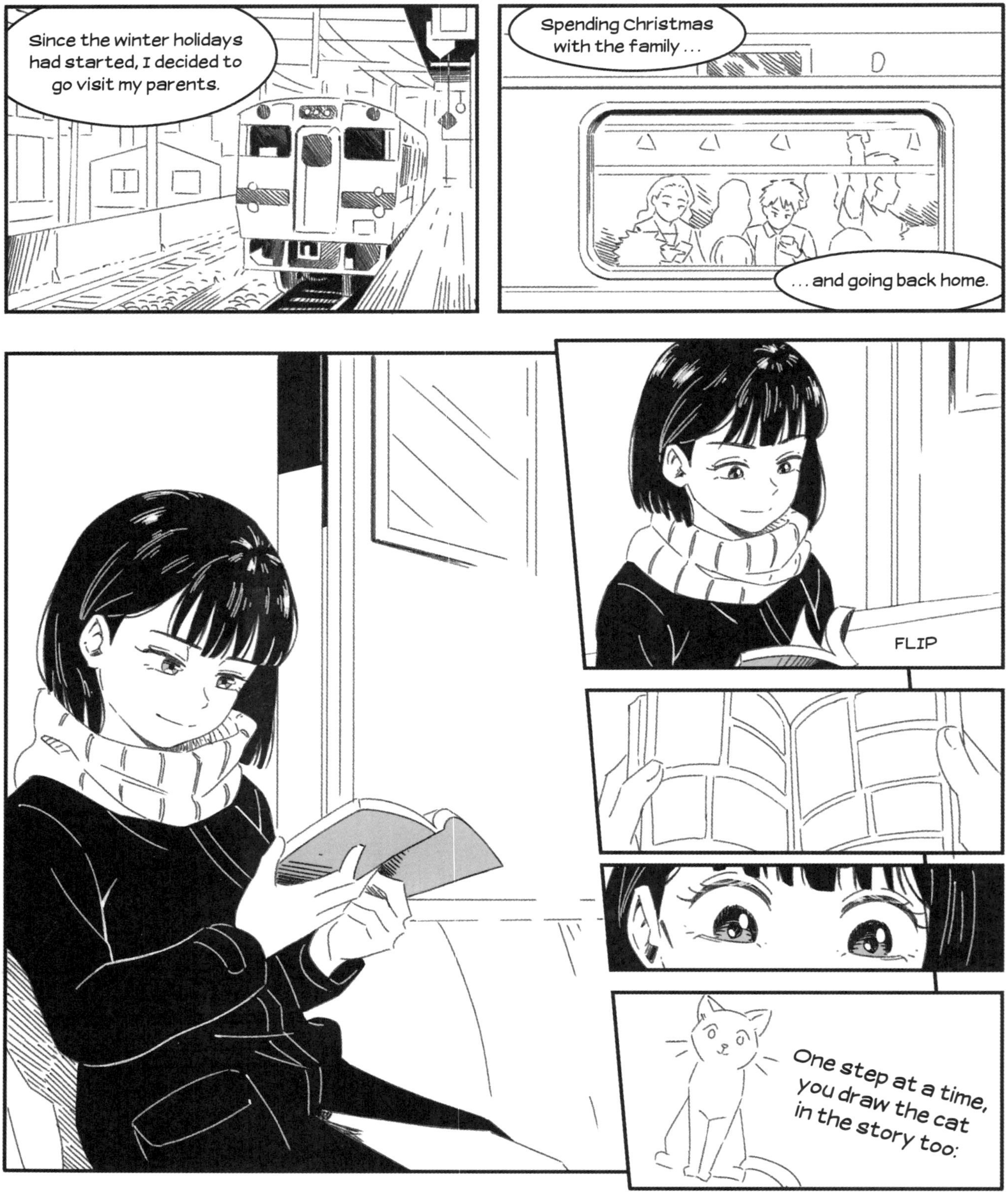

Since the winter holidays had started, I decided to go visit my parents.

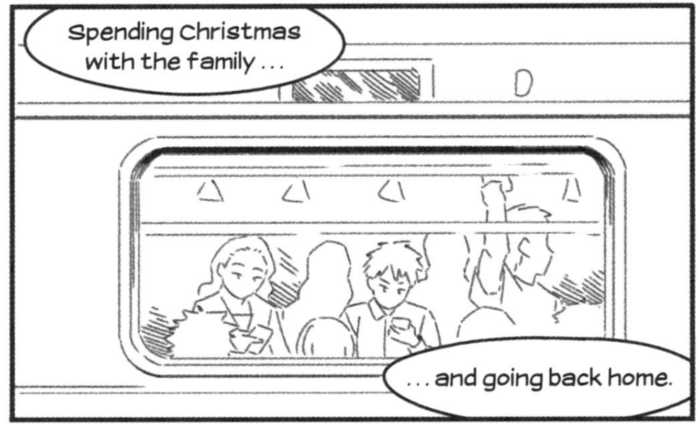

Spending Christmas with the family...
...and going back home.

FLIP
One step at a time, you draw the cat in the story too:

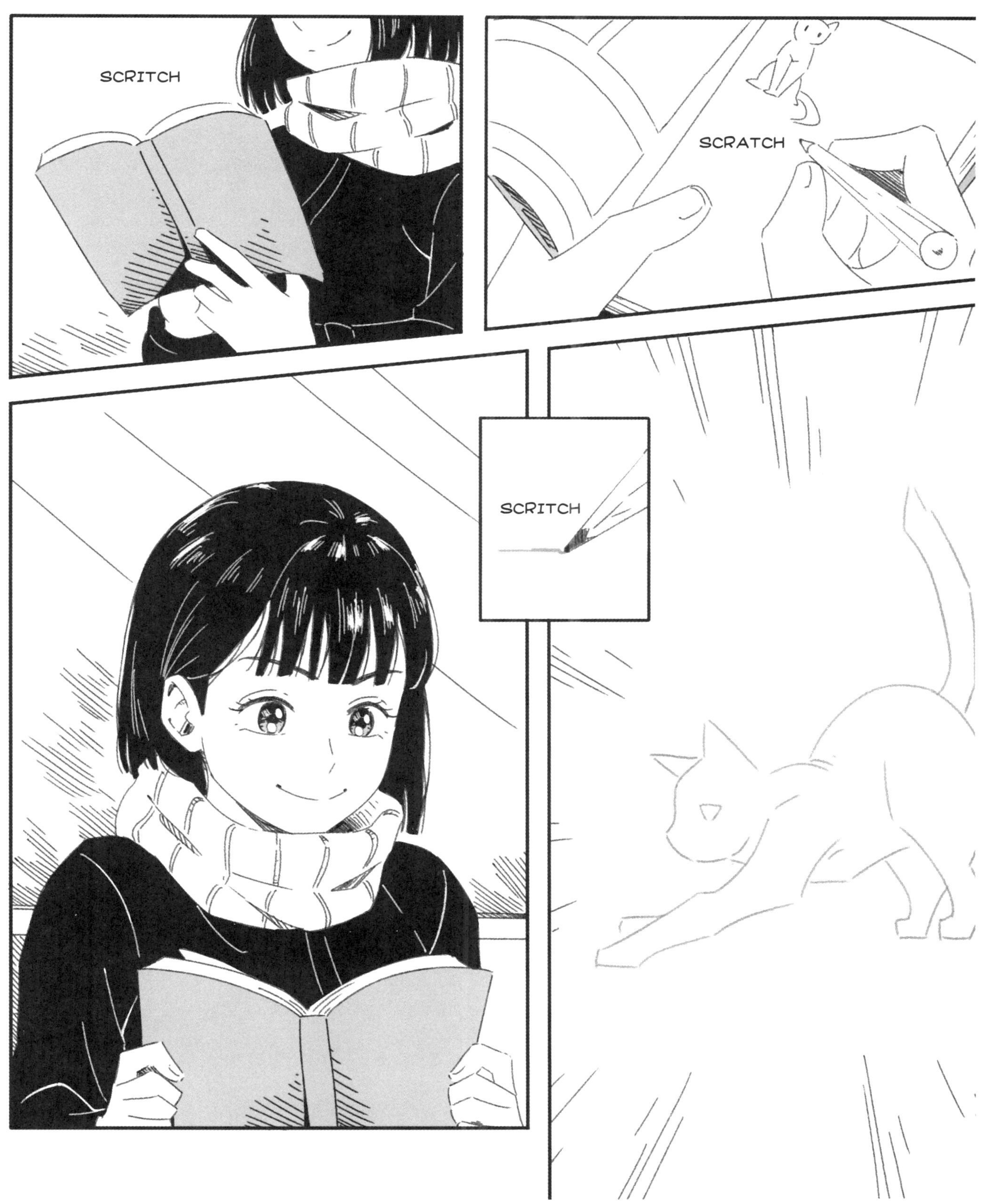

SCRITCH
SCRATCH
SCRITCH

The living world is not just
made up of human bodies.

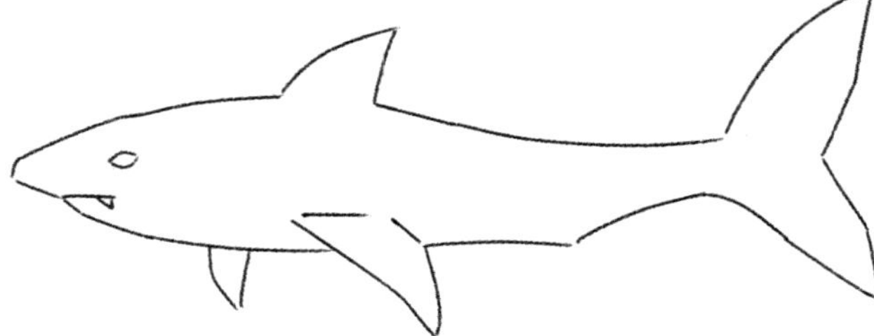

Animals come in such a huge variety of
shapes that it can be intimidating.

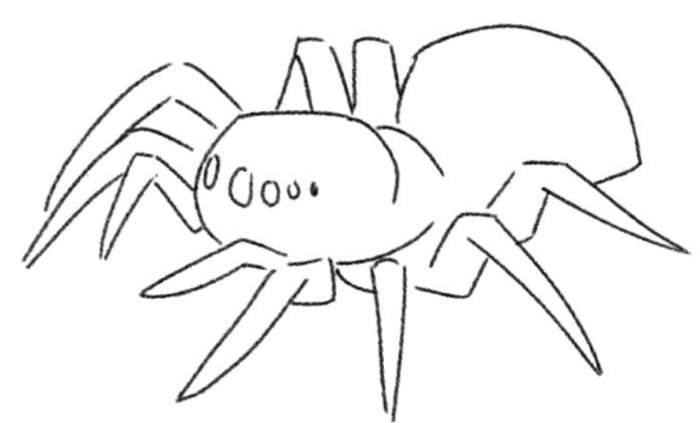

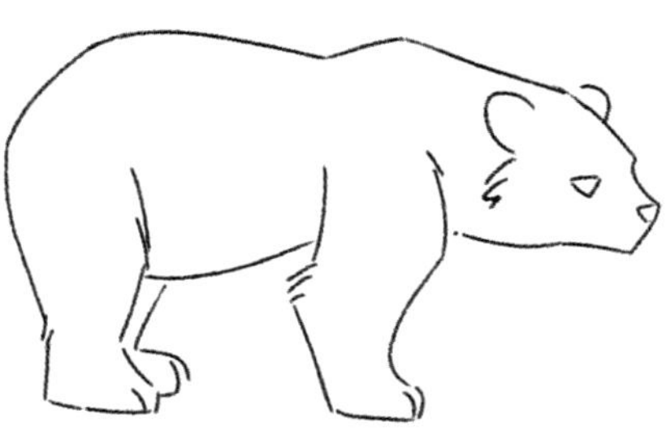

As with objects, though, you don't have
to learn how to draw them all separately
if you just use the basic rules that we
have already learned.

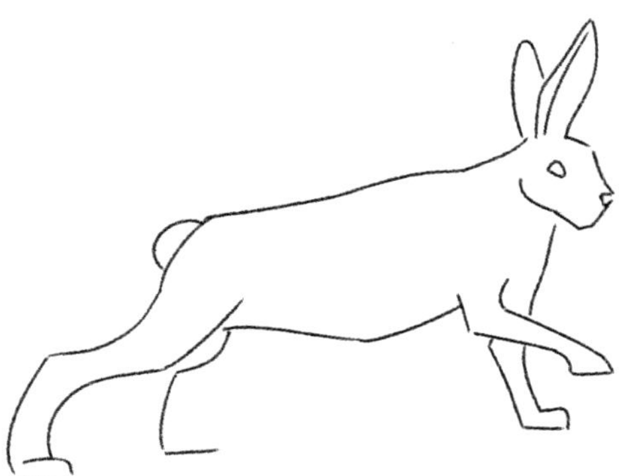

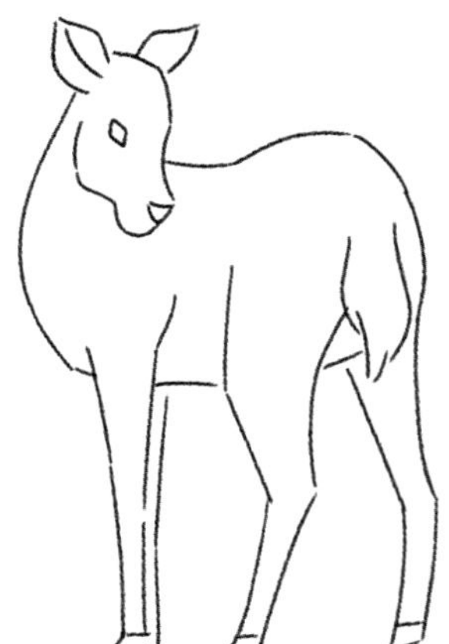

Just like with the human body, start your animal
drawings by using a structure made of simple shapes.

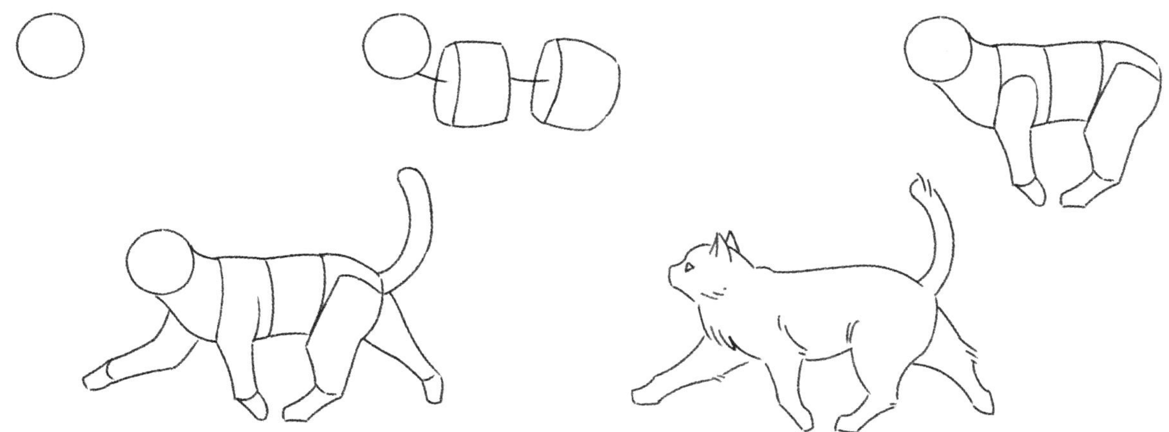

For mammals, we can go back to our structure of
two boxes, like we did for the human body.

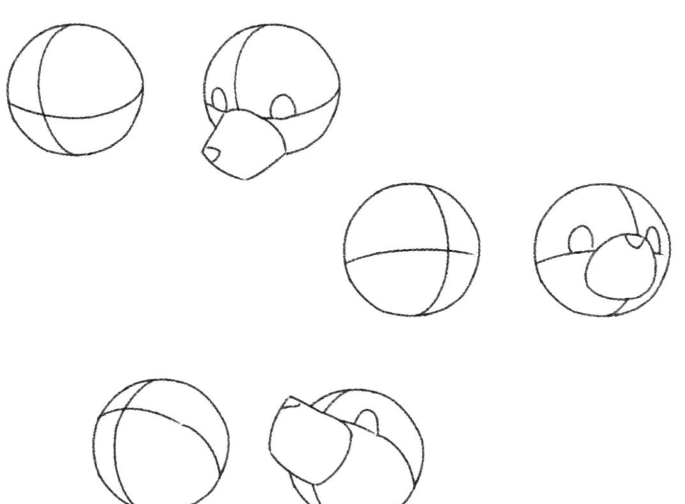

For the head, it's the same
principle as for humans.

Start with a sphere, and
show the direction it's looking in,
then add a block for the jaw.

Depending on the animal you
are drawing, the proportions
of the boxes will change.

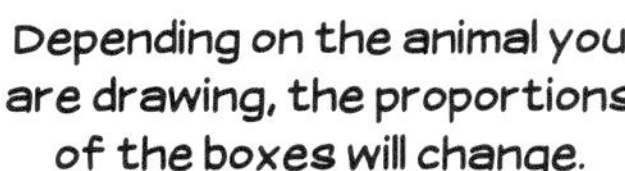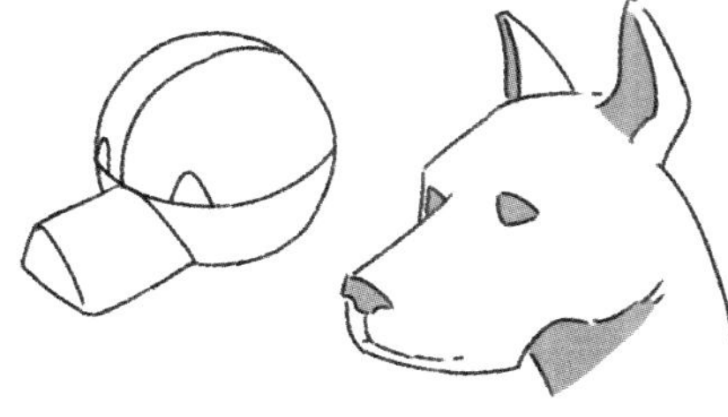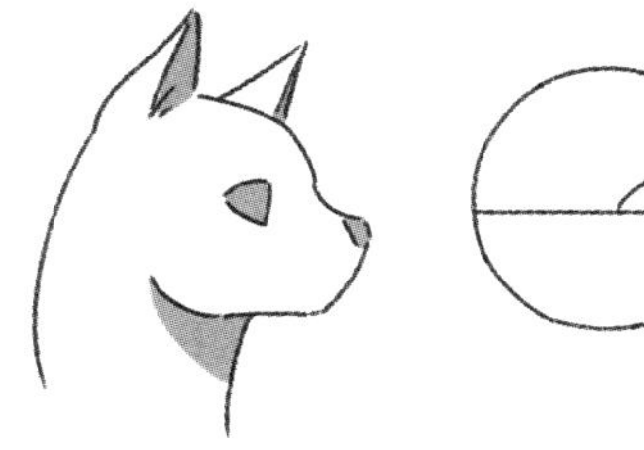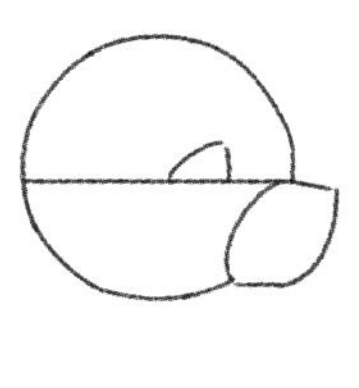

Modifying the proportions of the boxes is
what will give you different animals.

Now that you know how to put the animal
together using simple shapes, it is much easier
to draw it in different positions.

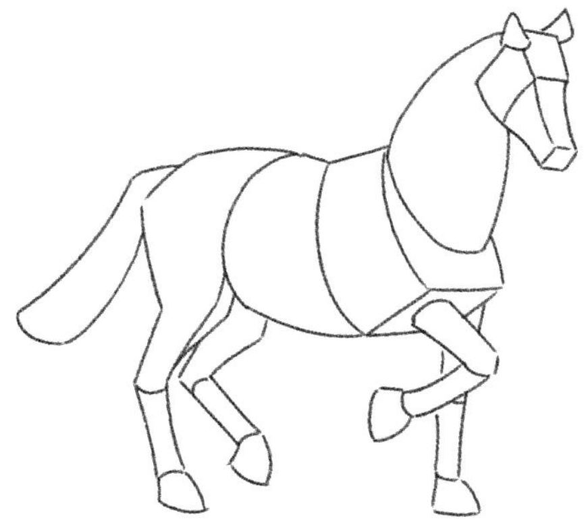

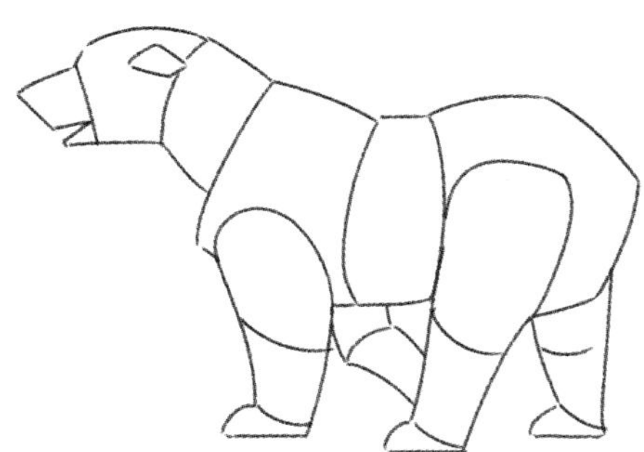

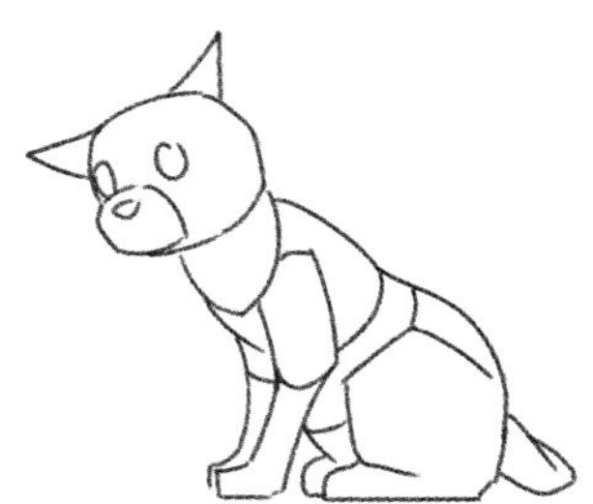

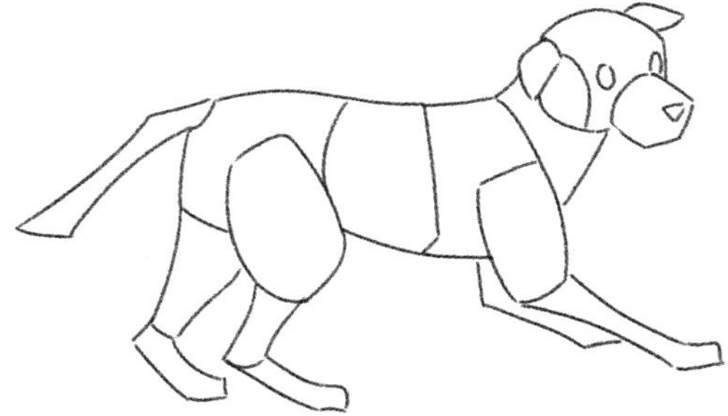

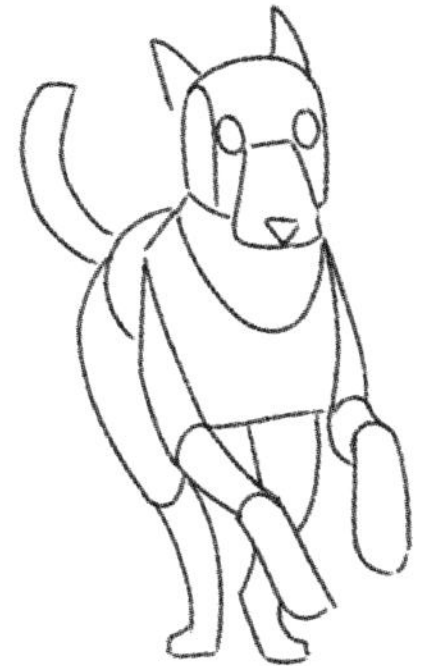

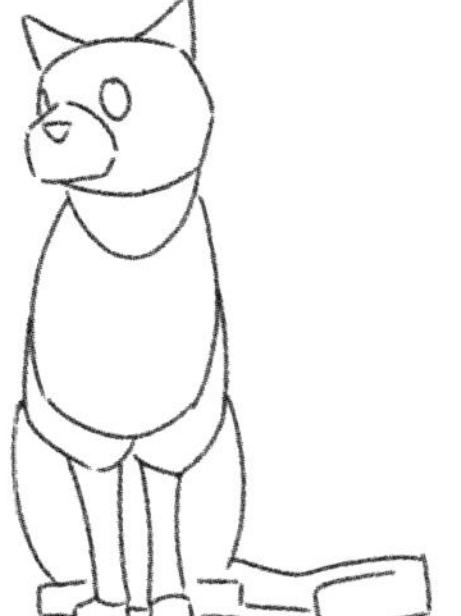

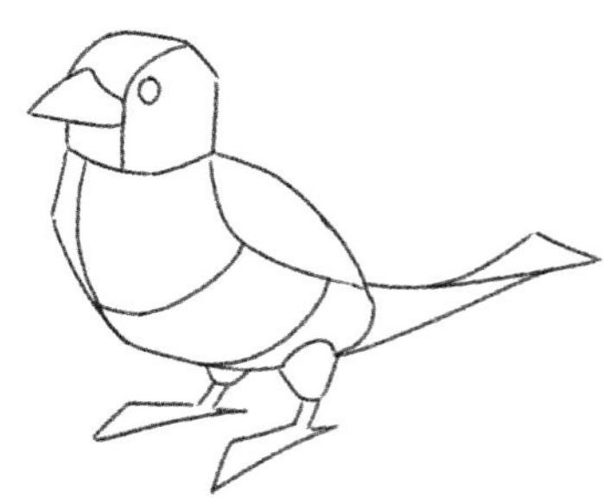

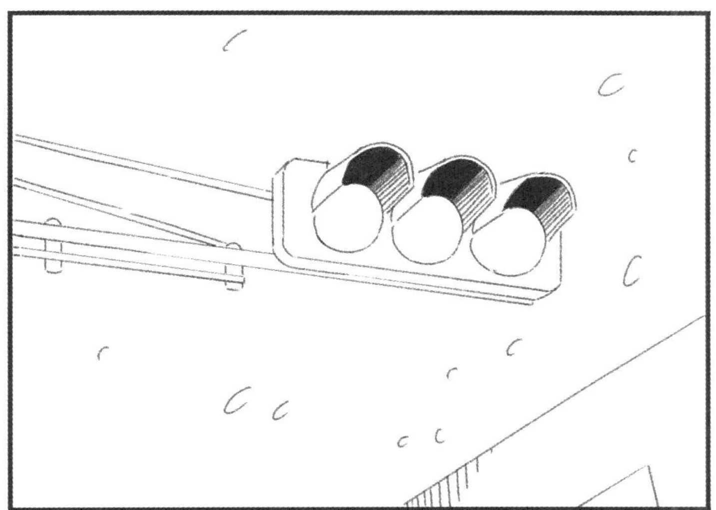

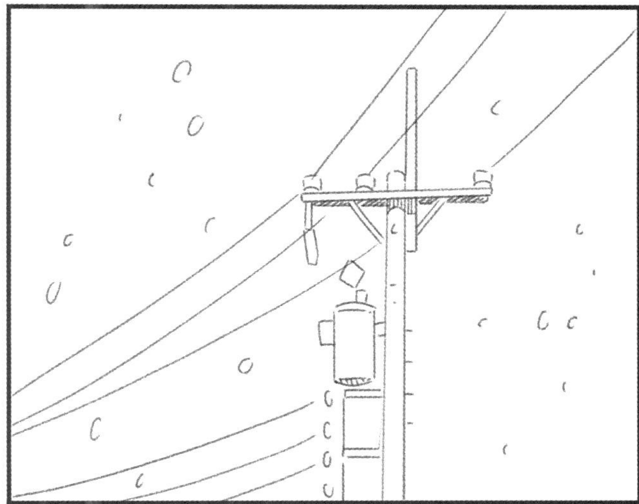

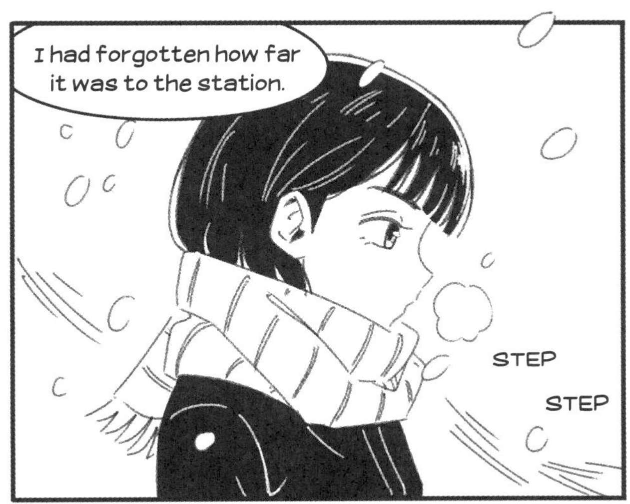
I had forgotten how far it was to the station.
STEP
STEP

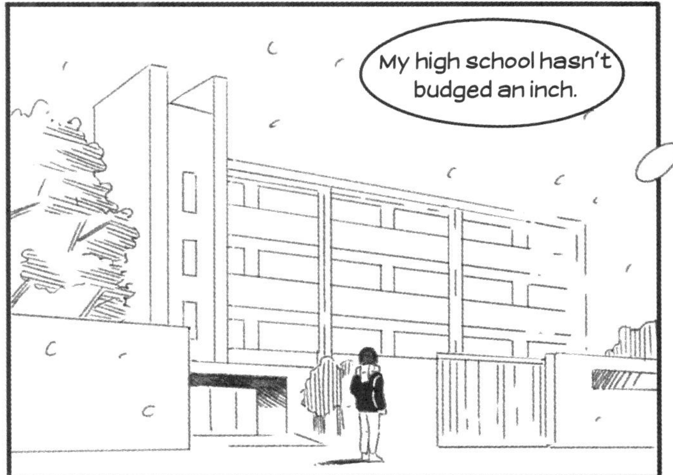
My high school hasn't budged an inch.

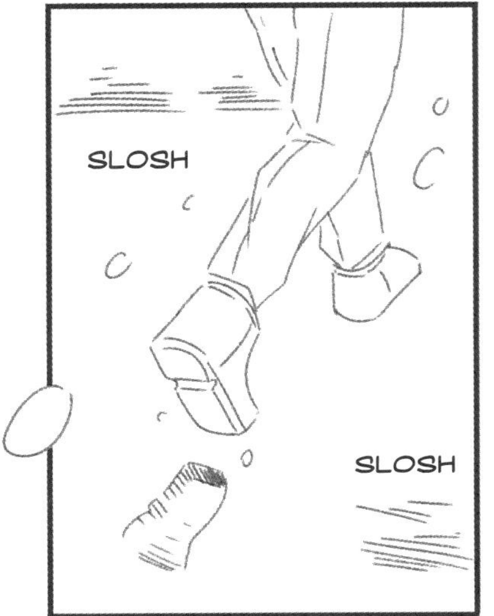
SLOSH
SLOSH

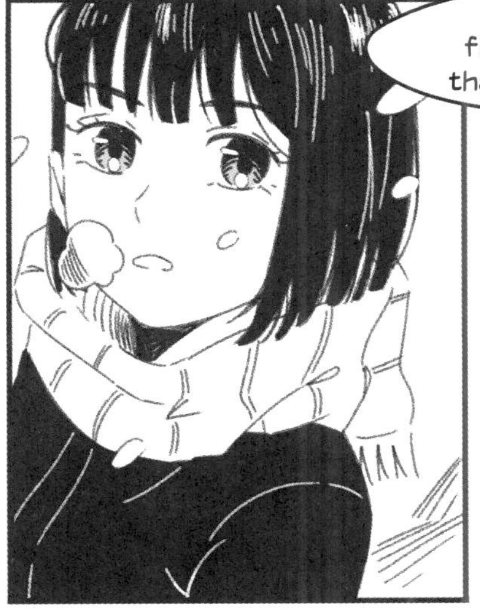
It looks like they finished the building that was being built...

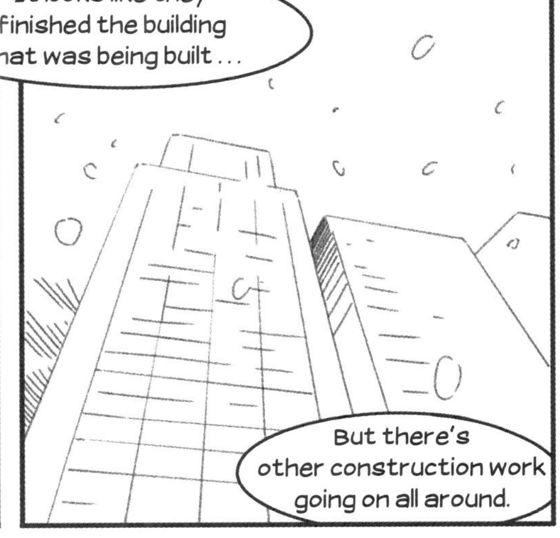
But there's other construction work going on all around.

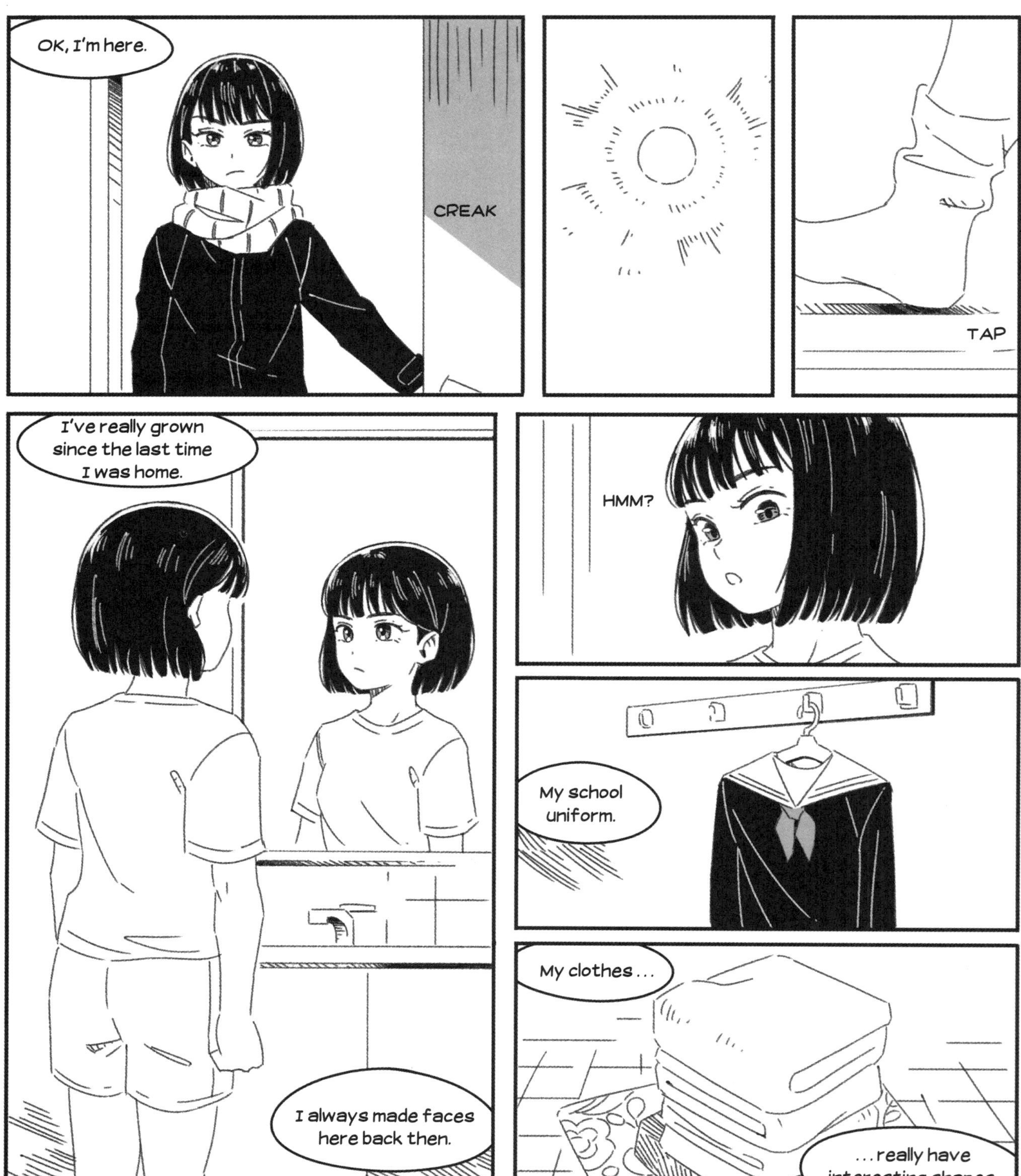

OK, I'm here.
CREAK
TAP
I've really grown since the last time I was home.
HMM?
My school uniform.
I always made faces here back then.
My clothes...
...really have interesting shapes.

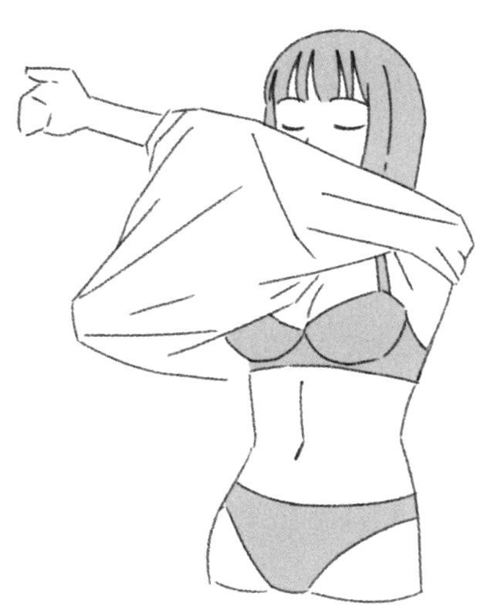

Clothes are another essential component
of the drawing of a character.

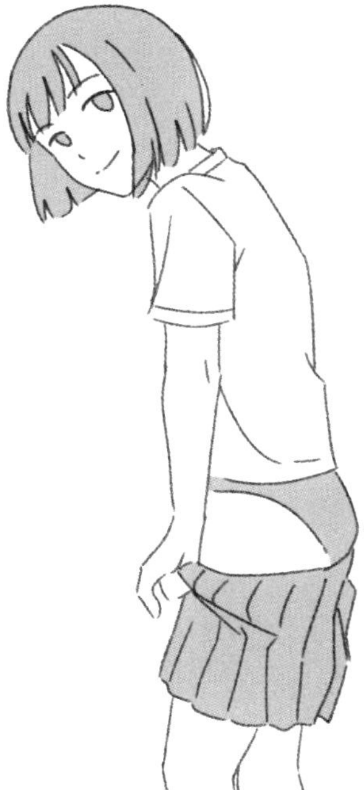

The clothes can help you round out their
appearance a little more thoroughly.

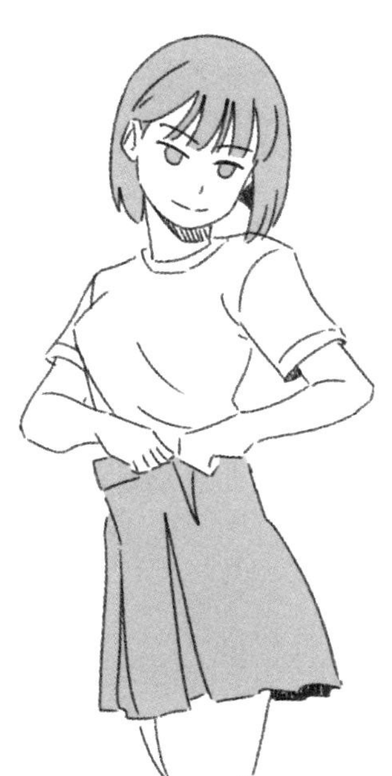

In addition, the way a person
dresses can say a lot about their
personality or their status.

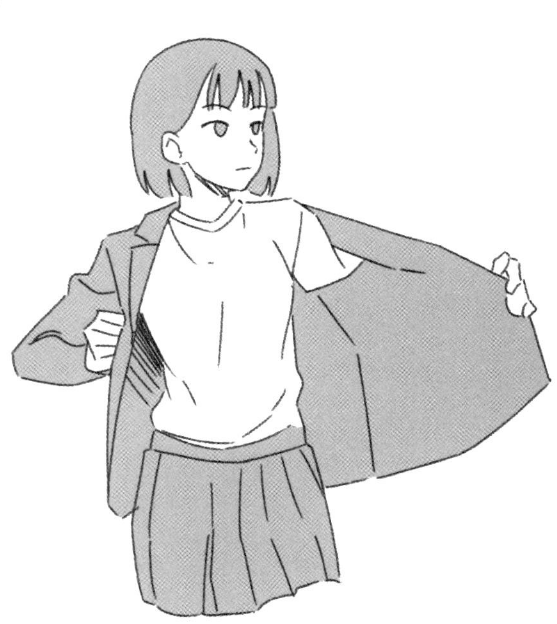

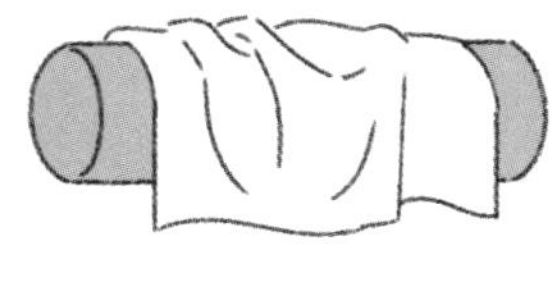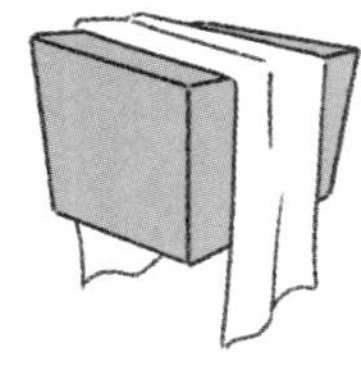

A piece of clothing is a flexible shape with a certain thickness. It conforms to the shape it covers, a little bit like water flowing over an object.

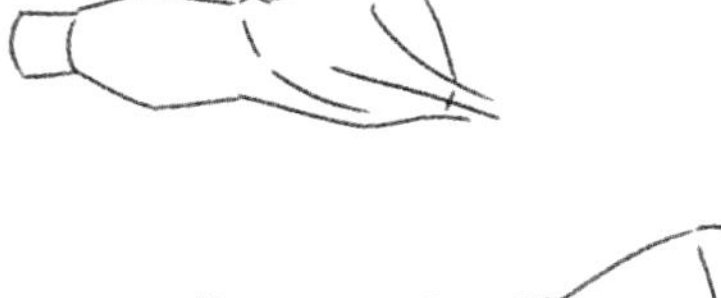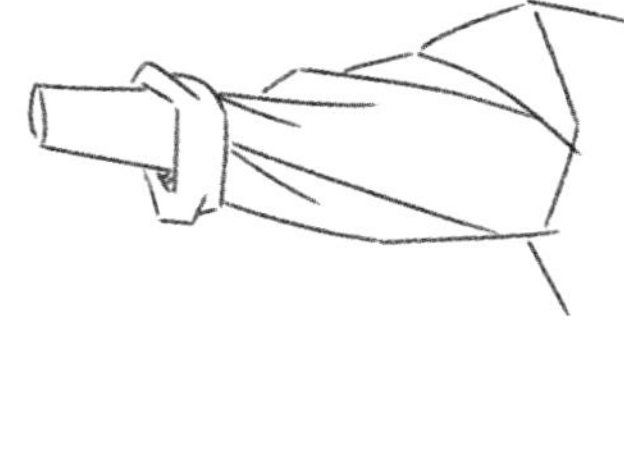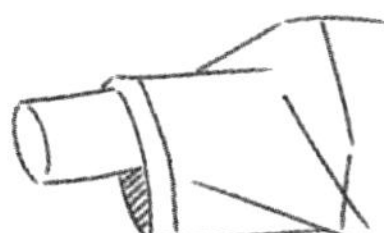

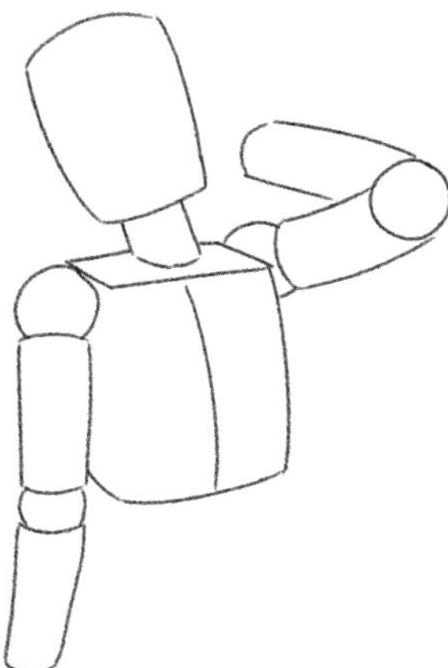

Because the fabric conforms to the shape of the body, it is important to start by drawing the body before adding the clothing on top of it.

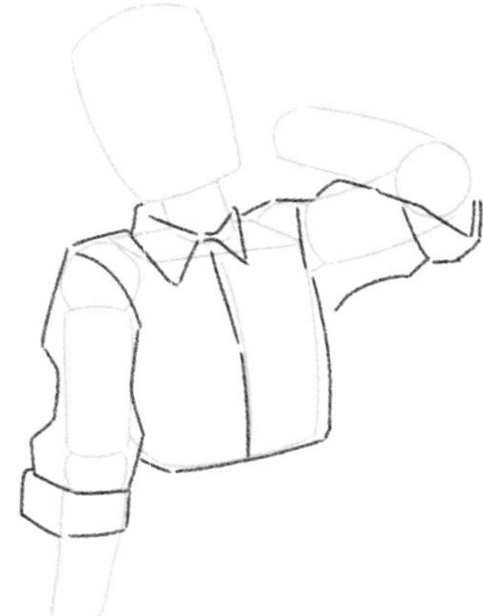

As with every other thing you draw, start by creating the "skeleton" of the piece of the clothing. First draw its overall shape, making sure that it conforms to the shape of the body.

This first draft will allow you to concentrate on the proportions of the garment.

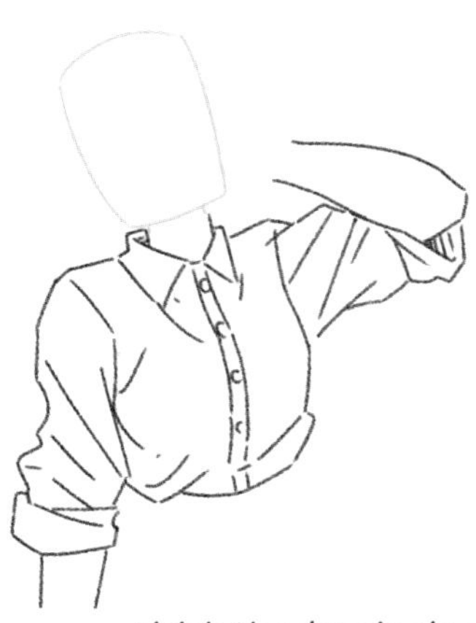

Finish the drawing by adding folds.

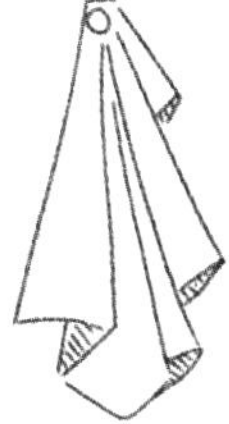 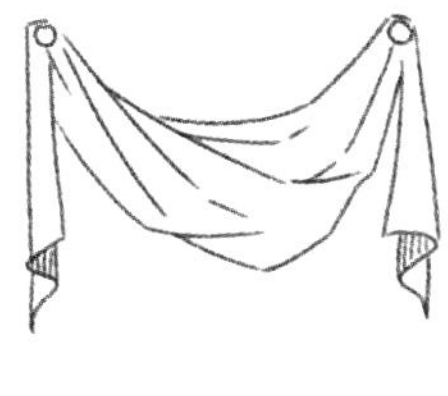

A tension point is a force that works against gravity. By attaching a piece of fabric to a wall, you are, of course, preventing it from falling. You create a point of tension from which it hangs.

Tension points are often created naturally by certain elements: elbows and knees, for example, but also the way the garment is sewn.

When you find the tension points, it makes it much easier to draw the folds. The main folds converge toward the tension points, following the movement.

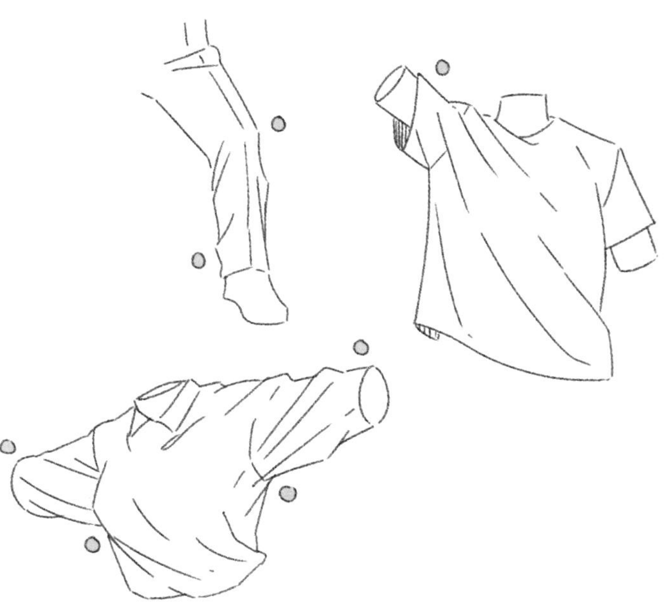

There is also a principle of compression. For example, when you bend an arm, the fabric of the garment will be compressed and create a new tension point in the hollow of the elbow, thus generating new folds.

The same phenomenon can be observed when you place an object on top of a piece of clothing. For instance, a hand, when our arms are crossed.

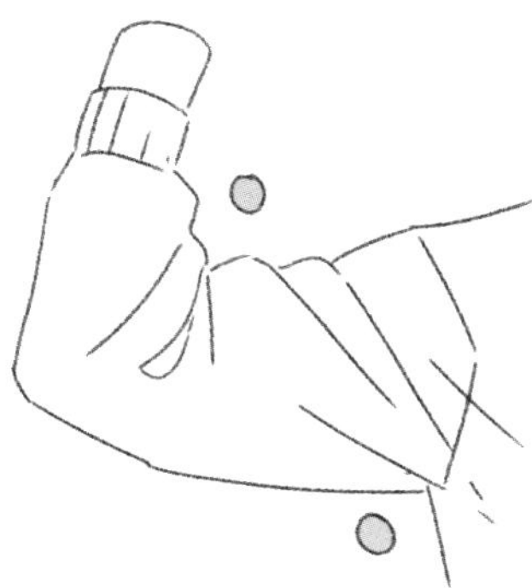 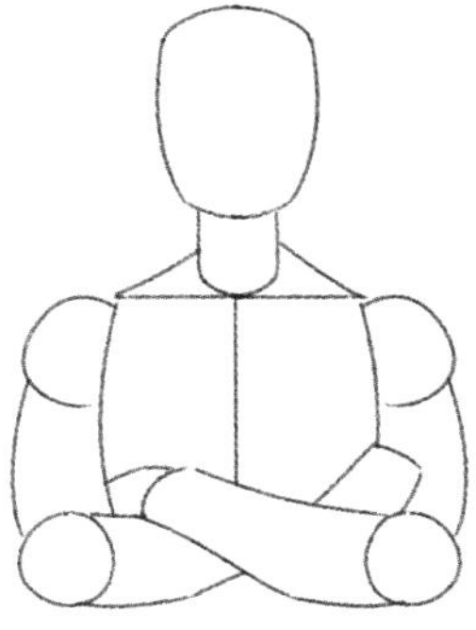 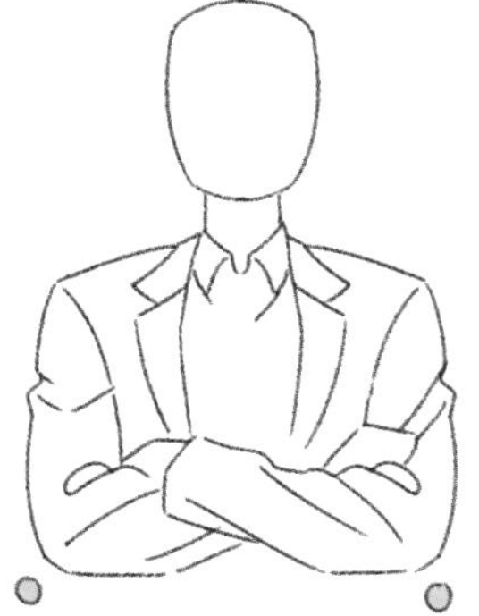

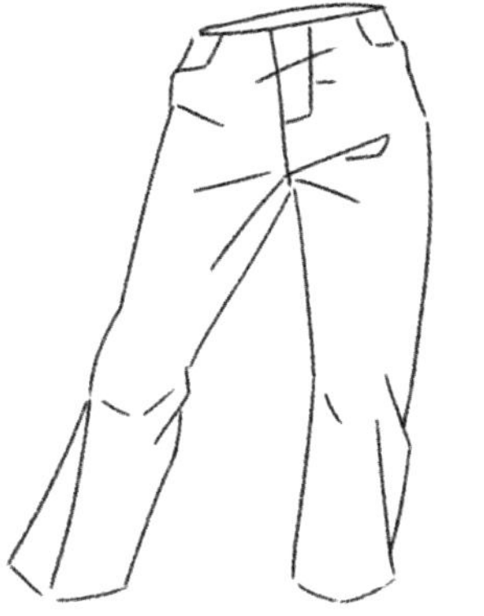 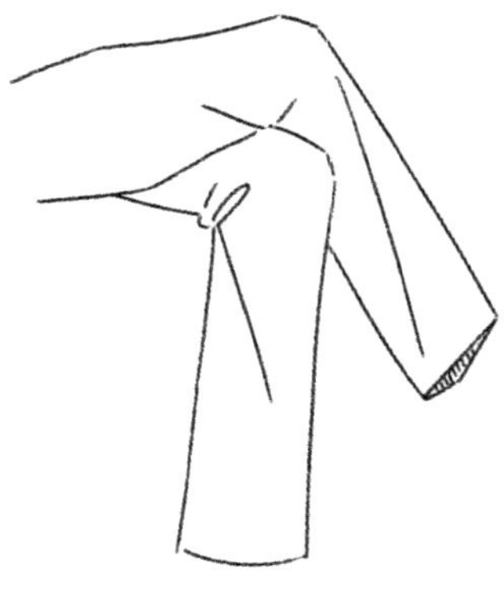 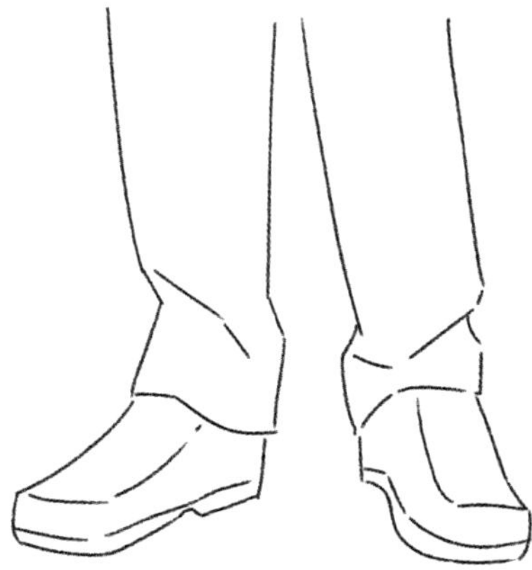

Pants work according to the same rules as other clothing. In particular, folds will form at the crotch and at the knees.

Pants will usually create an area of folds that fall over the foot.

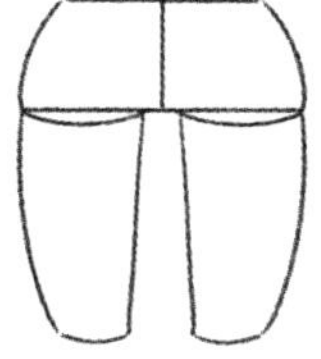 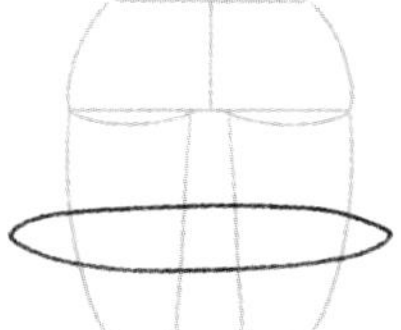 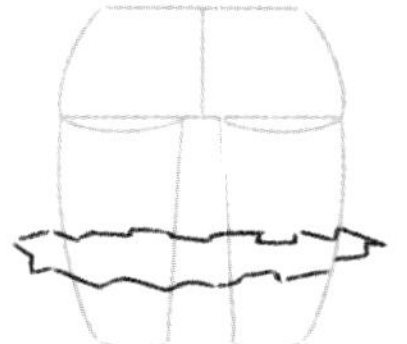

For pleated skirts, which are very common in Japan, we use a slightly different method.

Start by drawing the ellipse that is formed by the lower opening of the garment.

Then change up the ellipse with some zigzags.

Then you can draw the shape of the skirt and draw lines up from the corners of the zigzags toward the top of the skirt.

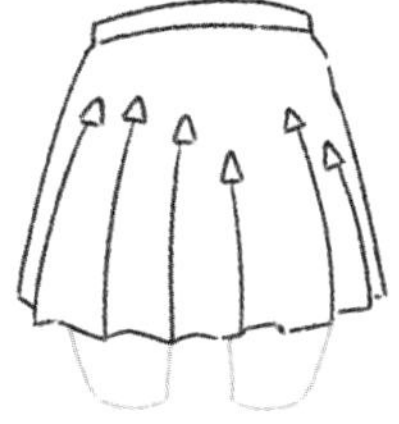 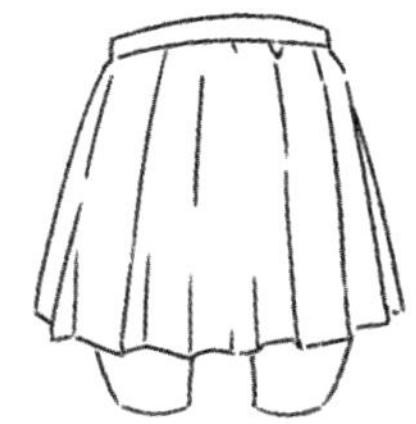

By using the tension point method and adding some details, you can then create lots of different shapes!

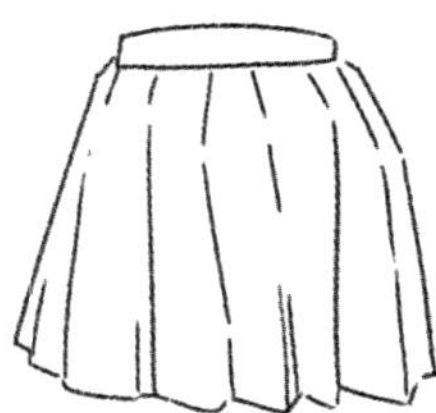 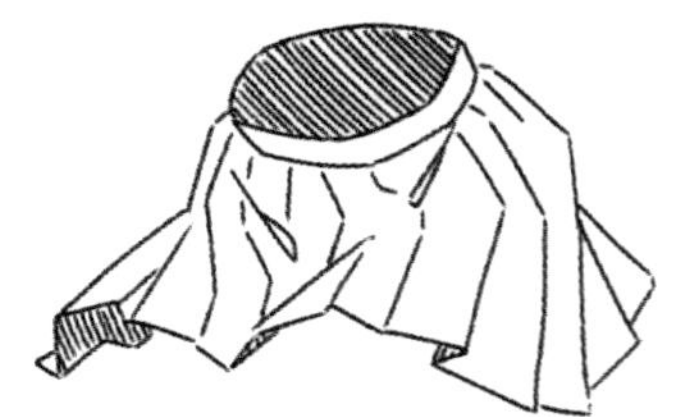

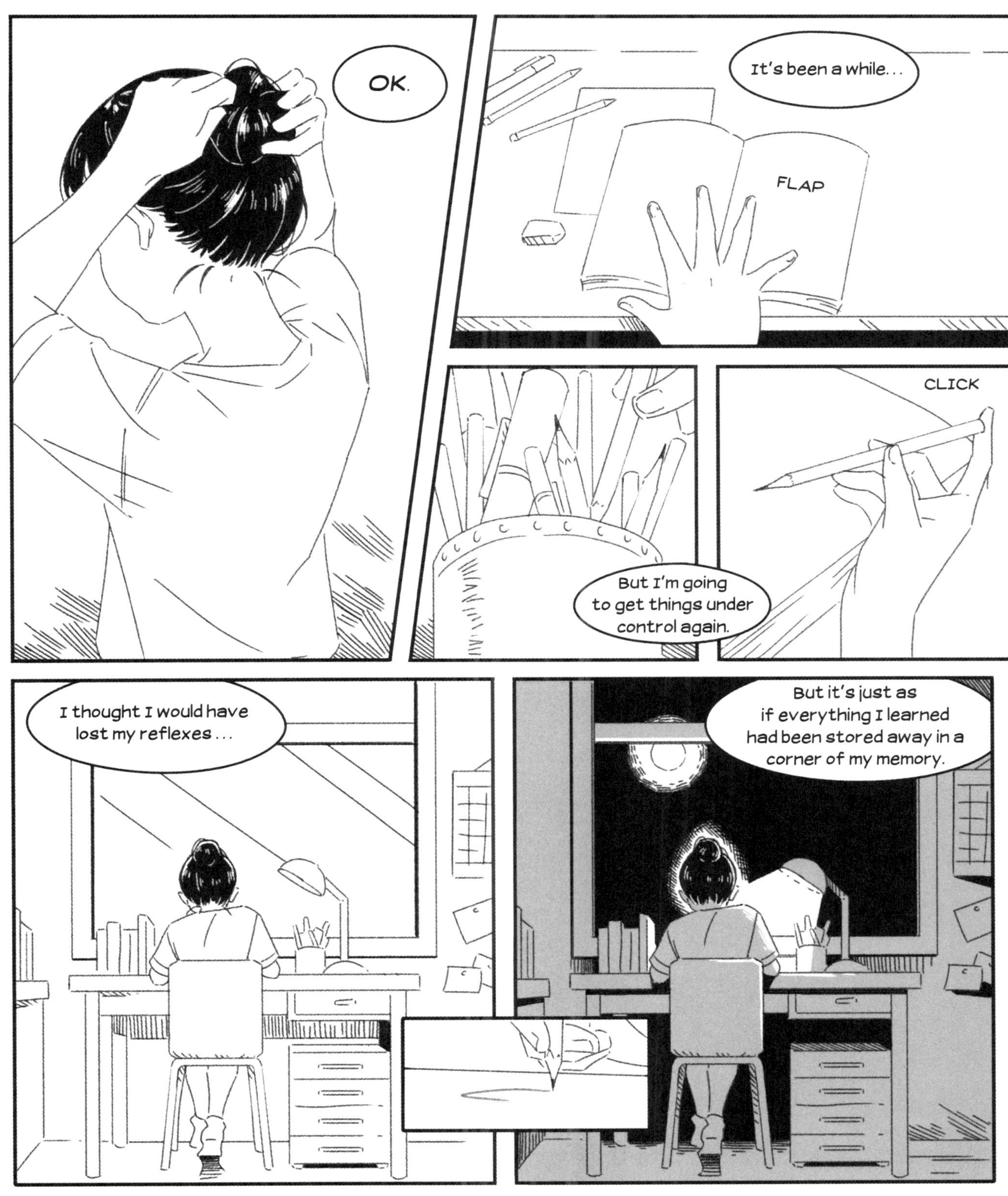

OK.
It's been a while...
FLAP
CLICK
But I'm going to get things under control again.
I thought I would have lost my reflexes...
But it's just as if everything I learned had been stored away in a corner of my memory.

Shadows and light allow you to give a drawing some volume. Without that, it can look flat.

In addition, and especially in the manga drawing style (because it is in black and white), the use of shading helps to define the appearance of settings and characters.

It can also offer a different reading of the scene by creating a certain atmosphere. By adjusting how much or how little contrast you include, you can bring tension to an image.

There are many ways to shade a drawing in a manga style.

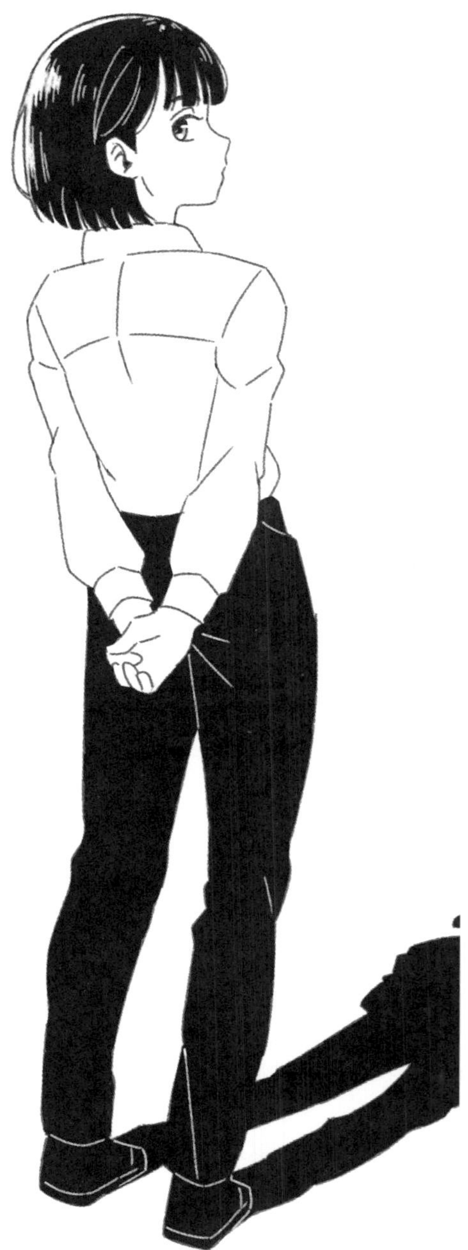

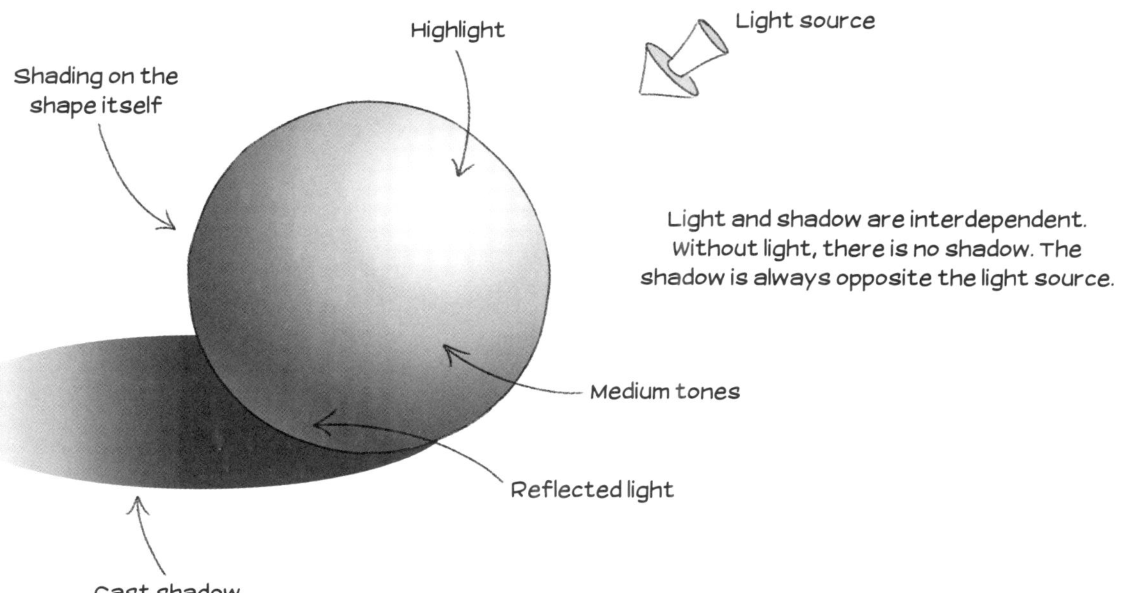

Light and shadow are interdependent. Without light, there is no shadow. The shadow is always opposite the light source.

Rounded forms tend to have soft shadows, while angular forms have hard ones.

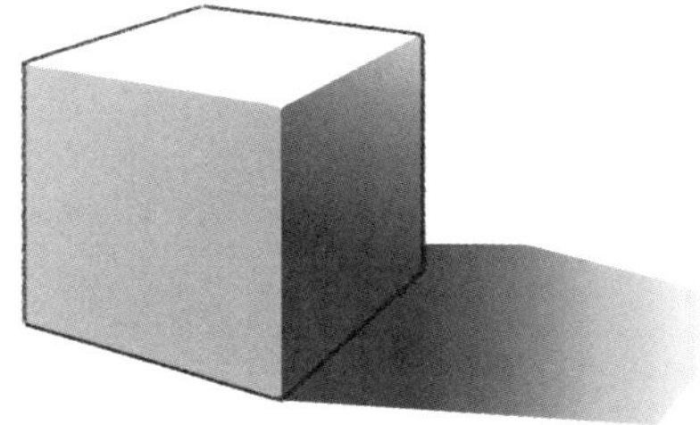

The cast shadow is opposite the light source.

If the object is in the air, its cast shadow is no longer touching it.

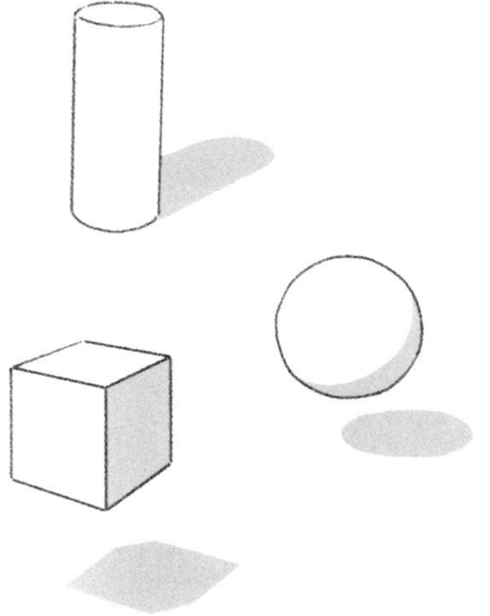

Screentones are patterns and textures
that can be applied to a drawing.

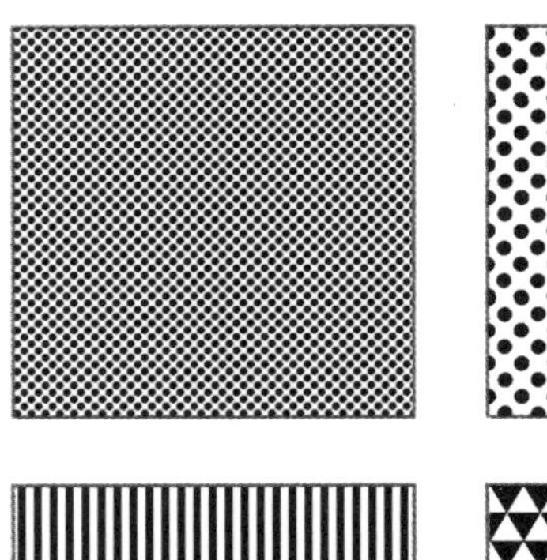

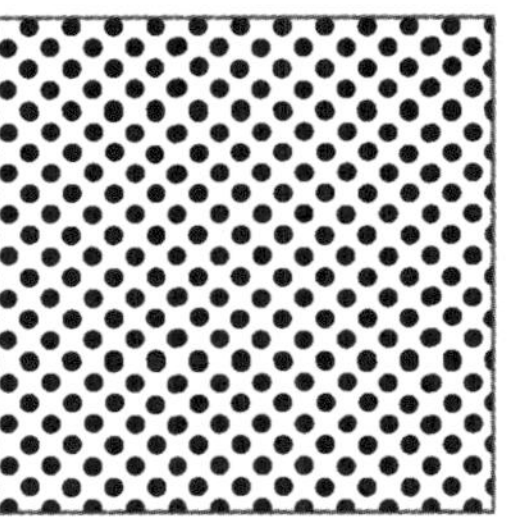

To shade a manga, we usually use grids
of different sizes and patterns.

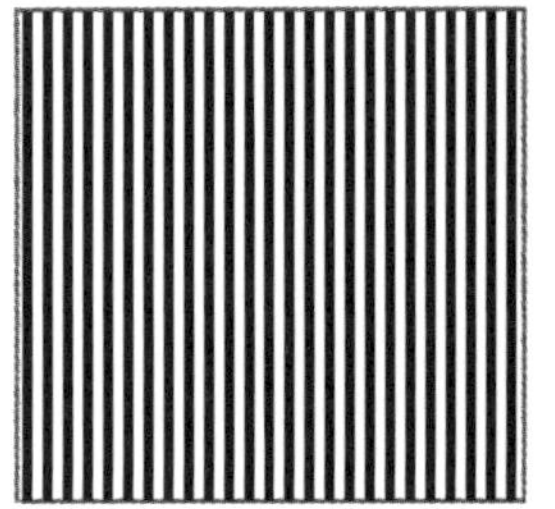

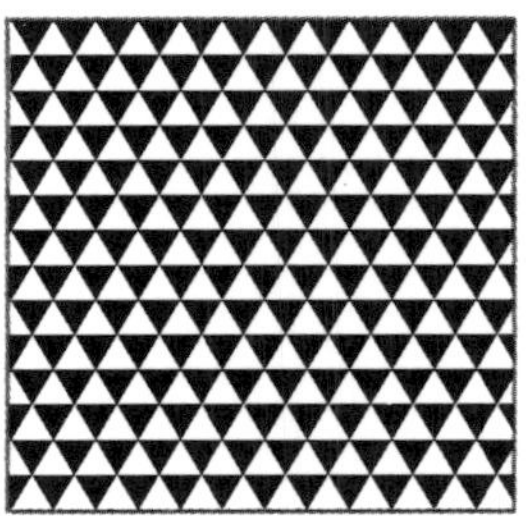

The grids add nuance to the drawing.

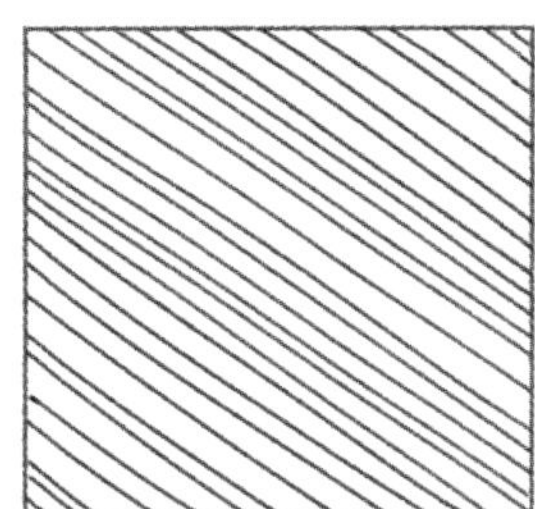

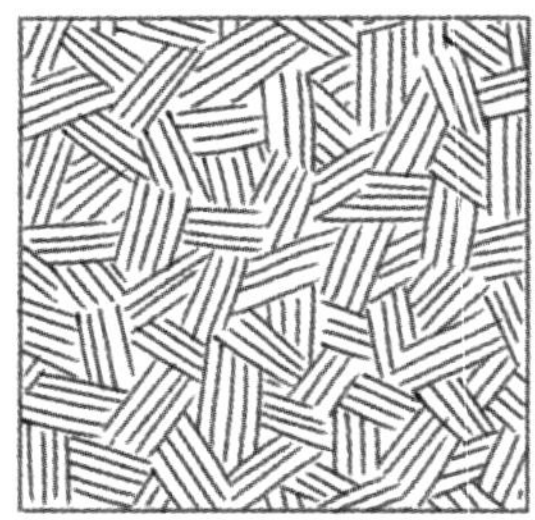

Hatching techniques use
patterns of lines to create
textural effects or nuances.

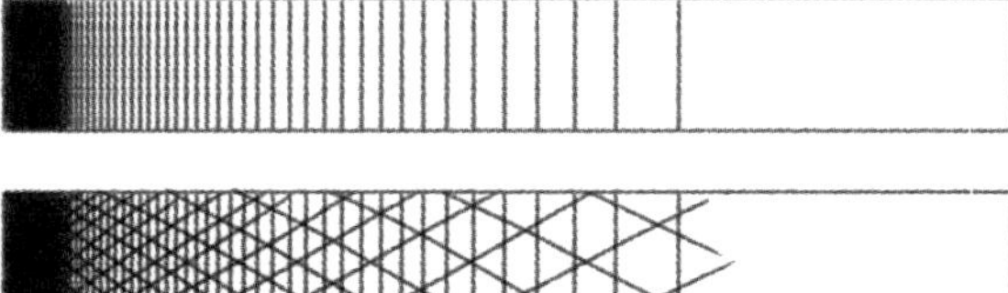

You can choose to overlay line
strokes going in different directions,
using the crosshatching technique.

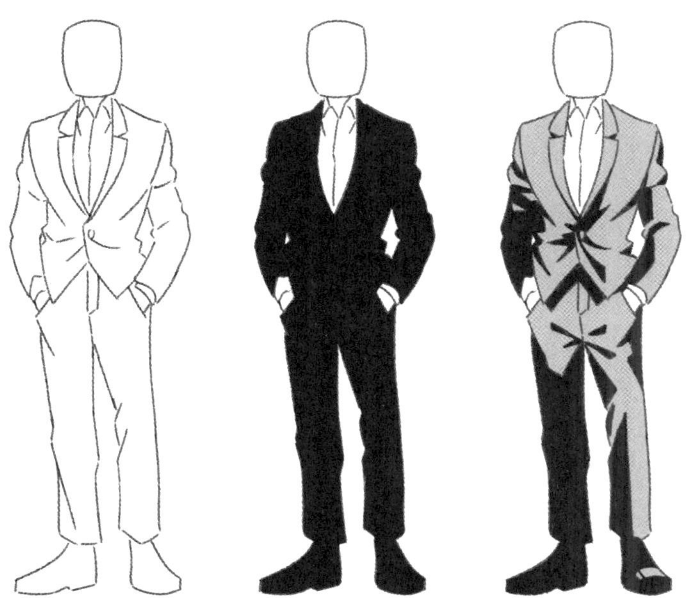

There are two techniques for shading dark items.

You can fill everything with black, which helps add contrast to the drawing.

You can also color the clothing gray (or use grids) and shade certain areas. The effect is more realistic, but it is also harder to achieve.

Some examples of shading on the face:

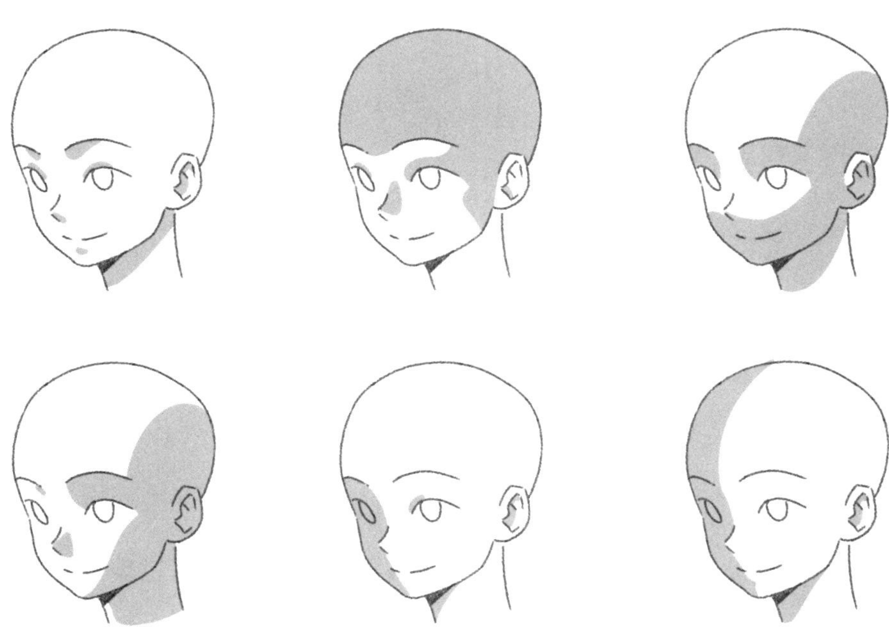

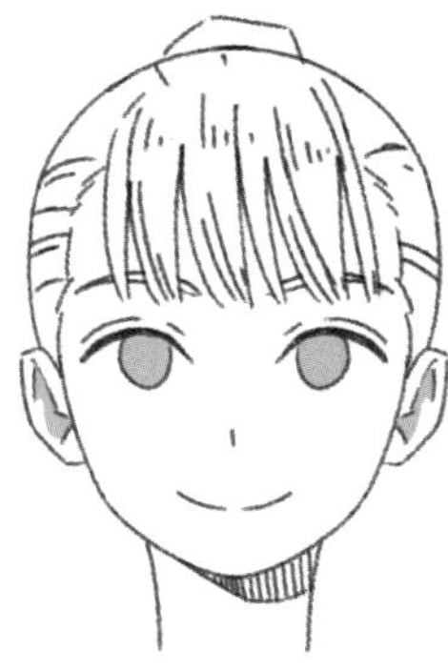 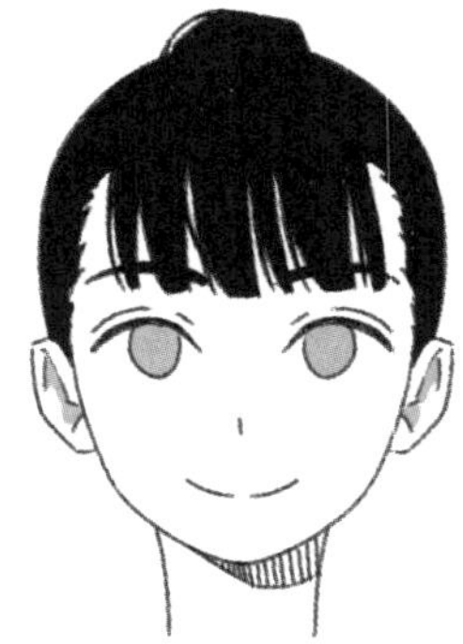

As we do with clothing, light-colored hair is left white and hair in medium tones is colored gray or with grids.

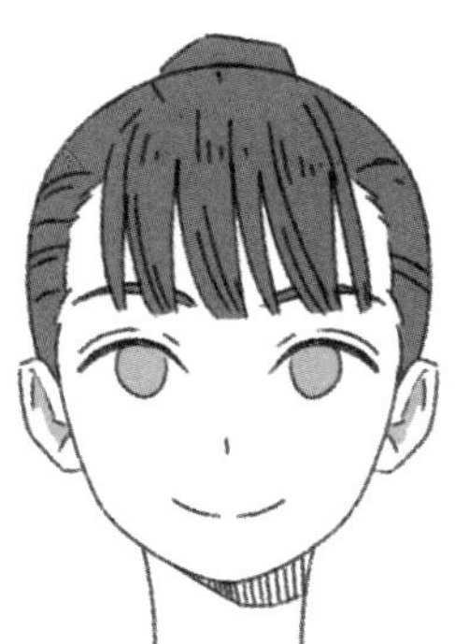 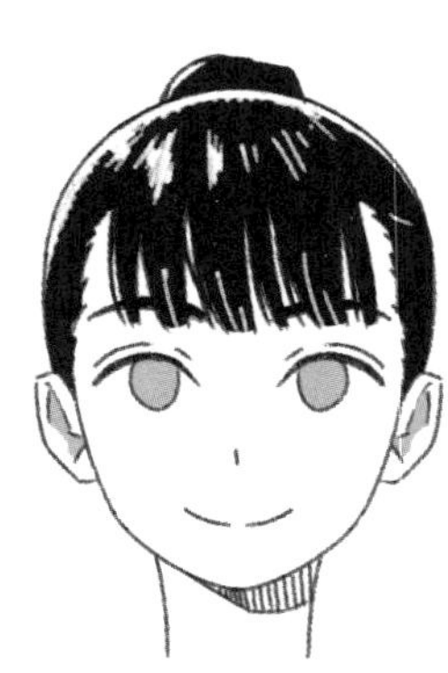

Dark hair is usually colored black, sometimes with a few white reflections.

Play with the coloring of clothing items to create contrasts and, as a result, more interesting characters.

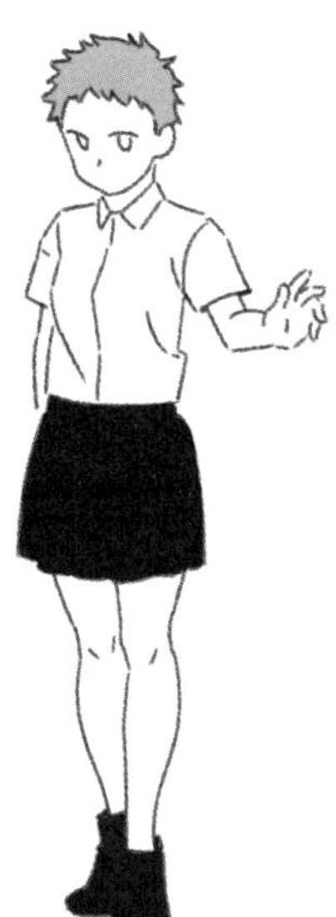 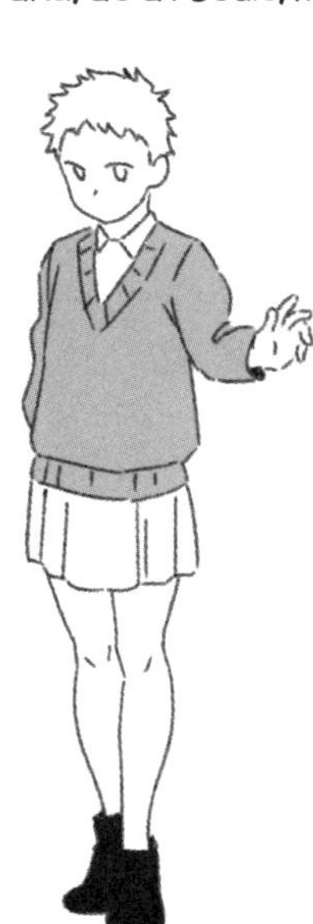 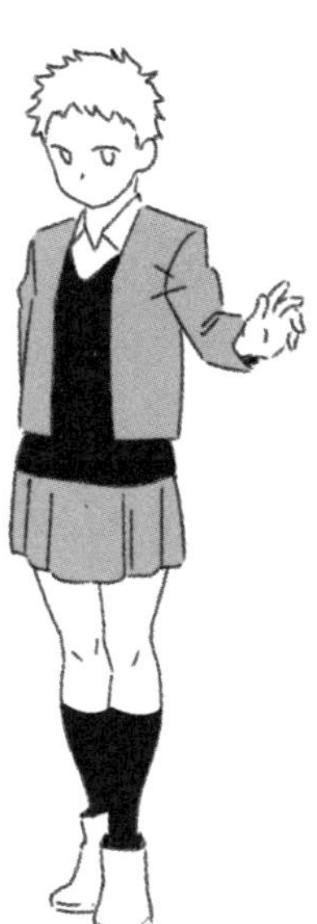 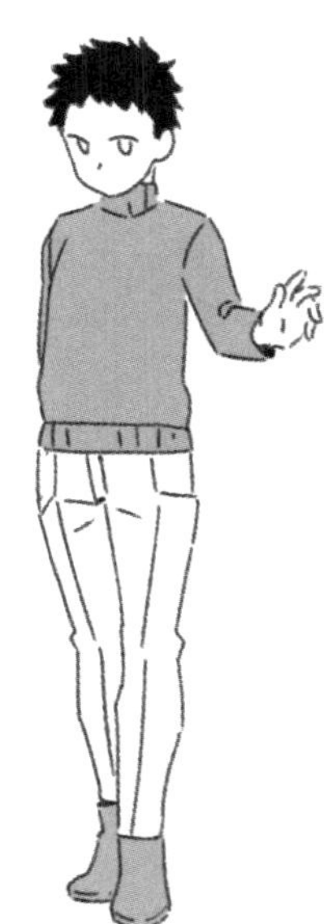

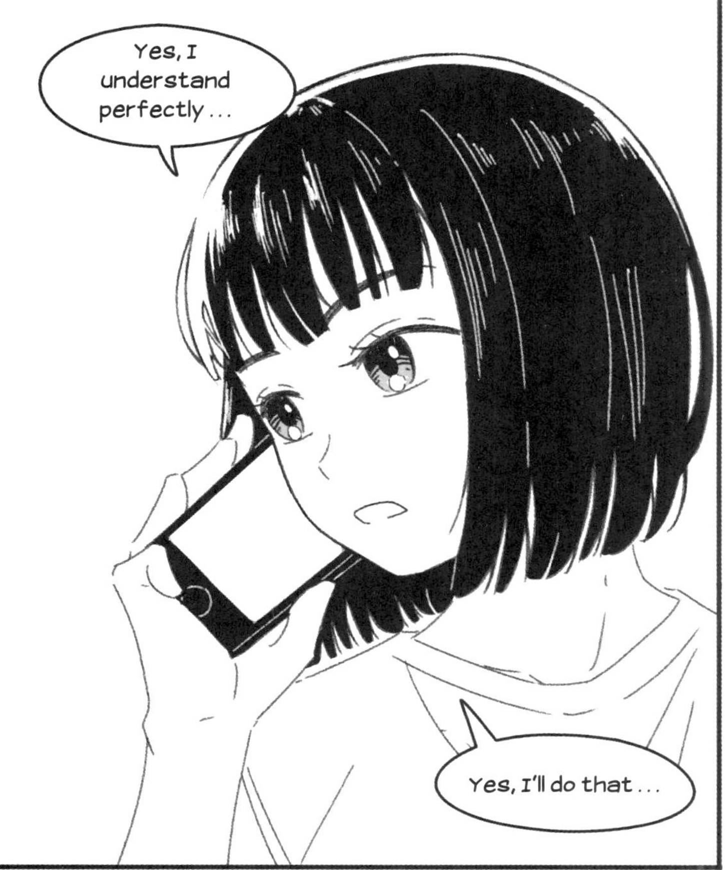

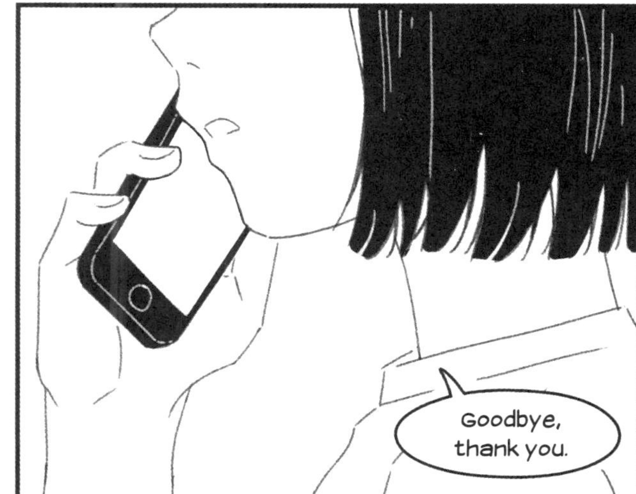

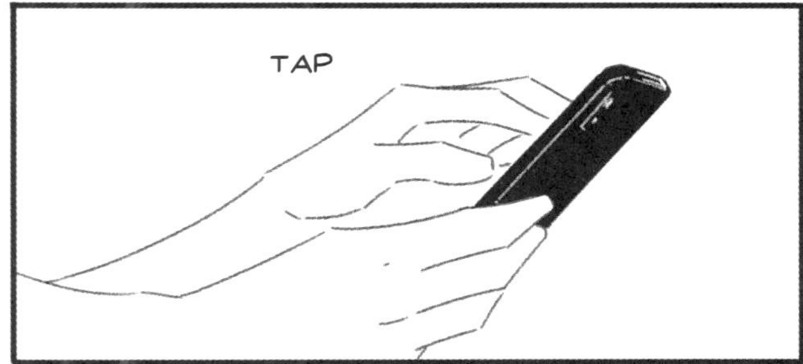

I started writing and drawing a story.

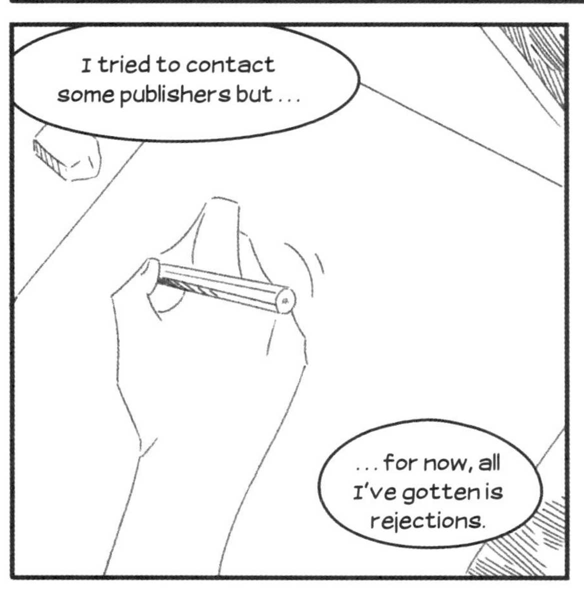

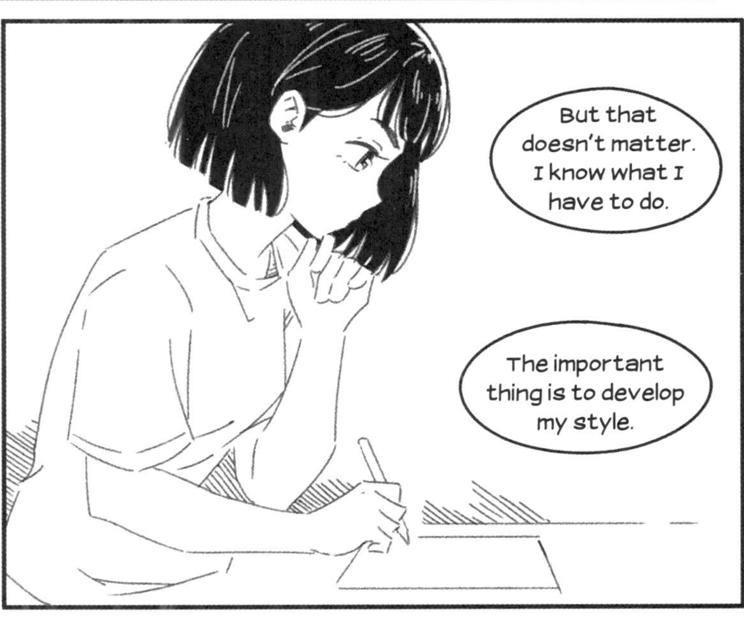

The way you design and draw your characters
is important. Depending on the body's shape and
proportions, we can already get an impression of the
character's role in the story and their temperament.

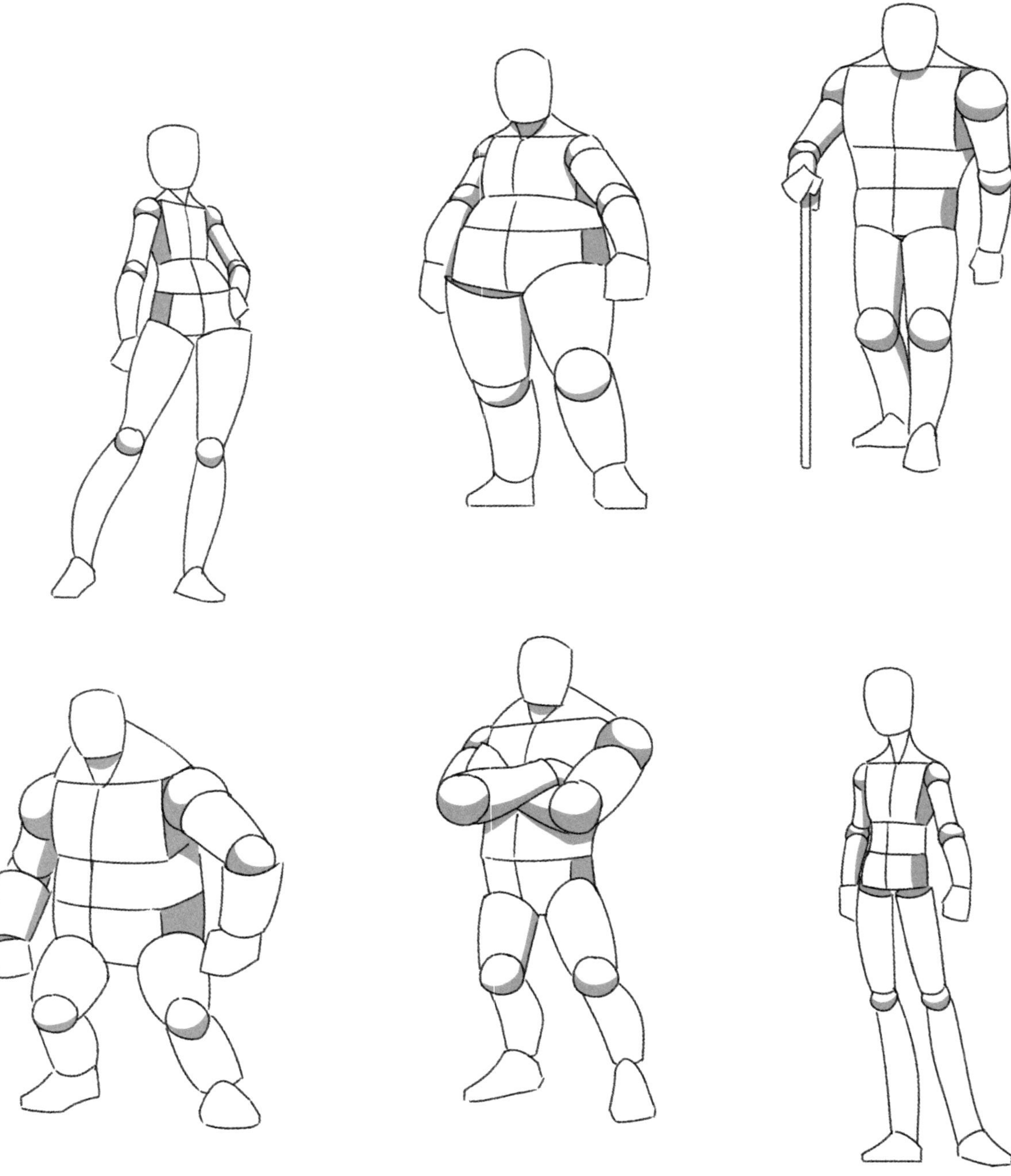

Whatever you do, start your drawing
with an outline. We will apply a particular
style of drawing to this outline.

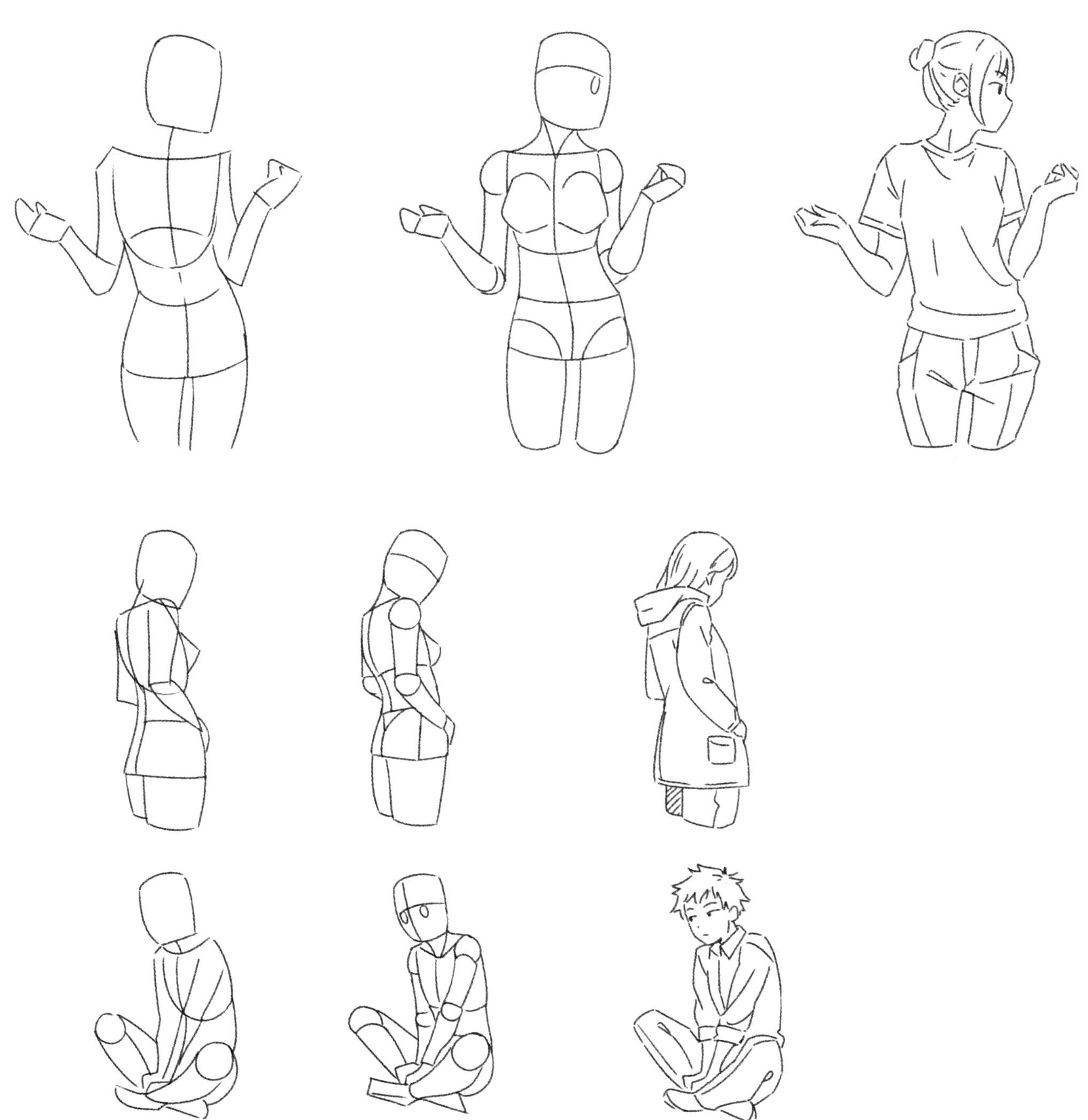

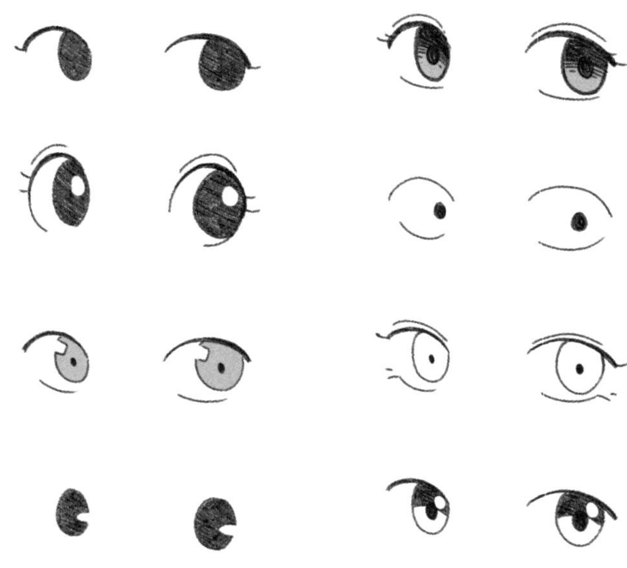

The style of the eyes is very important for differentiating between characters.

Depending on how the eyes are drawn, they can say a great deal about the personality of the character: shy, grumpy, seductive, stern, sly …

The way lines are drawn also changes from one style to another. You have to find what you are most comfortable with.

You may prefer fine, sharp lines, or bold, thick ones. Or you might prefer a more jittery line, like in a sketch, or even a black outline drawn around the outside of the character.

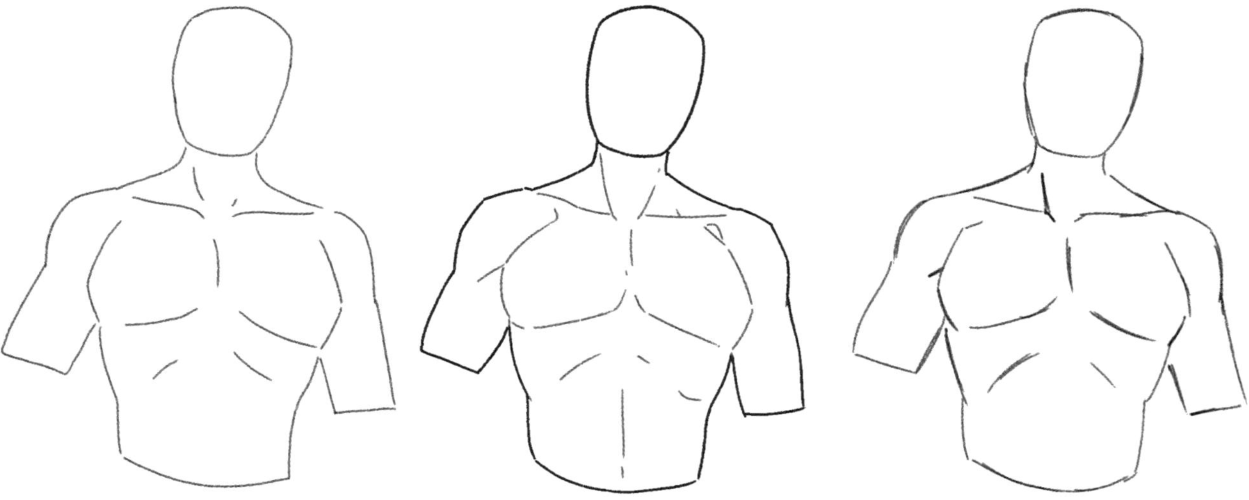

Here are some different styles:

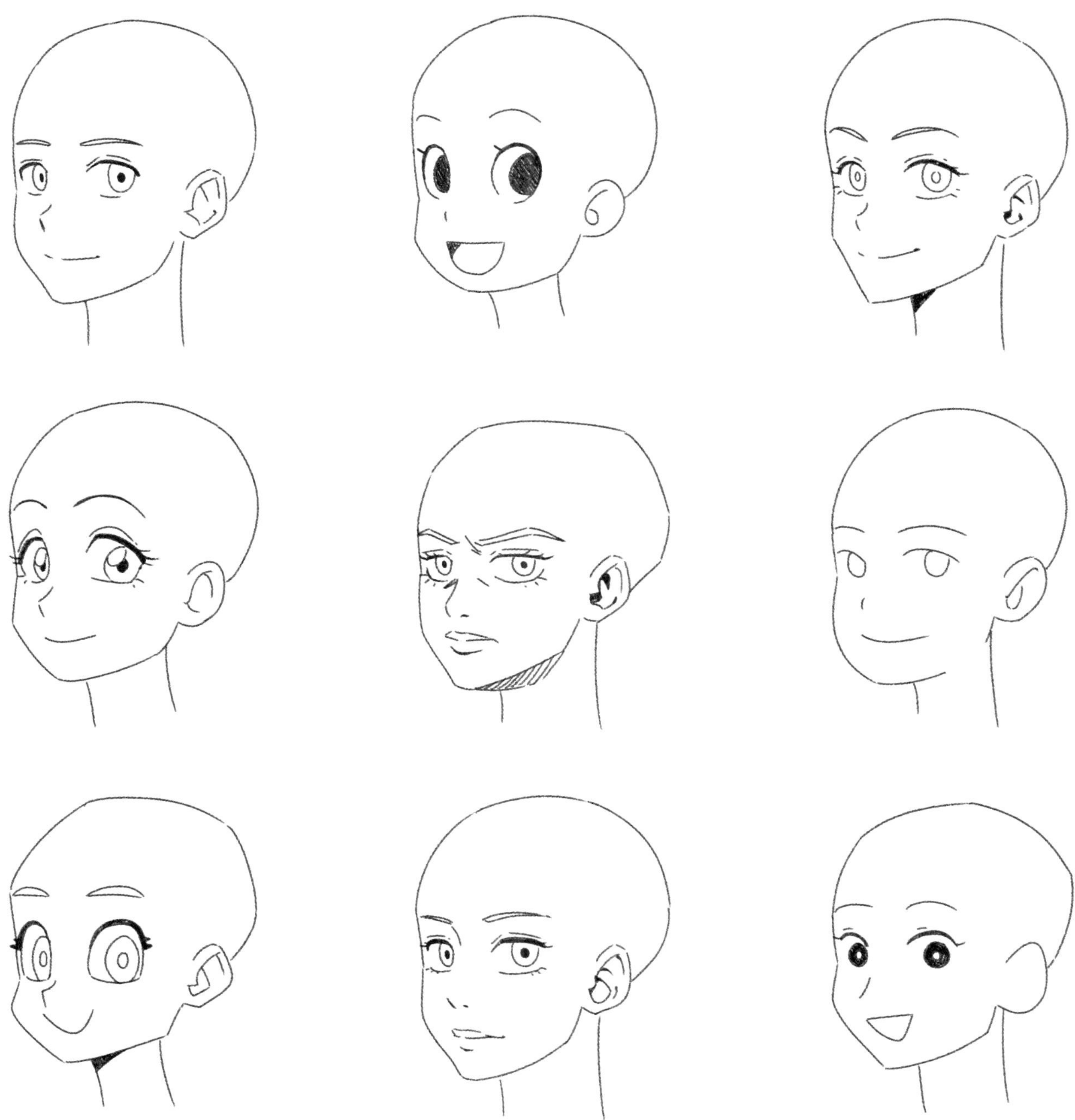

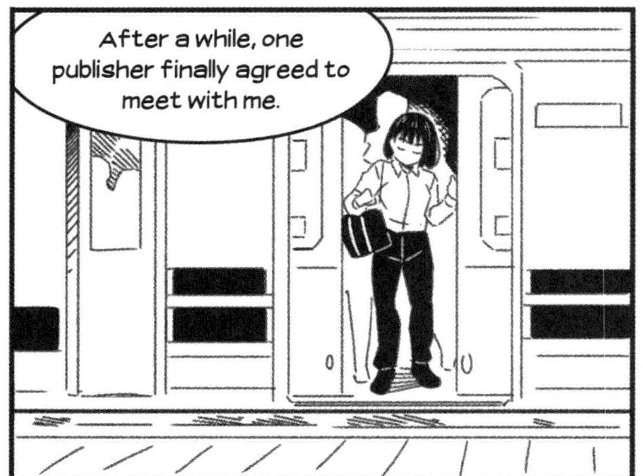

After a while, one publisher finally agreed to meet with me.

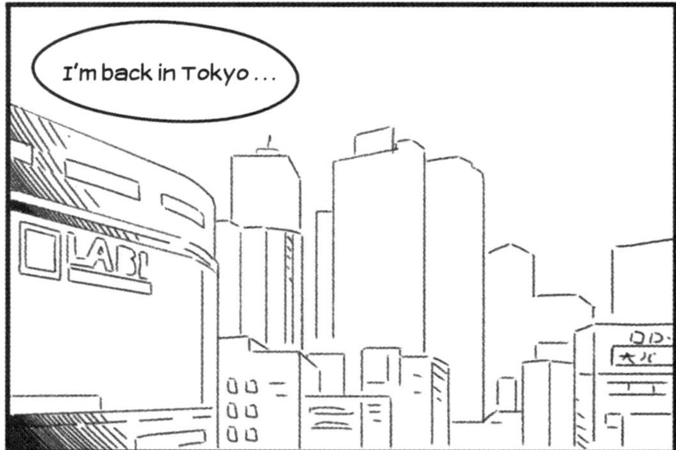

I'm back in Tokyo...

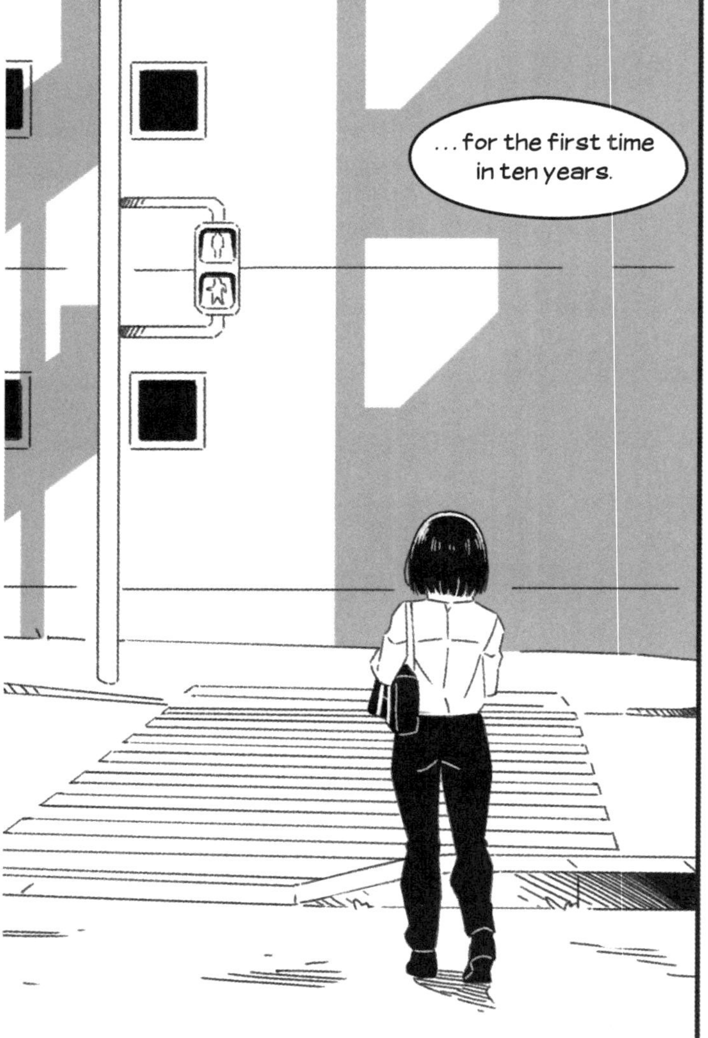

...for the first time in ten years.

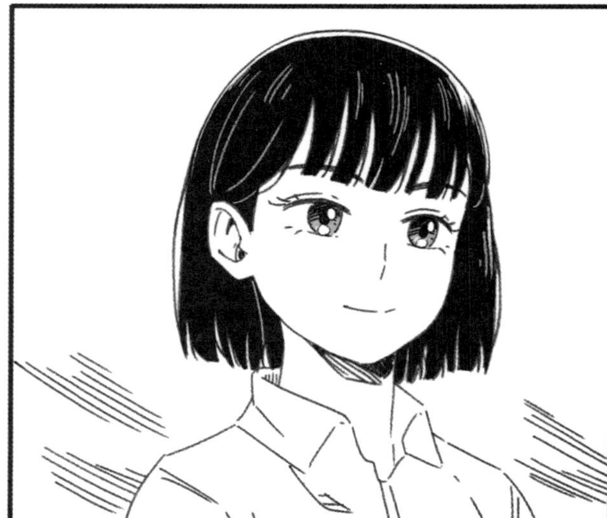

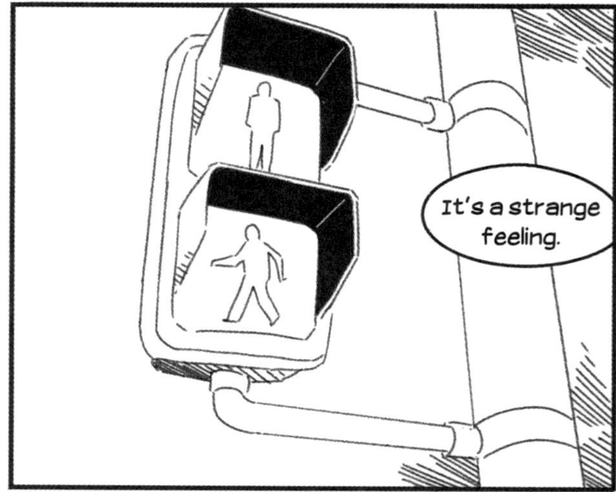

It's a strange feeling.

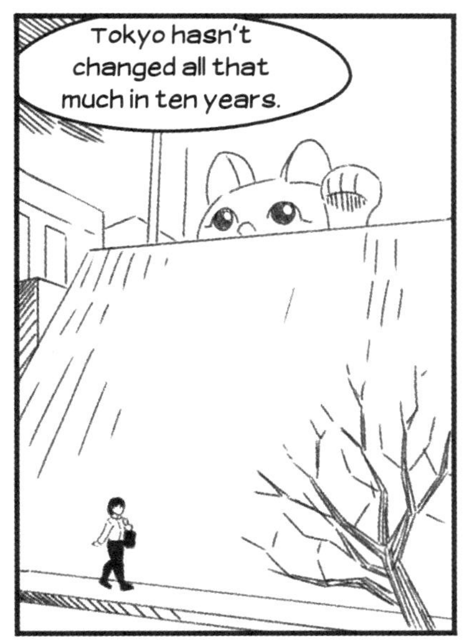

Tokyo hasn't changed all that much in ten years.

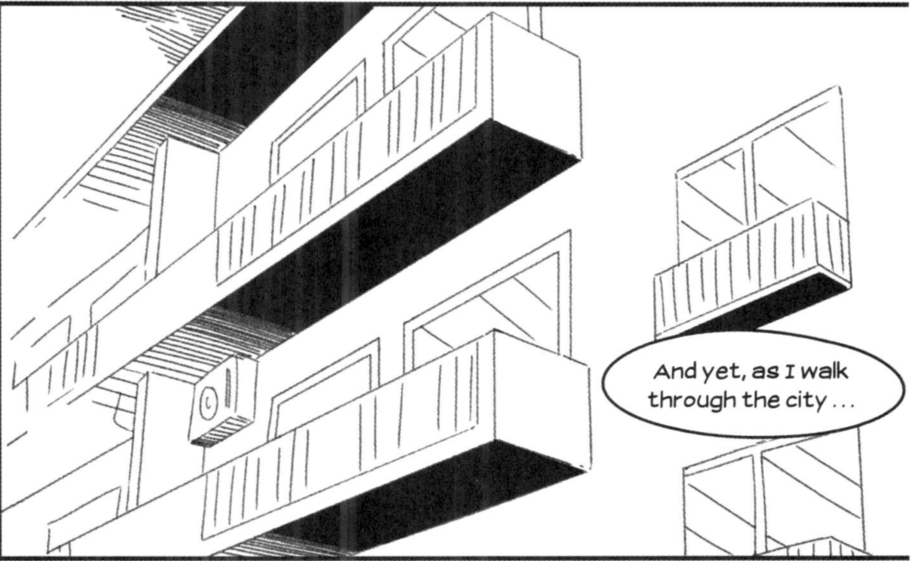

And yet, as I walk through the city...

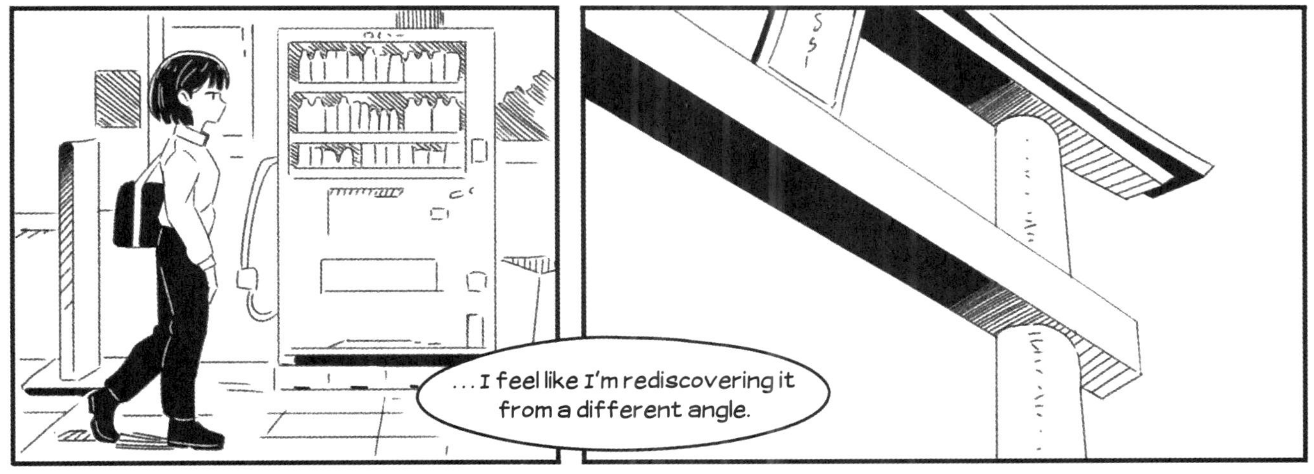

...I feel like I'm rediscovering it from a different angle.

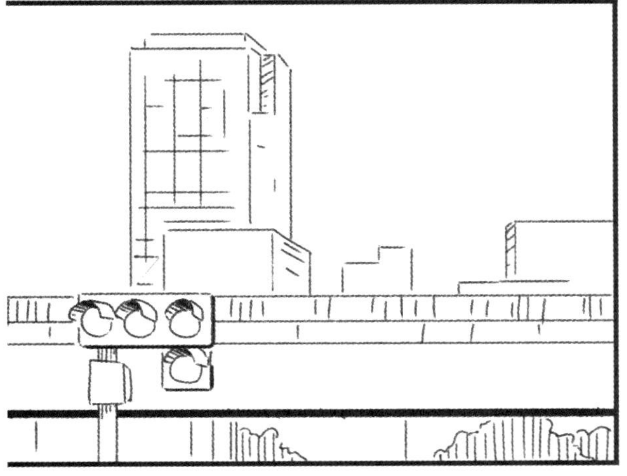

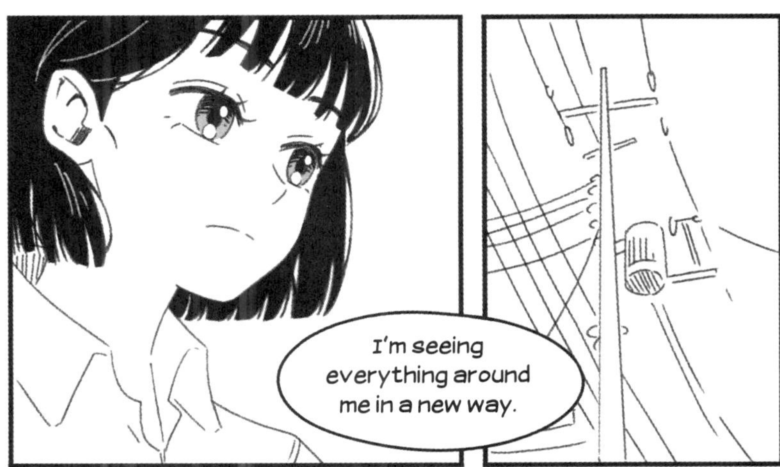

I'm seeing everything around me in a new way.

In a manga drawing, composition is crucial. You can
see each frame as its own separate illustration.

A little bit like in photography,
you want to find the best
framing that you can.

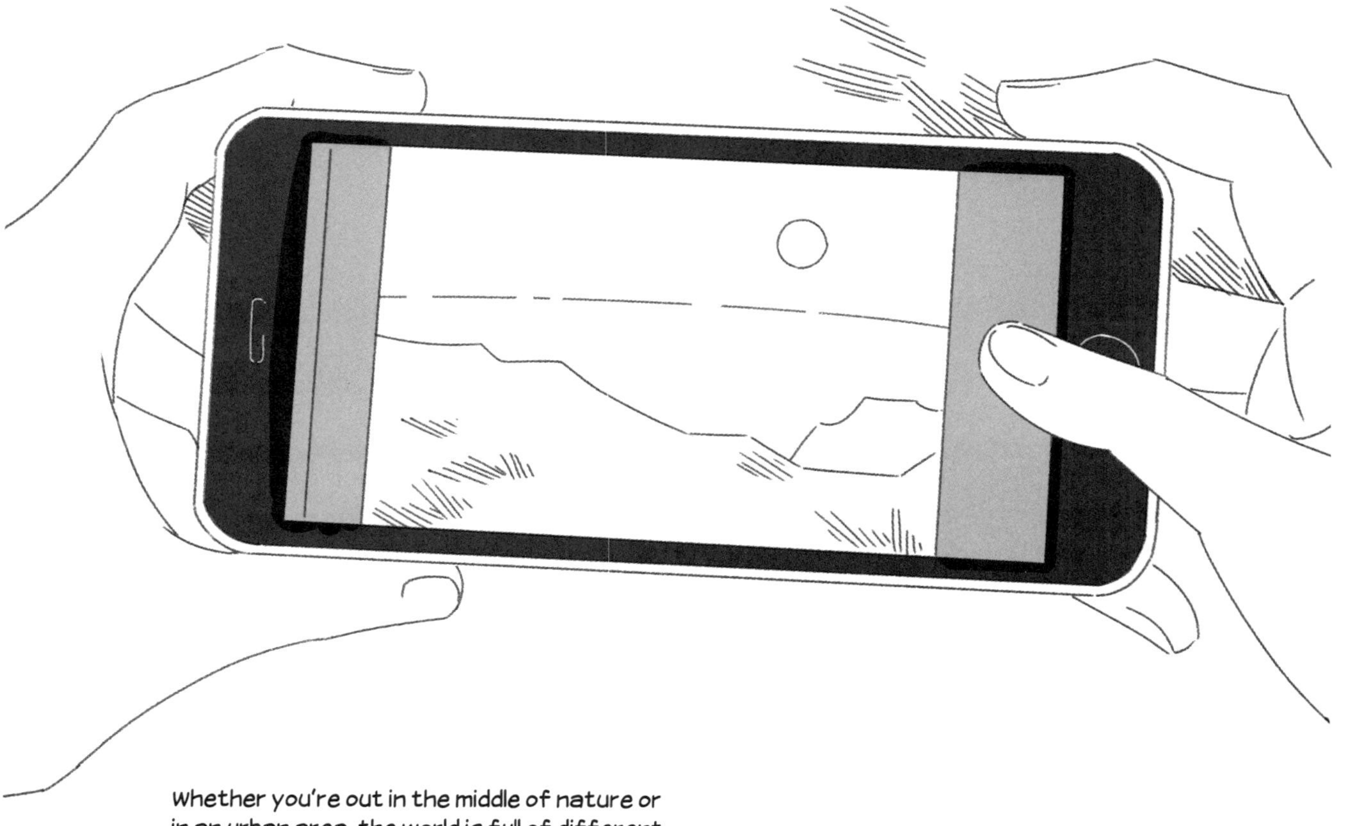

Whether you're out in the middle of nature or
in an urban area, the world is full of different
environments and landscapes.

And there are ways of
showcasing them.

The rule of thirds means that you divide the frame into three equal parts, both in width and in height.

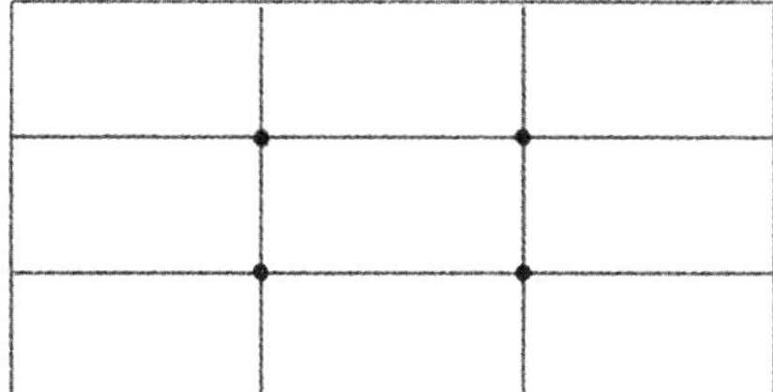

The intersections of these lines form strong points. These points are good places to put the subject of your drawing.

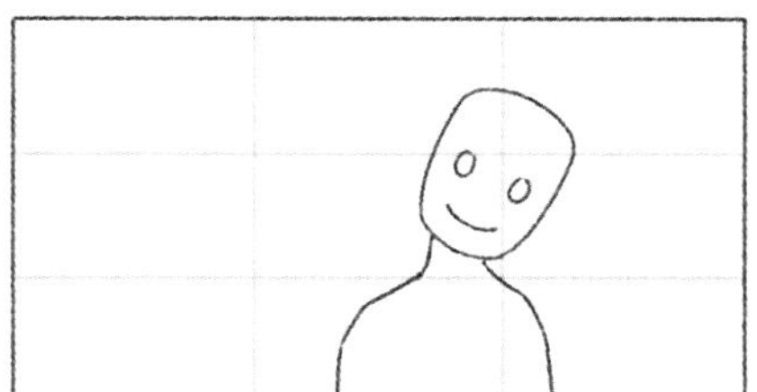

Here are some compositions that use the rule of thirds:

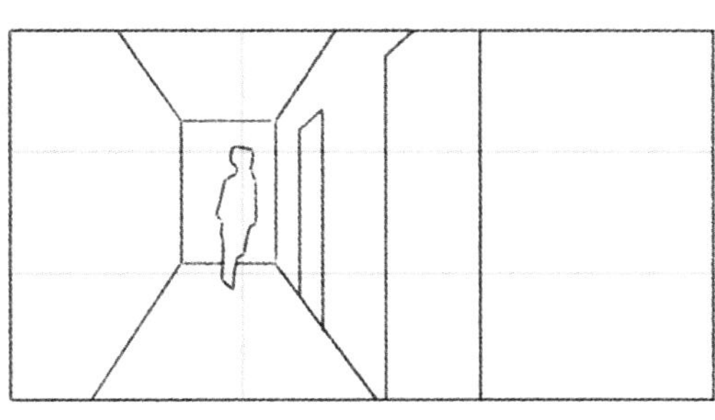

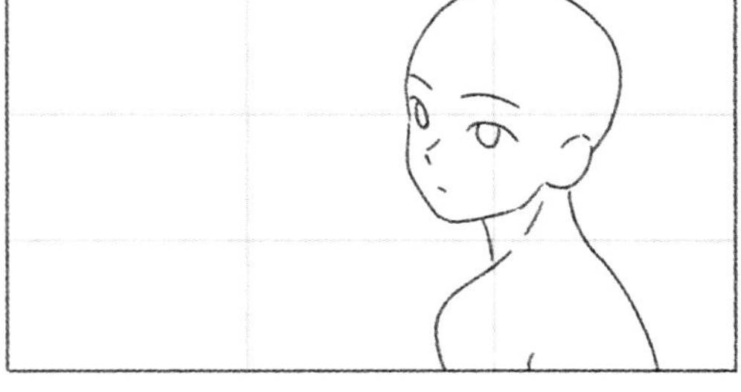

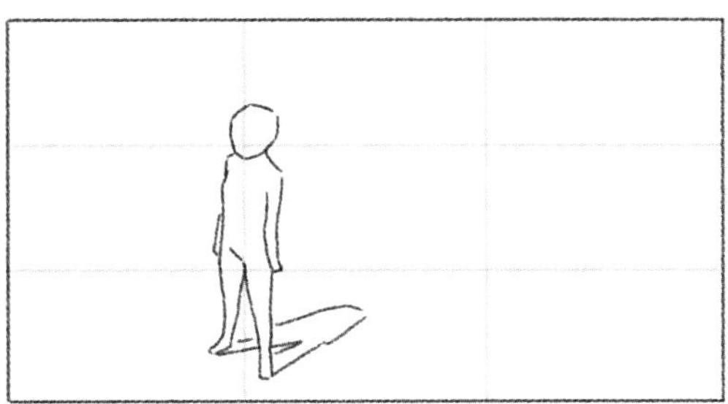

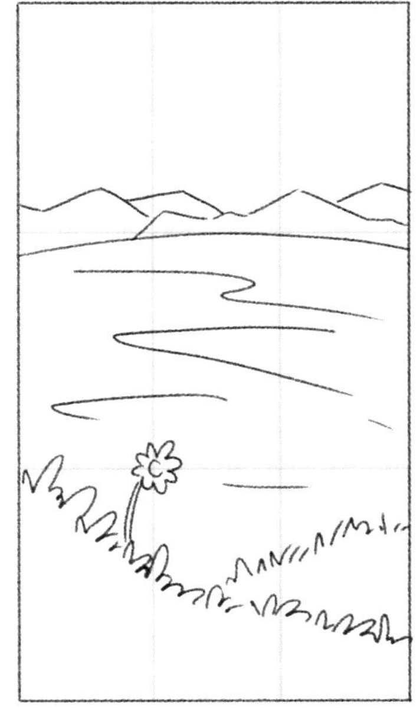

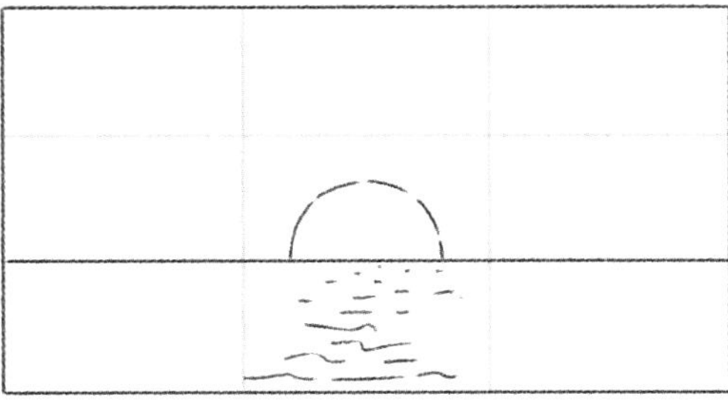

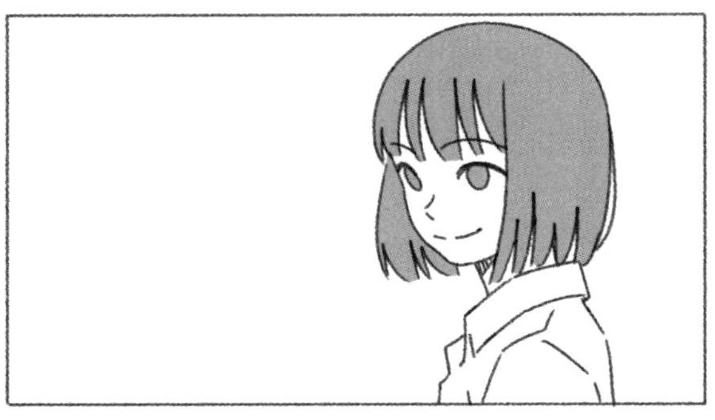

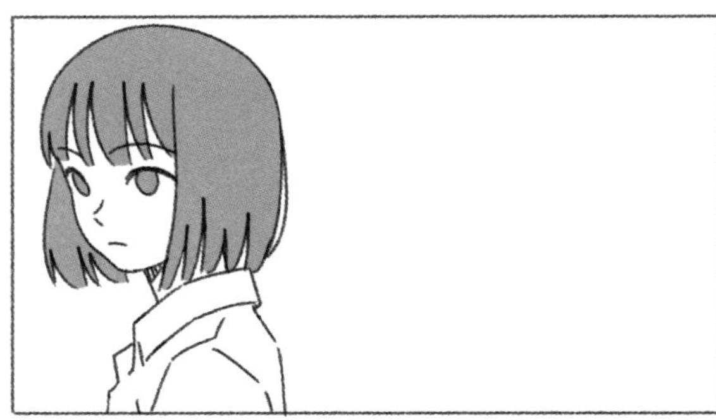

When you're drawing a character within a frame, you can leave some blank space in the direction of the character's gaze. This gives the composition some air.

If you do it the other way around, the character seems to be shut up within the frame. This can be a useful technique for when the character feels lost or blocked.

A character positioned right in the middle of the frame produces a sense of solitude.

This is also why we generally prefer to place characters on the strong points.

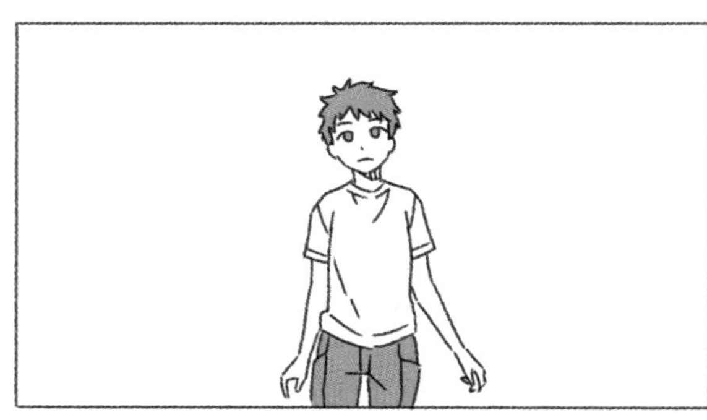

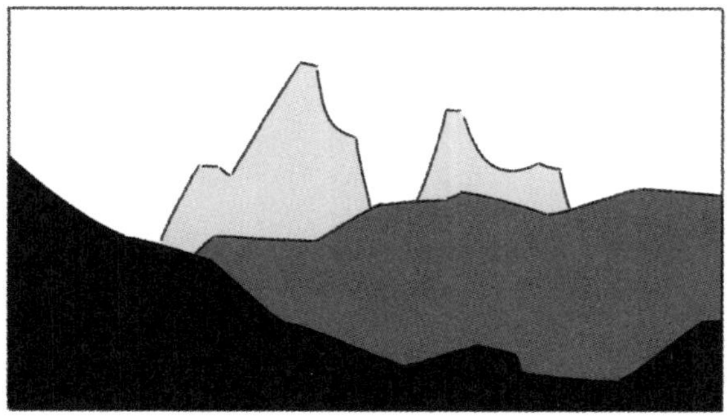

When we are constructing an image, it can be a good idea to place certain elements of the scene in the foreground. This creates more depth in the image.

In general, the elements that are in the foreground are darker, becoming lighter and lighter the further back one looks toward the horizon.

Here are some examples of compositions:

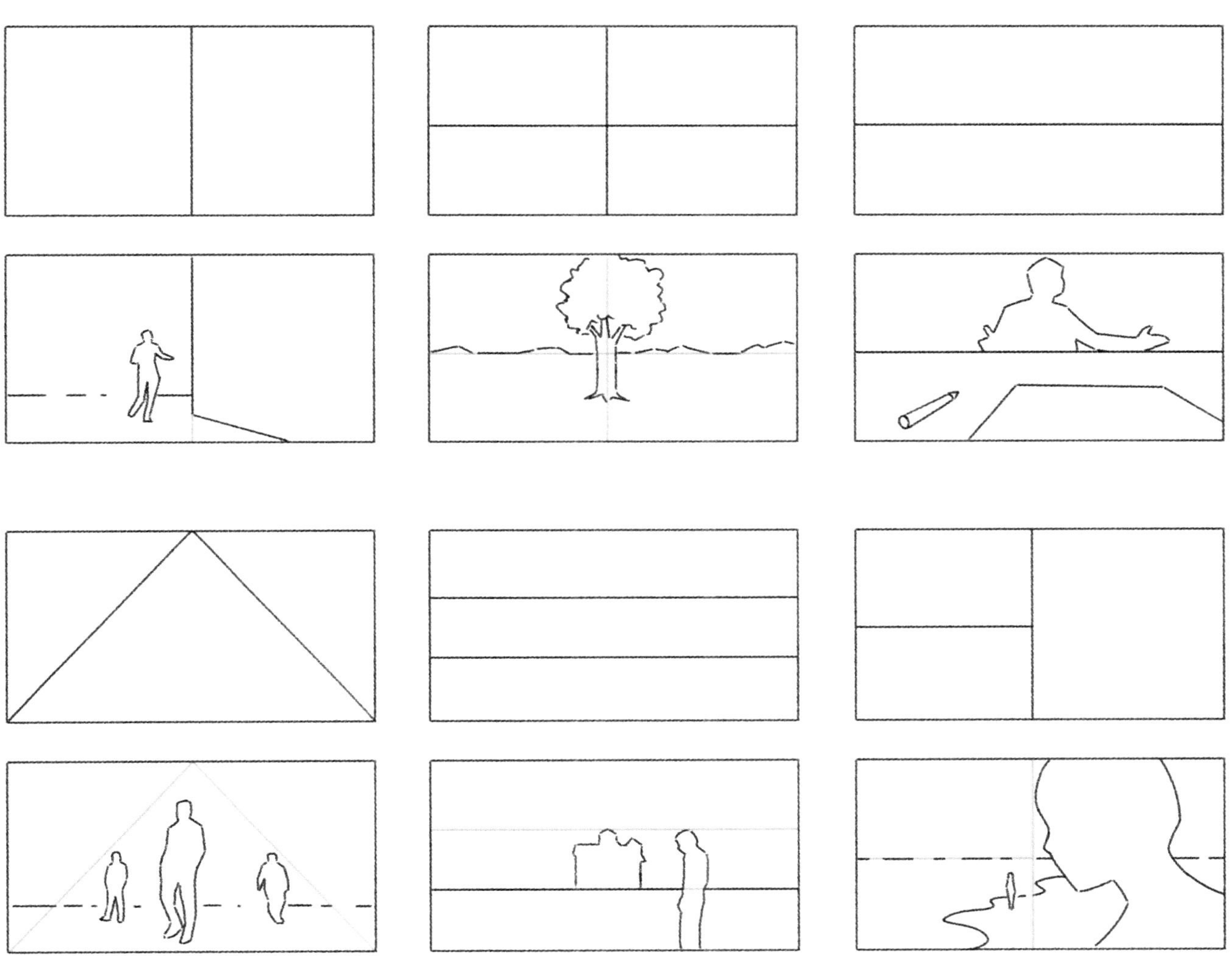

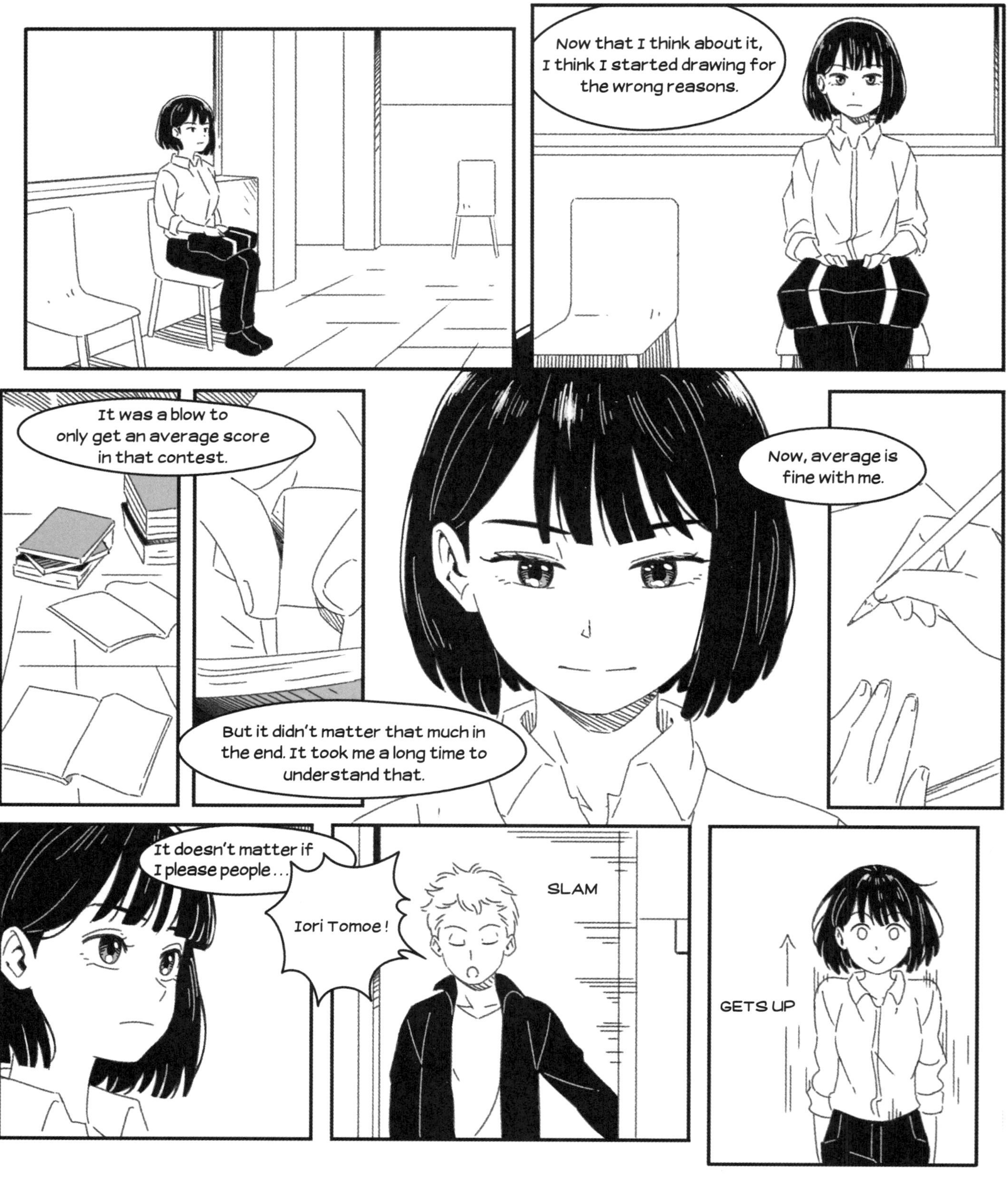

Now that I think about it, I think I started drawing for the wrong reasons.
It was a blow to only get an average score in that contest.
Now, average is fine with me.
But it didn't matter that much in the end. It took me a long time to understand that.
It doesn't matter if I please people...
Iori Tomoe!
SLAM
GETS UP

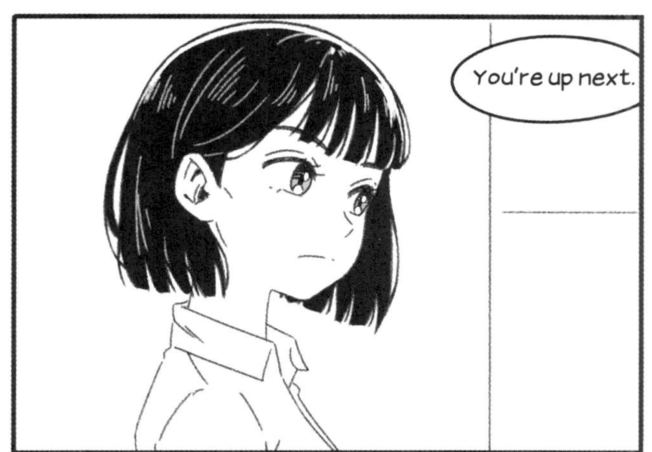

You're up next.

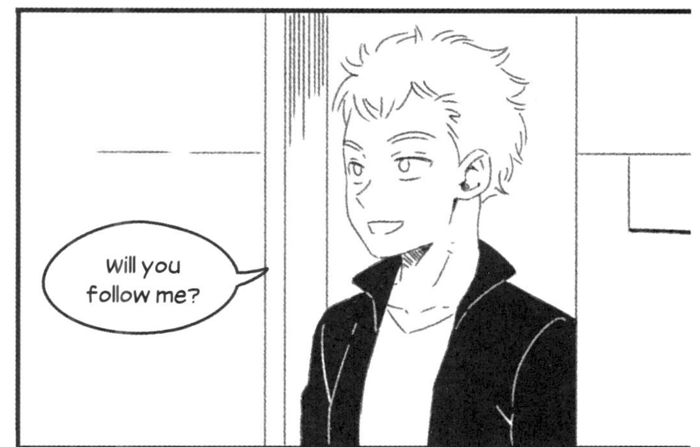

Will you follow me?

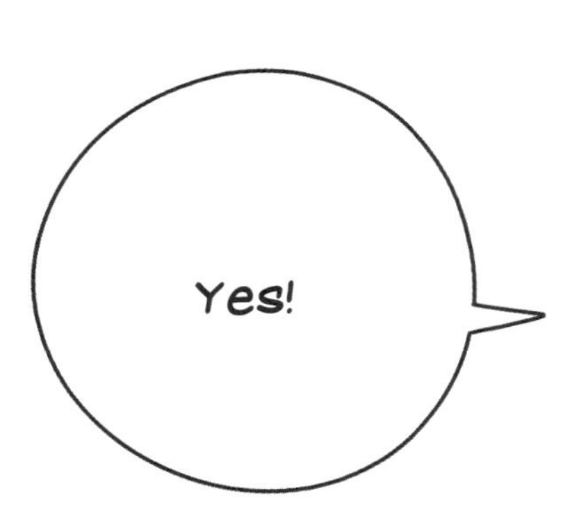

Yes!

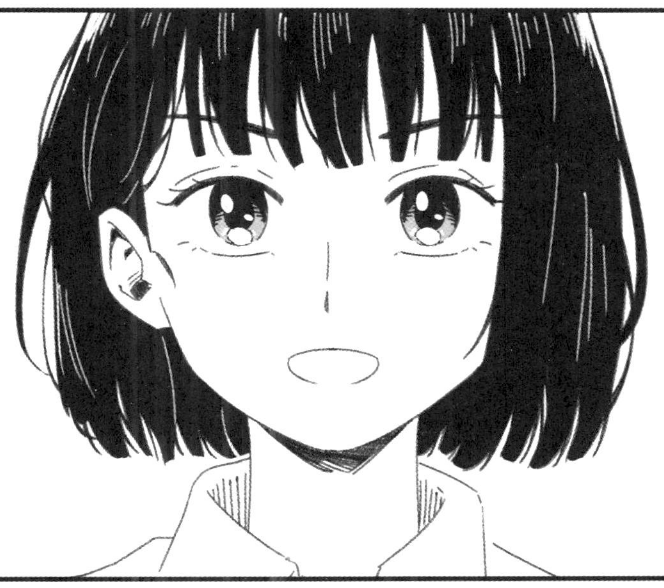

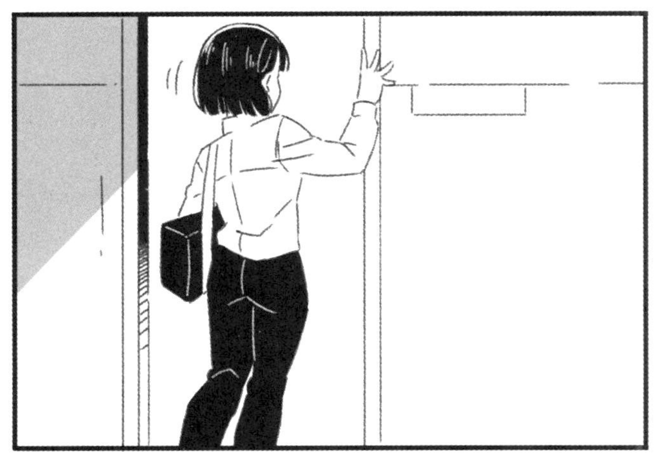

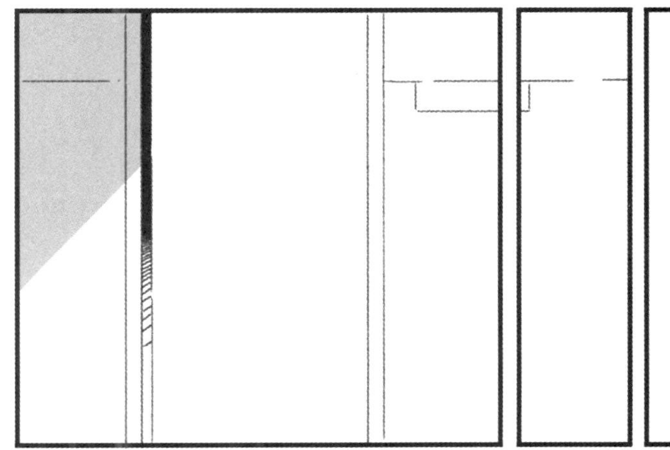

Drawing Manga: A Graphic Novel on How to Create Your Own Manga
Eliott Lerner

Project editor: Jocelyn Howell
Project manager: Lisa Brazieal
Marketing coordinator: Katie Walker
Artistic direction: Chloé Eve and Clarisse Delande
Layout: Maureen Forys
Cover: Max Marcil

ISBN: 979-8-88814-225-7
1st Edition (1st printing, September 2024)

English language edition © 2024 Rocky Nook, Inc.
Authorized translation from the French edition
Original French title: Manga: Récit illustré d'un apprentissage
© First published in French by Mango, Paris, France – 2023
(French ISBN: 978-2-31703-237-0)

Rocky Nook Inc.
1010 B Street, Suite 350
San Rafael, CA 94901
USA
www.rockynook.com

Distributed in the UK and Europe by Publishers Group UK
Distributed in the U.S. and all other territories by Publishers Group West

Library of Congress Control Number: 2024936844